Everyman, I will go with thee,
and be thy guide

THE EVERYMAN
LIBRARY

*The Everyman Library was founded by J. M. Dent
in 1906. He chose the name Everyman because he wanted
to make available the best books ever written in every
field to the greatest number of people at the cheapest possible
price. He began with Boswell's 'Life of Johnson';
his one-thousandth title was Aristotle's 'Metaphysics',
by which time sales exceeded forty million.*

*Today Everyman paperbacks remain true to
J. M. Dent's aims and high standards, with a wide range
of titles at affordable prices in editions which address
the needs of today's readers. Each new text is reset to give
a clear, elegant page and to incorporate the latest thinking
and scholarship. Each book carries the pilgrim logo,
the character in 'Everyman', a medieval morality play,
a proud link between Everyman
past and present.*

Arthur Schopenhauer

THE WORLD
AS WILL AND IDEA

Abridged in One Volume

Edited by
DAVID BERMAN
Trinity College, Dublin

Translated by
JILL BERMAN

EVERYMAN
J. M. DENT · LONDON
CHARLES E. TUTTLE
VERMONT

David Berman is Consultant Editor for the
Everyman Philosophy series

Introduction and other critical apparatus © J.M. Dent 1995

This edition first published in Everyman in 1995

15 17 19 20 18 16

J.M. Dent
Orion Publishing Group
Orion House
5 Upper St Martin's Lane
London WC2H 9EA
An Hachette UK company
and
Tuttle Publishing
Airport Industrial Park, 364 Innovation Drive,
North Clarendon, VT 05759-9436, USA

Typeset by CentraCet Ltd
Printed in Great Britain by
Clays Ltd, Elcograf S.p.A.

British Library Cataloguing-in-Publication Data is available
upon request.

ISBN 978-0-4608-7505-9

The Orion Publishing Group's policy is to use papers that
are natural, renewable and recyclable products and
made from wood grown in sustainable forests. The logging
and manufacturing processes are expected to conform to
the environmental regulations of the country of origin.

CONTENTS

THE WORLD AS WILL AND IDEA

NOTE ON THE AUTHOR,
EDITOR AND TRANSLATOR

ARTHUR SCHOPENHAUER was born in Danzig on 22 February 1788. His family were wealthy merchants, and it was intended that he would enter the family business. However, after his father's death Schopenhauer was able to pursue an academic and scholarly career. His first publication, originally his doctoral dissertation, was the *Fourfold Root of the Principle of Sufficient Reason* (1813). In his magnum opus, *The World as Will and Idea* (1819), he presents an idealism based on the will and an ethics rooted in pessimism and Eastern philosophy. A second edition of the work, with a supplementary volume, was published in 1844. He further elucidated his philosophy in *On the Will in Nature* (1835), *The Two Fundamental Problems of Ethics* (1841), and a miscellany, *Parerga and Paralipomena* (1851). Schopenhauer spent most of his adult life in Frankfurt am Main, where he died in September 1860. Although his philosophy was largely ignored until the 1850s, by the end of the century it had achieved wide recognition, profoundly influencing, among others, Wagner and Nietzsche.

DAVID BERMAN is Associate Professor of Philosophy and Fellow of Trinity College, Dublin. He is author of *A History of Atheism in Britain from Hobbes to Russell* (1988) and *George Berkeley: Idealism and the Man* (1994), and has edited *George Berkeley's Alciphron in Focus* (1993).

JILL BERMAN teaches German literature of the 18th and 19th centuries, and has written chiefly on Schiller.

CHRONOLOGY OF SCHOPENHAUER'S LIFE

Year	Life
1788	22 February: birth in Danzig (now Gdansk) of Arthur Schopenhauer, the son of Heinrich Floris Schopenhauer and of Johanna, née Trosiener
1793	Family moves to Hamburg, prompted by imminent occupation of Danzig by Prussian forces
1796	Schopenhauer family moves into das Haus Am Neuen Wandrahm 92 in Hamburg
1797	Birth of sister, Adele. Schopenhauer accompanies his father to Paris and then to Le Havre where he remains for two years with the family of Grégoire de Blésimaire. Friendship with Anthime, the son of the family
1799	Returns to Hamburg; attends Runge's private school for four years
1800	Travels to Prague, meeting Schiller in Weimar

CHRONOLOGY OF HIS TIMES

Year	Artistic Events	Historical Events
1788	Birth of Byron Kant, *Critique of Practical Reason*	
1789		Storming of Bastille marks beginning of French Revolution; American Constitution
1790	Goethe, *Faust: A Fragment* Kant, *Critique of Judgement*	
1791	Mozart, *The Magic Flute* Death of Mozart	
1792	Birth of Shelley	French invasions of Germany
1793		Louis XVI guillotined; Poland is re-divided, Danzig becomes Prussian
1794		Robespierre guillotined
1795	Schiller, *Letters on Aesthetic Education* Birth of Keats	
1796		Napoleon's Italian Campaign; death of Catherine the Great
1797	Births of Schubert and Heine Death of Burke	
1798		Napoleon First Consul; begins campaign in Egypt
1799	Birth of Balzac	
1800		French invade Bavaria
1801	Death of Novalis	Danish occupation of Hamburg ends
1802	Birth of Victor Hugo	

Year	Life
1803	Agrees to enter commerce, rather than pursuing a scholarly career – the reward for which is that he accompanies his parents on travels in Holland, England, France and Austria, beginning in May. Boards at the Rev. Thomas Lancaster's School in Wimbledon from June to September
1804	August: end of travels; apprenticed to Danzig merchant, Kabrun, from September to December
1805	Apprenticed to Jenisch, Hamburg merchant. 20 April: father dies, probably by suicide. Johanna sells family house in Hamburg
1806	Mother and sister go to Weimar, where Johanna sets up salon and becomes friendly with Goethe
1807	Abandons training as merchant – against his late father's wish, but supported by mother – for that of university; enters Gotha Gymnasium. Moves to Weimar; receives private tuition. Falls in love with Karoline Jagemann, the actress
1809	Enters Göttingen University, where he studies science and then philosophy: becomes friendly with W. B. Astor
1810	Johanna's biography of Fernau
1811	Leaves Göttingen for Berlin University, where he attends lectures of Fichte and Schleiermacher
1812	Travels via Weimar and Dresden to Teplitz
1813	Leaves Berlin because of war. Visits his mother in Weimar; leaves after quarrelling with her. Stays at Rudolstadt nearby. Publication of his doctoral dissertation *On the Fourfold Root of the Principle of Sufficient Reason*. Returns to his mother. Conversations with Goethe on colour and vision
1814	Final break with mother; leaves Weimar; lives in Dresden until 1818. Work on *The World as Will and Idea* (*W.W.I.*)
1816	His *On Seeing and Colours* printed
1818	Completes *W.W.I.*; begins travels in Italy
1819	Publication by Brockhaus of *W.W.I.*; returns to Germany because of financial crisis in family investments. Disagreements with sister. Returns to Dresden. Is appointed to a lectureship at Berlin University

Year	Artistic Events	Historical Events
1803	Death of Herder Erasmus Darwin's *Temple of Nature*	Britain declares war on France
1804	Death of Kant	Napoleon becomes Emperor
1805	Death of Schiller Beethoven, *Eroica*	Nelson defeats French at Trafalgar
1806		Battle of Jena; Napoleon enters Berlin
1807	Beethoven, *Fifth Symphony* Hegel, *Phenomenology of the Spirit, Part One*	Napoleon dismembers Prussia
1808	Goethe, *Faust, Part One*	
1809	Death of Haydn Goethe, *Elective Affinities*	
1810	Births of Chopin and Schumann	
1811	Birth of Liszt	
1812		Napoleon's Russian Campaign; burning of Moscow
1813	Births of Wagner, Verdi and Kierkegaard	Napoleon defeated at Leipzig
1814	Death of Fichte	Napoleon exiled to Elba; Congress of Vienna
1815		Battle of Waterloo; Napoleon banished to St Helena; birth of Bismark
1816	Rossini, *The Barber of Seville*	
1817	Death of Jane Austen	
1818	Mary Shelley, *Frankenstein*	Birth of Marx
1819	Death of Jacobi; births of Keller and Fontane	

Year	Life
1820	His lectures are poorly attended
1821	Falls in love with singer Caroline Medon. Assaults seamstress, who sues him
1822	May: travels to Italy again
1823	Returns from Italy to Munich, where he stays for a year; ill and depressed
1824	In Bad Gastein, Mannheim, and Dresden; poor reception of his philosophy. Plan to translate Hume's *Natural History of Religion* and *Dialogues concerning Natural Religion* into German, also unsuccessful
1826	In Berlin, again lecturing without success
1829–30	Plan to translate Kant into English, also abortive
1831	Leaves Berlin because of cholera epidemic; moves to Frankfurt-am-Main
1832–3	Living in Mannheim
1833	Resides in Frankfurt from this time until his death in 1860
1835	*On the Will in Nature* published
1838	Death of Mother
1839	Awarded prize by Scientific Academy in Norway for the best essay on freedom of the will
1840	Is not awarded prize by Danish Academy for essay on the foundation of morality
1841	Publishes these two essays in *The Two Fundamental Problems of Ethics*. Frauenstädt becomes Schopenhauer's student
1842	Adele visits
1843	Moves into house at Schöne Aussicht 17 in Frankfurt
1844	Second ed. of *W.W.I.* with second volume, containing fifty chapters elaborating on topics in Volume One
1847	Second edition of *Fourfold Root*

Year	Artistic Events	Historical Events
1820		Death of George III; birth of Engels
1821	Births of Dostoevsky, Flaubert and Baudelaire	Death of Napoleon
1822	Deaths of Shelley and E. T. A. Hoffmann	
1823	Beethoven, *Ninth Symphony*	Monroe Doctrine
1824	Death of Byron	Birth of Anton Bruckner
1825		Birth of Ferdinand LaSalle
1827	Death of Beethoven	
1828	Death of Schubert Birth of Tolstoy	
1829	Death of F. von Schlegel	
1830		July revolution in Paris; Death of George IV
1831	Hegel dies of cholera	
1832	Deaths of Goethe and Sir Walter Scott	
1833	Birth of Brahms	
1834	Death of Schleiermacher	
1835	Death of W. von Humboldt	
1837		Accession of Queen Victoria; Morse devises system of signals
1839		Birth of Mussorgski
1840	Births of Zola and Tchaikovsky	
1842	Death of Stendhal	
1843	Death of Hölderin	
1844	Birth of Nietzsche	
1845	Death of A. von Schlegel	

Year *Life*

1849 Death of Adele

1851 *Parerga and Paralipomena* (miscellaneous collection of essays, dialogues, aphorisms, etc.) published; positive reviews

1853 J. Oxenford's review-essay on his philosophy in *Westminster Review* marks beginning of his fame

1854 Second edition of *Will in Nature*; Frauenstädt's *Letters on Schopenhauer's Philosophy*

1857 His philosophy taught at Bonn University

1858 Declines invitation to be a member of Berlin Royal Academy
1859 Third ed. of *W.W.I.*
1860 Dies 21 September, and is buried on 26 September, in Frankfurt

Year	Artistic Events	Historical Events
1848		*Communist Manifesto*; uprisings in Europe
1849	Death of Chopin	German Constitution is adopted in Frankfurt
1850	Death of Balzac	
1851		Great Exhibition at the Crystal Palace
1852	H. B. Stowe's *Uncle Tom's Cabin*	Louis Napoleon proclaimed emperor
1854	Death of Schelling	Crimean War begins
1855	Death of Kierkegaard	Paris World Exhibition
1856	Birth of Freud Death of Heine	
1857	Flaubert, *Madame Bovary* Death of Comte	
1860		Unification of Italy; American Civil War

INTRODUCTION

I. *Biographical Background*

Born in Danzig on 22 February 1788, Schopenhauer was named
Arthur for cosmopolitan reasons. His father, Heinrich Floris, a
wealthy merchant and a keen traveller, wanted a name for his
son which would be recognizable in most European languages.
He had also planned that the baby should be born in England,
where he and his young wife, Johanna, were then travelling. As
Johanna later expressed it: a child born in England, 'though of
foreign parents, becomes thereby an Englishman ... entitled to
all the unpurchasable immunities ... so valuable to a merchant'.
But, she continues, 'as my desire was to return [home] to
Danzig', the plan was frustrated – to the great annoyance of her
Anglophile husband.[1] Yet Schopenhauer did receive part of his
schooling in England – a formative experience for him – where
his parents were visiting once again between 1803 and 1804.
Here he became fluent in English and developed a life-long taste
for things English.[2]

Schopenhauer's relationship with his parents was potent and
complex, as befits a man who anticipated many of Freud's
leading ideas.[3] He expressed great affection and reverence for
his father and disapproval of his mother, who was responsible,
it is thought, for his low opinion of woman in general. He
claimed to regard women as undeveloped men, situated somewhere between children and men.[4] His mother, who became a
successful writer and friend of Goethe, in turn had a low opinion
of him – at least of his temperament, which she thought
excessively morose. When Schopenhauer published his first
work, *On the Fourfold Root of the Principle of Sufficient
Reason*, she is said to have mischievously asked whether it was
something for druggists. This work, originally his doctoral
dissertation, was published in 1813, when he was twenty-five
years old. In this and other respects, Schopenhauer can be

compared to Berkeley and Hume – philosophers whom he greatly admired – whose major philosophical works were also published in their middle twenties. Schopenhauer's affinity with the classic British philosophers is evident, too, in his direct and clear style of writing – so uncharacteristic of the classic German philosophers, Kant, Fichte, Schelling and particularly of Hegel, the philosopher Schopenhauer most despised, and whom he describes variously as a charlatan, humbug, and windbag.[5]

Schopenhauer, it is clear, was no saint; and yet he put forward a philosophy of saintliness. Should he have practised what he preached? Not necessarily, he would say; for just as we do not demand that an artist who paints beautiful pictures should himself be beautiful, so, Schopenhauer holds, we should not require a moral philosopher to be exceptionally moral.[6] For Schopenhauer, philosophy is theoretical, concerned with knowing the truth; there is little connection between it and any practice. This is certainly true in his case. The philosopher who advocated denying the ego could hardly have been a greater egotist or more concerned with his personal and material well-being. He slept with loaded pistols by his bedside, and would not allow a barber to shave his neck. To avoid the possibility of drinking infected water he carried a leather water-flask; he would also lock away the stem and bowl of his tobacco pipe after he used it. He settled in Frankfurt (where he was to spend most of his later life) because of the high reputation of its doctors. And one could go on and on.[7]

His one redeeming human feature, it would seem, was his tenderness towards animals, and particularly to dogs. He was an early supporter of the movement for the 'Prevention of cruelty to animals'.[8] In later life he kept a French poodle, whom he called Atma (World-Soul), who was succeeded by another called Butt, whom the Frankfurters nicknamed 'Young Schopenhauer'. Whereas his kindness towards the poodles was touching, his relationship with his fellow human beings was prickly. Indeed, in a famous allegory he compares human social relations with those between porcupines – who, while wishing to be close for mutual warmth, cannot draw too close for fear of pricking each other.[9]

Schopenhauer had an uneven education. Despite his early productivity, he entered university relatively late because his father, a strong-minded man, wished his son to follow him in business. When Heinrich died – probably by his own hand – Schopenhauer was able, with his mother's help and after some hesitation, to give up the mercantile employment which he disliked to pursue a more scholarly and academic life. He went first to schools in Gotha and Weimar to study Greek and Latin, then to the University at Göttingen, where he first enrolled as a medical student. But after a year, in which he specialized in science, his interest changed to philosophy. At this point, he was advised by his teacher, G. E. Schulze, to concentrate on two philosophers: Plato and Kant, who are usually regarded as the main influences on his philosophical system. In his masterpiece, *The World as Will and Idea* (1819), the influence of Plato is most apparent in Book Three, on aesthetics; Kant's influence is evident in Book One, dealing with theory of knowledge, also in Book Three, and, most plainly, in the Appendix, a detailed 'Criticism of the Kantian Philosophy'. But there is much more to say about the forces which helped to shape Schopenhauer's work. His early interest in science, particularly biology and physiology, emerges importantly in Book Two, according to which all natural objects are expressions of will to life. There is also a pervasive British influence on his idealistic theory of knowledge and on his metaphysics of will. Another crucial influence on (or confirmation of) his philosophy is the eastern wisdom, especially as presented in the Upanishads and Buddhist texts, which Schopenhauer did much to popularize in Europe. This comes out most clearly in Book Four, which presents Schopenhauer's ethics and his pessimistic solution to the problem of life.

After receiving his Doctorate at the University of Jena, Schopenhauer obtained a lectureship at the University of Berlin, where Hegel, his *bête noire*, was then teaching. With typical arrogance, Schopenhauer fixed his lectures for the same time as those of Hegel, who was then at the height of his fame. The result was predictable: virtually no one attended Schopenhauer's lectures, and he eventually decided against an academic career. On account of his inheritance, which he shrewdly managed, he was able to live the life of an independent philosopher, gentleman and appreciator of the arts. Although his philosophical work was at first largely ignored – to his considerable chagrin – he eventually achieved philosophical fame late in life, as a result of his more popular essays, *Parerga and Paralipomena* (1851), and also of a review-article of his work, 'Iconoclasm in German Philosophy', originally published in the *Westminster Review* (1853), and then translated in a German periodical. When the 'misanthropic sage of Frankfurt' died seven years later, he was enjoying a reputation comparable even to Hegel's. By the 1890s he was described by one authority as more widely known than 'any other modern Continental metaphysician, except Kant'.[10]

II. *Philosophical Background and Starting-Point*

Probably the best way of approaching Schopenhauer's philosophy is to see the philosophical development which lead up to it; Schopenhauer places particular weight on his more immediate predecessors, and particularly (as we have seen) on Kant. But Kant's philosophy, as expressed in his great *Critique of Pure Reason* (1781), did not arise spontaneously: it 'sprung forth', as Schopenhauer says in a letter of 1831, 'from Locke's and Hume's speculations, or at least sets out from them'.[11] Schopenhauer is unusual amongst German philosophers in the significance he accords to the British development in philosophy. In the 1853 review, mentioned above, John Oxenford emphasized Schopenhauer's British orientation: 'Hobbes, Berkeley, and Priestley, whose existence has been almost ignored by modern German teachers, are at his [Schopenhauer's] fingers' end, and he cites them not only as kindred souls, but as authorities.'[12]

Locke is important, according to Schopenhauer, for the emphasis he places on epistemology, on the question of what we can know. Locke's answer in his *Essay concerning Human Understanding* (1690) is, in a word, ideas. What we immediately know of the world are ideas, either of sensation or reflection. This is important for Schopenhauer, because of its subjective starting point, although Locke is neither entirely original nor very clear or consistent in this standpoint. Descartes anticipates him; and Locke is notoriously ambiguous in his use of the term idea and about how ideas relate to objects in the world. However, Locke was moving in the right, subjectivist direction, according to Schopenhauer, as is shown in his celebrated account of primary/secondary qualities, which holds that the colour, taste, sound, and smell of objects are mind-dependent.[13] This development is taken further by Berkeley, who is more consistent than Locke. For Berkeley the physical world is known not just through sensible ideas, nor is it only sounds, smells, heat and cold that are mind-dependent: rather, the whole physical world is nothing more nor less than collections of ideas. All qualities, including solidity, extension, shape – which Locke held to be mind-independent qualities – exist only as they are perceived. As Berkeley famously puts it in his *Principles of Human Knowledge* (1710), Section 3, the existence of physical things consists in being perceived: their '*esse* is *percipi*'. In clearly presenting idealism for the first time in the history of philosophy, Berkeley has made a lasting contribution, says Schopenhauer, who is then quick to add that the rest of Berkeley's doctrines 'cannot stand the test of time' (*W.W.I.*, p. 4). Schopenhauer rejects Berkeley's metaphysics, his spiritualist account of the reality that lies behind ideas, according to which it is God who causes or imprints sensible ideas – which constitute the physical world – on our minds or immaterial substances.

It was Hume who identified the weaknesses in the Berkeleian or in any philosophical system which attempts to move from the world of ideas, or sensible impressions, to a spiritual cause and perceiver. The chief difficulty is that we do not perceive such substances or their (supposed) creative action; all we perceive are our perceptions or ideas. We also have no reason to believe that everything must have a cause. Nor can we be sure that we (*i.e.*, our minds) are anything more than collections of floating ideas. In short, for Hume, we can be rationally certain of our ideas, and little more.

It was this sceptical world-view which woke Kant, as he put it, from his dogmatic slumbers.[14] Prior to this, he had been a relatively complacent follower of the dominant Enlightenment world-view, which combined Newtonian science with the Rationalist metaphysics inspired by Leibniz. The awakened Kant was alarmed particularly at Hume's apparent undermining of science by the corrosive analysis of causality he presented most strikingly in his *Enquiry concerning Human Understanding* (1748), section 7.

Kant's response to Hume's sceptical challenge is set out in the first *Critique*, and involves a fundamental paradigm shift or new Copernican revolution. Formerly there had seemed to be only two ways of showing that causality always obtains in the physical world, and hence that our natural world is law-abiding, as assumed by science. First, one could argue this from experience or induction – for example, from observing that every time fire is applied to dry paper, the paper burns. Second, one could argue that the principle of universal causality is self-evidently true: that nothing in the world can exist outside the causal chain. However, Hume showed that each of these ways – characteristic of the empiricists and the rationalists, respectively – was flawed. Now Kant accepts Hume's criticisms; but he proposes a new, third way of justifying causality, whereby it is a feature not of the outer world, but is an inner, mental structure which we must impose on the world. So causality always and everywhere obtains in the physical world in much the same way that people with pink-tinted contact-lenses must always see the world in a pinkish light. It was in this novel way that Kant made science safe from the dangers of Humean scepticism.

Kant, in short, accepts idealism; although he is reluctant, as Schopenhauer sees it, to be as forthright in his idealism as was Berkeley. Yet this is the true tendency of his thought; for Kant showed that not only is causality a necessary mental structure in all minds that make judgements based on sense-experience, but that space and time are, as well. So what we perceive of the world are products of our spatial, temporal, and causal structuring, which takes place at an unconscious level – which Kant called the transcendental realm – and from which active structuring we get our orderly world of experience, or – as Berkeley called it – ideas.[15]

This, according to Schopenhauer, is the great contribution of Kant, who showed in systematic detail (which is absent in Berkeley's work) how the empirical world is objective, and distinguishable from the imaginary, yet is still a world of ideas or appearances: that it is (to use Kant's formula) empirically real but transcendentally ideal. Yet what, then, lies behind this ideal veil of appearances? Because our world is composed and bounded by our sense-experience, Kant holds, we cannot know. That unknowable something is what he called the *Ding an sich* (the thing-in-itself), or noumenon. Schopenhauer agreed with Kant that the thing-in-itself cannot be known either by pure reason, as rationalists like Descartes thought, or by empirical experience and reason, as some empiricists such as Locke believed, or by systematized experience, which is science. For each of these three approaches uses causality as though it were a bridge that can connect us to that which really exists independent of our experience – the things in themselves, unconditioned by our ways of knowing. But that is not tenable, as Hume and Kant showed.

So Kant safeguarded science, but at a price, namely, that science is valid only *within* the world of experience. Hence any rational or scientific attempt to move beyond the world of experience is ruled out. Thus neither the world-view of religion – with a God, immortal souls, an afterlife – nor the materialistic viewpoint, can be justified, at least not on rational or theoretical grounds. For since causality (as a transcendental form) is valid only within the empirical world of objects, it cannot carry us to that which transcends them.

III.   *World as idea and will*

Here, then, we have Schopenhauer's starting point in Book One of *The World as Will and Idea*. The idealistic view he outlines was first stated by Berkeley, purified by Hume, enriched by Kant, and is now finally corrected and simplified by Schopenhauer himself. In short, this is a world of orderly ideas or phenomena, in which science can reign unhindered, but which allows no scientific or theoretical access to that which lies beyond these appearances. Put in another way, Schopenhauer accepts, broadly speaking, the familiar positivist view of the world advocated by phenomenalists such as J. S. Mill and, in our own century, by Logical Positivists such as A. J. Ayer. On the other hand, Schopenhauer repeatedly rejects the forms of idealism of his contemporaries, Fichte, Schelling and Hegel, who, he scornfully claims, have simply ignored the positivistic implications of the British Empiricists and of Kant.

Of course, this is just the beginning of Schopenhauer's story, since he believes that he can go beyond positivism, beyond Kant's transcendental and agnostic idealism, yet in a way that does not violate the austere conditions for a metaphysics laid down by Kant and implied by Hume. In this respect, in his commitment to a metaphysical explanation, Schopenhauer is closer to his fellow German idealists than he is to Kant, and he is closer again to Berkeley than to Hume. And it is here, in Book Two, that he believes he is making his chief contribution to philosophy by identifying the thing which lies behind appearances. For there is a source, Schopenhauer argues, which previous philosophers had strangely ignored, given that it is so close to home – that is, our living bodies, through which, he maintains, we can gain some insight into the thing-in-itself.

My living body is, in Schopenhauer's view, a sort of Rosetta Stone.[16] I experience it in two ways: (1) objectively, as idea, as I experience all other objects in the world, but also (2) more directly as the most distinct manifestation or expression of the thing-in-itself. The crucial area here, at least initially, is that of motivation – a word which Schopenhauer introduced indirectly into the English language.[17] Thus when I reach for a drink to quench my thirst, I am doing one thing which can be known in two ways. First, it can be known by ordinary sense perception. You and I can both see my reaching and that it is prompted by thirst. But I, alone, am in a position also to experience this same motivated action inwardly – in a more direct, less mediated way. I do not have to see my parched lips to know that I am thirsty, or observe my hand moving to know that I have acted. What am I aware of here? What distinguishes this inner awareness from the outward perception that is accessible to all?

The best word, Schopenhauer maintains, to describe this familiar yet cognitively strange being or activity, is 'will'. Yet it is vital to appreciate that he is using the word in a novel and extended way: as the best term for something that had not previously been understood. For Schopenhauer, will is neither a cause nor an effect, neither spatial nor temporal: it is that metaphysical reality which underlies or grounds all phenomena, although our best apprehension of it is in the phenomenon of motivated action. This is so, because our awareness of such action is non-spatial; and being without one of the transcendental forms, our awareness is less structured and veiled.

Schopenhauer's conclusion is that my bodily actions are will objectified, will made physical by the structuring of time, space and causality. Hence that which had eluded Kant, and which he thought was intractably unknowable, can be known, Schopenhauer thinks, if we attend to our living bodies – which Kant and nearly all earlier philosophers had ignored. So our bodily feelings offer us the key or Rosetta Stone for deciphering the hitherto unknown language of reality.

What really exists, then, can be known not by objective means (as was thought by philosophers before Schopenhauer) but subjectively: by those intimate, personal feelings and sensations-longing, throbbing, hungering, which were hitherto dismissed with embarrassed relief. For Schopenhauer, human beings are not essentially rational, but are desiring, emotional animals, whose rationality was developed to serve and maximize the will to life. And it is not only our bodily actions that are essentially will, but so are our bodies themselves. Thus 'teeth, throat and intestines are objectified hunger, the genitals are objectified sexual desire' (*W.W.I.*, p. 41). This thesis, that human, and indeed all beings, are expressions of a blind, ceaseless will to life, is probably Schopenhauer's principal and most original philosophical contribution.

So while Schopenhauer wishes us to accept that the world is idea, he also tries to show us in Book Two that his first position (the idealism of Book One) is not complete. Unaccounted for is the inner meaning to things, which we all feel in an immediate, inchoate way, but which before Schopenhauer had not been given clear philosophical articulation. One main way by which he tries to move us in this metaphysical direction – which again shows his affinity with Berkeley – is through his use of solipsism, the extraordinary theory that only myself or modifications of myself exist.[18] For our adhering consistently to idealism, as set out in Book One, will lead, he argues, to a form of solipsism in which the whole world has reality only as idea, as a dependent object for me, as pure knowing subject.[19] The world, in short, will be like a very orderly and vivid dream, although not one in which I (David Berman) am the dreamer but only one of the characters in the dream. I cannot be the dreamer, since then the dreamer would be an object, and hence no longer the subject having the dream.

This, according to Schopenhauer, is the philosophical position which underlies scientific positivism, even though most scientists are either unaware of it or would prefer not to think about it. It equates what *is* with what can be *experienced*, and refuses to go beyond experience or appearances to *that* which appears. Yet such agnostic naturalism, although it is formidable scientifically, does not fit our sense of ourselves as subjective, acting human beings. I feel that I am something more, something different, than mere idea or natural phenomenon. Although I cannot prove it, I feel intuitively and immediately that *my* body at least is something different. And this intuition is enforced by the awful facts of death and suffering, facts that resist any satisfactory scientific or naturalistic explanation. Perhaps if we were immortal and always healthy, we could ignore metaphysical questions about the meaning of life and death, but as we are all suffering, mortal beings, we cannot.

Thus I feel that I have an inner core, that I am something that cannot be adequately explained by science; and this, Schopenhauer argues, is will to life. But then, am I the only being that is more than idea, that exists in itself as will? To be sure, I cannot be immediately aware of anything else, or any other body, in this intimate way. But it is hard to believe that other human beings are only my ideas, rather than things in themselves, like me. Yet if I wish to be strictly rigorous, I can refuse to accept this. No one can disprove this metaphysical form of solipsism: that I (David Berman) alone exist, that everything else is a mode of me, that the world is my dream. However, as Schopenhauer says, this form of solipsism (which he calls 'theoretical egoism') is more suited for a madhouse than for philosophical refutation. Hence one should conclude that every other human being, and not just myself, is a wilful thing in itself.

Yet can we stop there? Wouldn't that be a sort of species-solipsism, where only human beings are fully real? This is a position which has been held by religious systems such as Christianity; but Schopenhauer, whose sympathies lie with the pantheistic religions of the East, tries to show that this species-solipsism cannot be sustained. And here his sympathy for the ancient Eastern wisdom unites with his interest in physiology and biology. For, as those emerging sciences were demonstrating, there is little that separates *homo sapiens* from the rest of the natural world, and in particular from the higher mammals. Perhaps the most striking literary expression of this idea – which has become familiar since Charles Darwin – is presented in Mary Shelley's *Frankenstein* (published a year before *The World as Will and Idea*) which describes the creation of a man by natural means. So human beings are not a different sort of being, distinguished by the supposed possession of an immortal soul, but are simply the last or highest development of nature – a lustful, aggressive animal, in Schopenhauer's view, that can reflect on itself by the use of concepts. Apart from this reflective ability, there is no significant difference between ourselves and the so-called lower animals: we are all expressions of the will to life. The differences are of degree rather than kind, as can be seen in the varying complexity of the nervous systems, which shows a continuity from the simpler to the more complex organisms. So if we are going to be consistent, we must attribute will to even the lowest animals. But neither can the process stop there, since between even the simplest animals, like the amoeba, and the more complex plants, such as the venus flytrap, there is too much in common to suppose that animals are essentially different from plants.

Yet neither is Schopenhauer prepared to draw the line at living beings. Here he goes further than even the Eastern thinkers, since he argues that even inanimate objects – particles of dust – possess an inward, noumenal nature. They, too, are expressions of will, although at a lower level of actuality. Hence the whole world is will. There is no turning back, no drawing the line in the face of solipsism. Either accept that this world is a dream, in which there is no dreamer or thing-in-itself (the epistemic solipsism of Book One), or that I alone am a thing-in-itself (Book Two's metaphysical solipsism), or allow that the whole world is will. Of course, in allowing this, we must realize that the concept of will has been and must be extended, since the way that will objectifies itself in me, in my complex body, will be different from its manifestation in a spider or a blade of grass. We must stretch our imagination to recognize that all nature is will in varying grades of objectification.

Hence there are two dangers or errors to be avoided. We must not understand will as so dilute that it loses its connection with our starting point: our bodily experience in motivated action. So we should not make the mistake of one recent commentator who supposes that the will is force or energy; for this is to reduce Schopenhauer's system to materialism.[20] Yet neither should we fix our concept too narrowly on our own root experience of human willing, as another commentator has done, for then we would be making Schopenhauer into an animist.[21]

Although he has arguments that indirectly confirm his main thesis that the world is will, it is important to recognize that for Schopenhauer there can be no proper philosophical argument for this thesis. This is so because all proper arguments or proofs are based on the principle of sufficient reason, a principle which obtains only within the phenomenal and not in the noumenal world, or between the two worlds. Ultimately his thesis depends on whether he has convinced us of the significance of our immediate inward feelings – that in hunger and lust we are most distinctly aware of ourselves as will, as that which appears less distinctly in ordinary perception.

One of his indirect or supporting arguments concerns sexuality – a subject rarely, if ever, discussed by traditional philosophers. Clearly anticipating Freud, Schopenhauer argues that sexuality dominates our mental lives, and that this makes sense if we are essentially will to life, rather than rational thinking beings.[22] Schopenhauer also believes that he can solve certain hitherto intractable puzzles, such as that concerning free-will. The puzzle was nicely stated by Dr Johnson when he said that 'All theory is against the freedom of will; all experience for it.'[23] Why, in other words, do most of us feel that we sometimes act freely, yet recognize, in retrospect, that our actions were predictable and determined? Schopenhauer's answer draws on his two-world theory. Our feeling of freedom is a feeling of our inner, noumenal will, which, being outside the principle of causality, is free and undetermined. But phenomenally, as an individual person in space, time and causality, we are rigidly determined (*W.W.I.*, pp. 45–6).

Schopenhauer also, characteristically, draws on various art-forms for confirmation of his thesis. Consider even the simplest fairy tales. Most of them concern a young hero or heroine, who, while beginning well enough, soon has to struggle to regain the happiness for which she longs. In *Cinderella*, for example, the story details her deprivations, ordeals and distress. But what happens when she finally realizes her desire and marries the handsome prince? Well, they live happily ever after, and the story ends. But why is so little space given over to their happy life ever after? Schopenhauer answers that it would be incredible, even to children; for life is not about happiness or satisfaction, but about desiring, striving, longing, craving, and hence suffering. Moving from low to high art, this is also the reason,

Schopenhauer suggests, why Dante's *Inferno* is far more convincing than his *Paradiso*. In short, the world is a struggling hell, not a blissful heaven.

IV. *Art*

Yet art has a more fundamental role in Schopenhauer's system than merely to provide illustrations for his main metaphysical thesis. Art is the subject of Book Three, the most optimistic part of his work, where he argues that in aesthetic perception we come closest to understanding the world as idea. In short, the artist and the aesthetic perceiver succeed in doing what the philosopher and scientist strive for in vain. Here Schopenhauer draws on Plato's theory of Ideas, according to which particular things in the empirical world are imperfect reflections of Ideas or archtypes. So particular spiders or roses are shadows of an archetypal Idea of spider or rose, an Idea that is entirely adequate. Whereas particular roses are in some stage of development – budding, blooming, wilting – the Idea of rose, as outside space, time and causality, is complete in itself. So when I have an aesthetic experience of a rose – either in a still-life or in nature – I am seeing through the empirical representation to the underlying Idea. This is made possible when an idea has been purged of its will-ful element, when it does not evoke in me any desire: when I do not wish to use it, possess it, grab or eat it. Aesthetic judgement, as Kant had argued in his *Critique of Judgement* (1790), is disinterested. It enables me to transcend my particular egoistic and pragmatic ways of seeing or apprehending the object. What I see is not a rose that relates to my specific needs or desires, but an eternal Idea of a rose that any human being in any time or culture could see. Yet this aesthetic object should not, Schopenhauer stresses, be confused with a concept of rose, because a concept abstracts from an empirical experience, whereas an Idea is that which precedes my ordinary experience of a rose, as the rose's archetype. Such Ideas, in short, are the patterns of empirical objects: they are the ideal grades or levels through which the will objectifies or manifests itself in nature. For this reason, there is no way that we can adequately describe our aesthetic experiences. We are convinced that they are profoundly meaningful, yet we cannot explain their meaning. Because science works with concepts, it cannot grasp the Ideas. It is like the king's men trying hopelessly to put Humpty Dumpty together. Only the artist can do this; but then, the artist cannot explain how he was able to do it. There can be no recipes for works of art. This is the price that art pays. Unlike science, it has no pragmatic, no technological uses.

In Book Three Schopenhauer systematically examines art in its various forms, starting with architecture, then moving to painting, sculpture, literature and, finally, to music – the highest art form, as he sees it. Whereas architecture makes transparent rather elementary Ideas, music expresses most distinctly (partly because of its non-spatial character) the inner nature of the whole world. Schopenhauer also draws a parallel between the main art forms and the grades of nature. Thus architecture adequately expresses the non-organic world, painting and sculpture the organic, literature the human, and music the will itself.

Probably no philosopher before Schopenhauer has assigned such an exalted place to art. For not only does it capture what has evaded scientists and philosophers and theologians, but it also enables us to experience moments of saintly virtue. For in our awareness of Ideas, we are will-less, which -- as we shall see – is the highest moral state. Given Schopenhauer's account of art, it is not surprising that artists have been at the forefront in admiring his writings.[24] His is very much an artist's philosophy, as is shown not only in his frequent quotations from poets and dramatists, but also in his extensive and brilliant use of metaphor, simile, analogy, allegory and other literary modes of expression. Here he himself is, consistently, doing philosophy in a more artistic way: philosophy as art.

V.   Pessimism and Salvation

Although art releases us from the servitude of the will, this release is only transitory. Aesthetic contemplation is bound to be interrupted – by a pang of hunger, for example, or by some other will-ful call of nature. Schopenhauer examines the way to a more lasting liberation in the final Book Four. Here in the second aspect of will he draws out the implications of Book Two. We are now made to see the moral consequences of overcoming solipsism. This book is headed: 'The Assertion and Denial of the Will to Life, when Self-Consciousness has been attained'. One way that Schopenhauer tries to make his readers self-conscious is by a graphic image which shows his Eastern sympathies. He imagines that we are all moving barefoot around a circle which is strewn with red-hot coals. In some places there are no coals, and it is these areas we self-deceptively describe as happy or satisfying. We look forward to them as we walk round, deceiving ourselves, once again, that we are going somewhere – that either individual or human history has a goal. We believe these coal-less areas are intrinsically positive and that they make life worth living. In fact, they are little more than the absence or suspension of pain – like the momentary respite from an itch or thirst.

This explains why we are always getting ready to live; why our happiness is always being projected into the future. There is no solid happiness now, in this life, because there is no real positive good or purpose in the substance of the world. It is essentially, in itself, just endless will, greedy desire for more and greater life. Nothing can satisfy desire, because in itself, noumenally, there is only desire. Hope springs eternally and diabolically in the human breast, for there is just enough satisfaction to keep the process going. Drawing on another circular image, Schopenhauer maintains that our life consists basically of desire, then of some satisfaction, then of boredom, which leads back again to desire. This is the endless cycle of life:

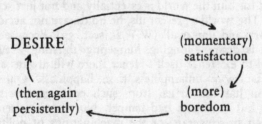

DESIRE   (momentary) satisfaction

(then again persistently)   (more) boredom

The world is a grisly place; for even the momentary satisfaction of desire is won at the expense of some other being in the world. The will to life is not just lustful and greedy but necessarily aggressive. Plants consume water and air; animals feed on plants; human beings prey on both plants and animals and also on each other. Even inert material things, like pebbles, by taking up space exclude other materials beings. Will to life goes with will to power. To exist is to be unjust, since it is impossible not to encroach on the will of another. Because we are the highest and most complete objectification of will, we human beings torture and suffer most. In this limited sense there is justice in the world: the torturer is itself tortured.

The world is something we should be sorry about, for at bottom it is something that ought not to be. We are now approaching the core of Schopenhauer's pessimism; although, as he is aware, his position is not entirely novel. Thus, as he points out: 'in the Gospel the words 'world' and 'evil' are used almost synonymously' (*W.W.I.*, p. 206). Yet Schopenhauer's pessimism goes beyond that of Christianity, since for him there is no next world, no afterlife, nor a God to redeem human beings or make them happy. Certainly Schopenhauer's philosophy is atheistic, if by God is meant a good and wise creator of the world.[25] For given the flawed nature of the world, it follows that God is too good to exist. To paraphrase the well-known joke: What would a nice God have to do with a world like this? In such a world, non-existence would be (*pace* the ontological argument) a perfection.

This, Schopenhauer held, is the worst of all possible worlds. If it were even slightly worse, it would fall into chaos. It is important to see how Schopenhauer's pessimism differs from other, earlier versions, such as that in Christianity. It is not merely that Schopenhauer subtracts the supernatural elements, but that for him the world is essentially and not just accidentally wrong. The world's present ills, he holds, are not accidental but 'necessary and universal' (*W.W.I.*, sect. 57). Because the thing in itself is desire – longing, hungering, thirsting – 'suffering is essential to existence itself'. Hence there will always and everywhere be more unhappiness than happiness. Our unhappy condition has not arisen from such contingent acts such as Adam's fall or Zeus's bad temper. Nor has it arisen through priestcraft or kingcraft, or the machinations of politicians, or the discordant relationship between means and modes of production, or alienation, or any inefficient management of society, or lack of good hygiene or diet or education. These would be accidental causes of human discontent, which could, at least in principle, be rectified.

Schopenhauer's pessimism is deeper and more radical, since for him the cause of our discontent lies in the substance of the world – in its being will to life. Life, in short, (1) is morally wrong, (2) has no meaning or purpose, and (3) will always have more pain than pleasure. So there is ultimately nothing we can do to alter this worst of all possible worlds – except to end it by strangling all desire, thereby achieving what the Buddhists call Nirvana, which is the state closest to pure nothingness.

VI The Everyman Edition

The aim of the present edition is to make Schopenhauer's major work, *Die Welt als Wille und Vorstellung* (*The World as Will and Idea*), accessible to a wide range of readers. For although Schopenhauer was essentially a philosopher, the interest of his work goes beyond professional or school philosophy which he often castigates. A great individualist himself, his appeal has been to individuals. Even in the realm of philosophy he has mainly attracted independent, indeed, anti-philosophical philosophers, most notably Nietzsche and Wittgenstein, who used, rather than followed, his philosophy.[26] Yet Schopenhauer's greatest impact has probably been on individuals outside philosophy – on artists such as Wagner, and psychologists such as Freud and Jung.[27]

One reason Schopenhauer's work has had this wide personal appeal probably lies in its directness and seriousness. He is not writing for fellow-philosophers; rather, he is confronting the deepest philosophical issues, of life, suffering and death, with an urgency absent from most professional philosophy. He combines Germanic seriousness with English lucidity – a distinction that he shares with that other great Anglo-Germanic philosopher, Wittgenstein.

And yet, having said that Schopenhauer has very high standards of clarity and argument, one must also admit that *The World as Will and Idea* is not the easiest book to read, and that he does not always make matters easy for his readers. Indeed, in some of his demands, he gives the impression that he is trying to make things harder. For example, he insists that the reader must first have read and mastered his *On the Fourfold Root of the Principle of Sufficient Reason*, and that it should be read as the Introduction to his major work.[28]

Schopenhauer also inflicts on the reader numerous digressions in which he excoriates his philosophical opponents. There is considerable repetition. He is fond, too, of displaying his undoubted erudition, so that the reader is treated to learned footnotes and lengthy quotations from ancient, medieval and modern sources – literary and scientific, as well as philosophical. Nor, often, is he satisfied with less than two or three illustrations for each point. Schopenhauer's work has often been compared to an elaborate musical composition. This rich diversity can be charming, but also bewildering and frustrating to the reader who wishes to see a clear line of thought. And there *is* a clear line. Indeed, Schopenhauer suggests that it is even simpler than a line of argument: that he is really trying to 'impart a single thought'.[29]

The aim of this edition is to abridge Schopenhauer's digressions, footnotes, repetitions, illustrations, and his attacks on Fichte, Schelling, Jacobi, Schleiermacher and Hegel, thereby enabling the reader to move more easily through his work. For this purpose, Schopenhauer's Prefaces have been omitted. The First Book has been the most radically abridged, since it is the most disjointed, and has probably discouraged many readers from reaching the more distinctively Schopenhauerian portions of the work, particularly in Book Two, which has here been left largely intact. To use the musical analogy: in this edition Schopenhauer's elaborate double concerto (for will and idea) has been simplified, with attention given more to the melody than to the orchestration.

Another principle operating in this edition, as it is more philosophical and interpretative, should also be mentioned. While few will quarrel with the excision of Schopenhauer's ill-tempered attacks on his philosophical brethren, some objection may be raised to the abridgement of his critical discussion of Kant, particularly of the long Appendix on Kant's philosophy. While it cannot be doubted that Kant was of major importance to Schopenhauer – a philosophical father-figure – it is also clear that Schopenhauer's extensive discussion of Kant is often tangled and narrowly scholarly. One such tangle is Schopenhauer's elaborate attempt in section 31 to display the similarities and 'inner agreement' between Kant's thing-in-itself and Plato's Ideas, an excursus which he then concludes in section 32 by admitting that they should not be equated.[30] This potentially confusing discussion has been here excised. One scholarly question, important to Schopenhauer but probably not to many present-day readers, is the (supposedly misleading) revisions Kant made to the second edition of the *Critique*, and Schopenhauer's proud discovery of the purer (as he saw it) first edition. This and other similar material has been abridged here.

It can also be argued that much that Schopenhauer claimed to derive from Kant was itself derived from Berkeley and Hume. Schopenhauer seems to have seen himself as in a middle position between English and German thought – which is shown in, among other things, his desire to translate Kant into English, and Hume into German. While it is doubtful whether he saw himself as either primarily in the British philosophical tradition, or – as one recent biographer has claimed – as an 'honorary Englishman', it should still be helpful, particularly for English readers, to appreciate the British context of his philosophical work.[31] This has been a guiding principle of the present edition, as can be seen straightaway in the title, *The World as Will and Idea*, which follows the 1883–6 translation of R. B. Haldane and J. Kemp.[32] In his 1958 translation, E. F. J. Payne castigates Haldane and Kemp in particular for their title, which he replaces with *The World as Will and Representation*.[33] Now one consequence of translating *Vorstellung* as 'representation' rather than 'idea' is to move Schopenhauer away from Locke, and away especially from Berkeley, according to whom ideas are what the mind experiences and thinks on. Payne, who recognizes that the issue is 'important', offers a number of reasons for rejecting 'idea', none of which seems convincing. Thus, probably following the 1889 English translation of the *Fourfold Root*, he points out that in this work Schopenhauer says that '"idea" should be used only in its original Platonic sense'.[34] But this is extremely misleading; for what Schopenhauer actually says is:

> My readers know that I accept the word Idea (*Idee*) only in its original Platonic sense, and that I have thoroughly discussed it especially in the Third Book of my chief work. The Frenchman and the Englishman, on the other hand, understand the words *idée* or idea in a very ordinary yet perfectly definite meaning. When, however, anyone speaks to the Germans about Ideas (*Ideen*) ... their heads begin to swim [as when] the notorious charlatan Hegel ... called his principle of the world ... the Idea (*die Idee*) ... (Chap. V, sect. 34).

What Schopenhauer opposes, in short, is the use of the German word *Idee* to refer to anything but Platonic Ideas. He specifically has no objection to 'idea' being used in English in the non-Platonic sense. That this is indeed his view is shown in his 1829 specimen for an English translation of Kant's *Prolegomena for any Future Metaphysics*. In three places Kant uses the term *Vorstellungen*, and, in all of these, Schopenhauer translates it by 'ideas'. To quote one example: '... the senses never ... manifest to our cognizance the things as they are in themselves, but merely as appearances, which are no more than mere ideas [*Vorstellungen*] of our sensitive faculty ...'.[35] Here we can see not only which translation Schopenhauer would prefer, but also his clear affinity with Locke and Berkeley. Following Schopenhauer, therefore, *Vorstellung* is here translated as idea, the lower case 'i' indicating its Berkeleian sense; *Idee* is translated Idea, the capital 'I' showing its Platonic sense.

In this edition, deletions of a sentence or more are indicated by the following: '[...]'; although the deletion of footnotes is not indicated. Schopenhauer's foreign-language quotations are given in English translations.

DAVID BERMAN

References

1. Johanna Schopenhauer, *My Youthful Life* (1847), vol. 2, p. 90.

2. See P. Bridgwater, *Arthur Schopenhauer's English Schooling* (London, 1988) for a detailed description of Schopenhauer's period at Wimbledon school.

3. In *An Autobiographical Study* (1925) Freud speaks of the 'large extent to which psycho-analysis coincides with the philosophy of Schopenhauer – not only did he assert the dominance of the emotions and the supreme importance of sexuality but he was even aware of the mechanism of repression ...', *Standard Edition of the Complete Psychological Works* (London, 1964), vol. xx, p. 59.

4. Essay 'On Woman', in *Parerga and Paralipomena*, translated by Payne (Oxford, 1974), vol. 2, pp. 614–15.

5. Thus Nietzsche speaks of Schopenhauer's 'sense for hard facts, his good will for clarity and reason, which so often makes him appear so

English and unGerman ...'; *Gay Science*, trans. by W. Kaufmann (New York, 1974), no. 99.

6. *The World as Will and Idea* (abbreviated as *W.W.I.*); all references, unless otherwise stated, will be to the present edition.

7. See W. Wallace, *Life and Writings of Arthur Schopenhauer* (London, circa 1890), p. 146; H. Zimmern, *Arthur Schopenhauer: His Life and Philosophy* (London, 1876), pp. 89–90, 146.

8. See Zimmern, *Arthur Schopenhauer*, pp. 154–5, 160 and my 'Spinoza's Spiders, Schopenhauer's Dogs', *Philosophical Studies*, xxix (1982), pp. 202–9.

9. See *Parega and Paralipomena*, vol. 2, pp. 651–2.

10. J. Royce, *The Spirit of Modern Philosophy* (Boston, 1892; repr. 1983), p. 228.

11. The letter is reprinted by Bridgwater (see note 2 above), p. 343.

12. J. Oxenford, 'Iconoclasm in German Philosophy', *Westminster Review* (1853), p. 394.

13. See *W.W.I.*, Supplement to Bk. One: 'The Standpoint of Idealism', pp. 18–19 and Locke's *Essay concerning Human Understanding* II.viii.

14. See *Prolegomena for any Future Metaphysics*, Preface.

15. Schopenhauer himself uses 'idea' to translate the key term *Vorstellung*; see below. pp. xxxv–xxxvi.

16. The discovery of the Rosetta Stone in 1798 enabled scholars to decypher the ancient Egyptian language, as the stone's inscription was in Greek as well as in hieroglyphics. In *W.W.I.*, sect. 17, Schopenhauer says that the world, considered only as ideas, stands 'before us like hieroglyphics which we do not understand'; also see pp. 29 and 162. In sect. 56, he also refers to a drawing by Tischbein which, like the Rosetta Stone, expresses one thing in two ways.

17. The earliest use of the term 'motivation', according to the *Oxford English Dictionary* (1989), was in an 1873 article which refers to Schopenhauer's account of the 'law of motivation'; see vol. 9, p. 1131. In the 1889 translation of Schopenhauer's *Fourfold Root*, the translator notes that 'Some readers may take exception at such expressions as ... motivation ...; for they are not ... English words [but] belong to Schopenhauer's own characteristic terminology ...' (p. xi). Yet Scho-

penhauer's contribution to the field of motivation goes deeper than merely coining the term.

18. See Berkeley, *Principles*, sects. 145–8 and my *Berkeley's Alciphron in Focus* (London, 1993), 87–92, 201.

19. *Ibid.*

20. See B. Magee, *The Philosophy of Schopenhauer* (Oxford, 1983), p. 161.

21. See D. W. Hamlyn, *Schopenhauer* (London, 1980), pp. 95–7.

22. See *W.W.I.*, Supplement to Bk. Four, 'On the Metaphysics of Sexual Love', pp. 263–6.

23. See J. Boswell, *Life of Samuel Johnson* (Dublin, 1792), vol. 3, p. 22.

24. Among these are Richard Wagner, Tolstoy, Thomas Mann, Samuel Beckett; for a lively account of Schopenhauer's impact on artists, see Magee; on the connection with Tolstoy, Hardy and Beckett, see von der Luft (ed.), *Schopenhauer: New Essays* (1988), chaps. 14, 17 and 19.

25. In *Gay Science*, no. 357, Nietzsche celebrated Schopenhauer as the first honest German atheist. Schopenhauer's most succinct argument for atheism is in *W.W.I.*, sup. chap. XLVIII; in short: a putative being with intelligence greatly superior to ours would be so sickened and bored by what it knew that it would cease to exist.

26. For some account of Nietzsche's use of Schopenhauer, see D. Berman, 'Nietzsche's Three Phases of Atheism', *History of Philosophy Quarterly* (1988); for his connection with Freud and Wittgenstein, see Gupta, 'Freud and Schopenhauer' and Engel, 'Schopenhauer's Impact on Wittgenstein', both reprinted in M. Fox (ed.), *Schopenhauer: his Achievement* (1980).

27. See below, 'Schopenhauer and his Critics', pp. 279–80.

28. See *W.W.I.*, Preface to the first edition. While Payne ignores Schopenhauer's demand, Haldane and Kemp compromise by printing an Abstract of the *Fourfold Root* as an Appendix (which is also included in this edition).

29. In the Preface to the first edition of *W.W.I.*, Schopenhauer writes that '... I intend to impart only a single thought'; also see *W.W.I.*, sect. 54.

30. Indeed, in sect. 35 Schopenhauer says that 'it is absolutely necessary to distinguish the will as thing-in-itself from its adequate objectivity ... the Ideas ...'.

31. See Bridgwater, p. 1; also see Richard Taylor, Foreword to *Schopenhauer: New Essays* (1988), p. xxiii.

32. Schopenhauer, *The World as Will and Idea*, trans. by Haldane and Kemp (London: Trubner & Co., 1883–6), 3 vols, (Bohn Philosophical Library, vols. xxii–xxiv.

33. Payne, *The World as Will and Representation* (Indian Hills, Colorado, 1958), 2 vols.

34. Payne, vol. 1, p. ix; see *Two Essays*, trans. by Hildebrand; see also Payne's helpful 'Schopenhauer in English' in the *Schopenhauer-Jahrbuch* xxxiii (1949/50), pp. 95–103.

35. Bridgwater, p. 337.

The editor and translator are grateful to Dr Christopher Janaway, Mr Vasilis Politis and Prof. Wolfgang Breidert for helpful comments.

TRANSLATOR'S NOTE

In undertaking this abridged edition of Schopenhauer's work our first, more modest, intention was to reprint, with some revision, the English version by R. B. Haldane and John Kemp (London, 1883–6), but in the course of revising we found ourselves recasting rather than refurbishing their text. It soon became clear that I should return to Schopenhauer's original German, and translate it anew. Fortunately, Everyman agreed. I translate from the edition by Arthur Hübscher (Mannheim, 1988), itself based on the edition by Julius Frauenstädt. Word for word I have compared my own version with the pioneering work of Haldane and Kemp and with the more recent and fluent translation by E. F. J. Payne (Colorado, 1958). To both I am grateful, even where I beg to differ.

The translator's task is not easy. Though Schopenhauer has a reputation as the fine stylist among German philosophers, this stylishness lies in his metaphor rather than in his syntax. Many of his sentences are long and involved; their urgency might be conveyed *viva voce* by an impassioned orator, but on the printed page their dynamic can falter. So I have divided these lengthy periods into shorter, simpler sentences; and I have divided long paragraphs, too, often at the single dash with which Schopenhauer has himself marked a new phase in his argument.

The resonances of metaphor are not easily conveyed in the second language; and here literary translation, even of this most literary philosopher, is at odds with a technical subject. While aiming to translate his work with fidelity and clarity, I have tried to resist the temptation to make Schopenhauer's thought more explicit then he has done. It would have been easy to make rough places smooth, but it could not be done without trespass. So, in deference to his intricate system, I have sometimes been rigorously literal rather than elegant. The pessimist's sternly didactic tone and occasional irascible impatience must, in any event, obtrude, as does his sometimes idiosyncratic choice of examples to illustrate an argument. Just as these characteristics should not be glossed over, neither should mechanical transition within the development of his thought.

Always, it is as teasing as it is humbling to ponder how Schopenhauer, an anglophile who tried his hand at translating Kant into English, might have chosen to present in this language his own *The World as Will and Idea*.

J. B.

BOOK ONE

The World as idea

The idea subordinated to the principle of sufficient reason: The object of experience and science

Emerge from your childhood, friend, and awake!

Jean-Jacques Rousseau

§ 1. 'The world is my idea': this is a truth which holds good for everything that lives and knows, though only man can bring it into reflected, abstract consciousness. If he really does this, philosophical discretion has evolved in him. It then becomes clear to him, and certain, that he knows not a sun, and not an earth, but only an eye that sees a sun, a hand that feels an earth; that the world which surrounds him exists only as idea – that is, only in relation to something else, the one who conceives the idea, which is himself.

If any truth can be enunciated *a priori*, it is this; for it expresses the form of all possible and thinkable experience: a form which is more general than all others – than time, or space, or causality – for they all presuppose it. Each of these, which we have recognised as so many particular modes of the principle of sufficient reason, is valid only for a particular class of ideas, whereas the division into object and subject is the common form of all these classes and is the only form under which any idea – of any kind, abstract or intuitive, pure or empirical – is at all possible and conceivable. Thus no truth is more certain, more independent of all others, and less in need of proof, than this: that all that is there for the knowing – that is, this whole world – is only object in relation to the subject, perception of the perceiver – in a word, idea. Of course, this is true of the present just as it is true of every past and of every future, of what is most remote as well as of what is near at hand; for it is true of time and space themselves, in which alone these distinctions arise. Everything that in any way belongs, or can belong, to the world is inevitably affected by this: it is conditioned by the subject, and exists only for the subject. The world is idea.

This truth is by no means new. It was inherent in the sceptical reflections from which Descartes set out. But Berkeley was the first to articulate it positively, and for that his contribution to philosophy will not be forgotten, even though the rest of his doctrine cannot stand the test of time. Kant's initial mistake was to neglect the principle. On the other hand, how early this truth was recognised by the wise men of India, in that it features as the fundamental tenet of the Vedânta philosophy ascribed to Vyasa, is pointed out by Sir William Jones in the last of his essays, 'On the Philosophy of the Asiatics' (*Asiatic Researches*, vol. iv. p. 164): 'The fundamental tenet of the Vedânta school consisted not in denying the existence of matter, that is, of solidity, impenetrability, and extended figure (to deny which would be lunacy), but in correcting the popular notion of it, and in contending that it has no essence independent of mental perception; that existence and perceptibility are convertible terms.' These words amply convey the compatibility of empirical reality and transcendental ideality.

In this first book, then, we consider the world only from this aspect, only in so far as it is idea. The inner reluctance with which anyone supposes the world to be merely his idea, tells him that this view of it, irrespective of its truth, is nevertheless one-sided, and must have been conjured up by some arbitrary abstraction; and yet it is a hypothesis from which he can never free himself. The one-sidedness of this view will be compensated in the next book by means of a truth which is not so immediately certain as the one from which we start here. Only deeper research and more difficult abstraction, the separation of what is different and the amalgamation of what is identical, can lead us to this truth. This truth is solemn, and must for everyone be, if not frightening, then certainly sobering and serious; for it states that each and every one of us can say and must say, 'The world is my will.' But for the present, in this first book we must give our full, undivided attention to that aspect of the world which is the point of departure for our study – the aspect of the knowable – and accordingly we must without reluctance regard all objects which are in any way present – indeed, even our own bodies, as we shall discuss more fully below – only as ideas, and call them mere ideas. In so doing we always abstract only from will (as we hope everyone will be convinced later), which by itself constitutes the other aspect of the world. For as the world is in one aspect entirely *idea*, so in another it is entirely *will*. However, a reality which is neither of these two, but an object in itself (into which even Kant's thing-in-itself has unfortunately degenerated in the course of his work), is the absurd product of a dream, and its credence in philosophy is a treacherous will-o'-the wisp.

§ 2. That which knows all things, and is known by none, is the subject. Accordingly it is the support of the world, is the condition (that is universal and always presupposed) of all phenomenon, of all object; for whatever exists, exists only for the subject. Everyone finds himself to be this subject, but only in so far as he knows, not in so far as he is an object of knowing. But his very body is object, so that even that, from this point of view, we call idea. For the body is an object among objects, and must submit to the laws of objects, although it is an immediate object. Like all objects of perception, it lies within the forms of knowledge – time and space – through which there is plurality. The subject, on the contrary, which is always the knower, never the known, does not come under these forms, but has always been, rather, presupposed by them; so it has neither plurality nor its opposite, unity. We never know *it*, but wherever anything is known, *it* is the knower.

So then the world as idea, the only aspect in which we consider it at present, has two essential, necessary, and insepar- able halves. The one half is the *object*, the forms of which are space and time, and through these plurality. The other half is the subject, which is not in space and time, for it is whole and undivided, in every percipient being. So that any one percipient being together with the object, constitutes the whole world as idea just as fully as do the existing millions; but if this one were to disappear, then the world as idea would cease to be. Thus these halves are inseparable even in thought, for each of the two has meaning and existence only through and for the other, each exists with the other and vanishes with it. The one borders directly upon the other; where the object begins, the subject ends. The mutuality of this limitation is shown by our being able to discover and fully know the essential and hence universal forms of all objects – which are space, time, and causality – even when without knowledge of the object itself, our point of departure is the subject; that is to say, in Kantian language, they lie *a priori* in our consciousness. That he discovered this is one of Kant's principal achievements, and it is a very great achievement. Taking this further, I maintain that the principle of sufficient reason is the collective term for all these forms of the object of which we are *a priori* conscious; and that therefore all that we know purely *a priori* is nothing but the content of that principle and what follows from it; in it all our certain *a priori* knowledge is expressed. In my essay *On the Fourfold Root of the Principle of Sufficient Reason* I have shown in detail how every possible object is subordinate to it; that is, stands in a necessary relation to other objects, on one hand as determined, on the other as determining: this is of such wide application that the whole existence of all objects, in so far as they are objects, ideas and nothing more, derives from their necessary relation to each other, consists only in it, and is thus entirely relative; but of this we shall say more later.[1] [. . .]

§ 3. The difference between the intuitive and the abstract is the chief factor in our distinguishing between our own ideas. Abstract ideas constitute just *one* class of ideas, namely concepts, and on earth these are the property of man alone. The capacity for these, which distinguishes him from all the animals, has always been called *reason*. Later we shall consider these abstract ideas by themselves, but first we shall talk exclusively about the *intuitive ideas*. These comprehend the whole visible world, or the sum total of experience, along with the conditions under which experience is possible. It is, as we have already said, a highly important discovery of Kant's that these very conditions, these forms of the visible world — that is, the absolutely universal element in its being perceived, the property common in the same way to all its phenomena: space and time — even when taken by themselves and apart from their content,

---

[1] [What Schopenhauer means by the principle of sufficient reason is chiefly the cognitive form whereby the material of our senses is connected and organised, thereby enabling us to perceive an orderly world of things. The four ways in which he sees the principle operating are by (1) the law of causality: if the cause is given, the effect must follow; (2) the logical principle that if a premise is given, then the conclusion must follow; (3) the principle relating space and time; and (4) the principle of motivation: that given a motive, an action will ensue. See Appendix for an abstract of Schopenhauer's *Fourfold Root*.]

can be not only thought in the abstract, but also perceived directly; and that this perception or intuition is not some kind of phantasm by recurrence borrowed from experience, but is so entirely independent of experience that, on the contrary, experience should be considered dependent on it, in that the qualities of space and time, as they are known in *a priori* perception or intuition, are for all possible experience valid as laws to which such experience must conform everywhere. Accordingly, in my essay *On the Principle of Sufficient Reason* I have treated space and time, in so far as they are perceived as pure and empty of content, as a special and independent class of ideas. Now this quality of the universal forms of intuition as discovered by Kant – that they may be perceived in themselves and apart from experience, and that they may be known by conformity to law on which mathematics, with its infallibility, is based – is certainly very important, but no less remarkable is the other quality of time and space whereby the principle of sufficient reason – which determines experience as the law of causation and of motive, and determines thought as the law of the basis of judgement – appears here in quite a special form, to which I have given the name *ground of being*. In time this is the sequence of its moments, and in space the position of its parts which reciprocally determine one another *ad infinitum*.

Anyone who from the introductory essay has clearly seen the complete identity of the content of the principle of sufficient reason, despite the variety of its forms, will also be convinced that to know the very simplest of these forms is important to his insight into his own inmost nature. We recognise the simplest form of the principle to be time. Each moment in time exists only in so far as it has effaced the preceding one, its progenitor, and only to be itself in turn as quickly effaced. The past and the future (if we may disregard the consequences of their content) are empty as a dream, and between them runs the present as a mere boundary-line without extension and without duration. Likewise in all the other forms of the principle of sufficient reason we shall find the same emptiness, and shall see that space and time and the whole content of both – that is, all that proceeds from causes and motives – has a merely relative existence, has existence only through and for another like it, that is in its turn only just as permanent. The essence of this viewpoint is old: Heraclitus lamented the eternal flux of things;

Plato degrades the object to that which is ever becoming, but never being; Spinoza called it the doctrine of mere accidents of the one existing and persisting substance. What is thus known as the mere phenomenon, Kant opposes to the thing-in-itself. Lastly, the ancient wisdom of the Indian philosophers declares, 'It is Mâyâ, the veil of deception, which covers the eyes of mortals, and makes them see a world of which one cannot say either that it is, or that it is not: for it is like a dream; it is like the sunshine on the sand which from afar the traveller mistakes for water, or the piece of rope cast to the ground, which he mistakes for a snake.' (These similes are repeated in innumerable passages of the Vedas and the Puranas.) But what all these thinkers mean, and what they are talking about, is nothing more than what we, too, at this moment are considering – the world as idea subordinated to the principle of sufficient reason.

§ 4. [. . .] But as in general the object exists only for the subject, as its idea, so every special class of ideas exists only for an equally special quality in the subject, which is called a faculty of perception. This subjective correlative of time and space in themselves as empty forms, Kant has named pure sensibility; and we may retain this term, as Kant was the first to explore this territory, although it does not fit perfectly, for sensibility presupposes matter. The subjective correlative of matter or of causation (for these two are the same) is understanding, which is nothing more than this. To know causality is its one function, its only power; and it is a great power, embracing much, of manifold application, yet of unmistakable identity in all its manifestations. Conversely all causation, and thus, all matter, hence the whole of reality, is only for the understanding, through the understanding, and in the understanding. The first, simplest, and ever-present manifestation of understanding is the perception of the actual world. This is knowledge of the cause from the effect: hence all perception is intellectual. Nevertheless, it could never attain to perception, were not some one effect immediately recognised, thereby serving as the point of departure. But this is the effect on the animal bodies. So far, then, the animal body is the *immediate object* of the subject; the perception of all other objects becomes possible through it. The changes which every animal body experiences are immediately known, that is, felt; and as these effects are at once referred to their causes, the perception of the latter as *objects* arises. This relation is no conclusion in abstract conceptions; it does not arise from reflection, nor is it arbitrary, but immediate, necessary, and certain. It is the cognitive method of the *pure understanding*, without which there could be no perception; there would only remain a dull plant-like consciousness of the changes of the immediate object, which would succeed each other in an utterly meaningless way, except in so far as they might have a meaning for the will, either as pain or pleasure. But as when the sun emerges, the visible world lies before us, so, at *one* stroke, the understanding, by means of its one simple function, converts dull, meaningless sensation into perception. What the eye, the ear, or the hand feels, is not perception; it is merely data. Only when the understanding passes from the effect to the cause does the world lie before us as perception extended in space, varying in respect of form, persistent through all time in respect of matter; for the understanding unites space and time in the idea of *matter*, that is, effective activity. The world as idea exists only through the understanding and likewise it exists only for the understanding. [. . .]

The process by which children learn to see, as do people who, having been born blind, have had their sight restored by surgery; our seeing singly what has been (by two eyes) doubly sensed; the double vision and double touching which occur when the organs of sense have been displaced from their usual position; the way objects appear the right way, whereas their image in the eye is inverted; the attributing of colour to external objects, whereas it is merely an inner function, a division through polarisation, of the eye's activity; and, lastly, the stereoscope – all these are firm and incontrovertible evidence that perception is not merely of the senses, but is intellectual: that is, *pure knowledge through the understanding of the cause from the effect*. Consequently it presupposes the law of causality, and on the knowledge of this depends all perception, and thus all experience, by virtue of its primary and only possibility. The contrary view – that knowledge of the law of causality results from experience – is false. This was the scepticism of Hume, which was first refuted by this argument [of Kant's]. [. . .]

§ 9. Concepts form a distinct class of ideas, existing only in the mind of man, and entirely different from the ideas of perception which we have considered up till now. We can therefore never attain to a perceptive and, properly speaking, evident knowledge of their nature, but only to a knowledge which is abstract and discursive. Hence it would be absurd to demand that they should be verified in experience, if by experience is meant the real external world which consists of ideas of perception, or that they should be brought before the eyes or the imagination like objects of perception. They can only be thought, not perceived, and only the effects which people produce through them are properly objects of experience. Such effects are language, deliberate and planned action, and science, and all that results from these. Speech, as an object of outer experience, is obviously nothing more than a very comprehensive telegraph which communicates arbitrary signs with the greatest speed and subtlety. But what do these signs mean? How are they interpreted? When someone speaks, do we at once translate his words into pictures in the imagination, which fly past us, quick as lightning, intertwine, move, change shape, draw in the detail according to the deluge of words and their grammatical inflections? What a tumult there would be in our heads while we listened to speech, or read a book! But that is not what actually happens. The meaning of speech is immediately grasped, accurately and distinctly comprehended, without, as a rule, the intervention of fantasies. It is reason which speaks to reason, keeping within its own province. What it communicates and receives are abstract conceptions, ideas that cannot be presented in perceptions, which are formed once and for all, and are relatively few in number, but which yet encompass, contain, and represent all the countless objects of the actual world. This alone explains why an animal can never speak or comprehend, although it has the organs of speech and ideas of perception in common with us. But precisely because words denote this particular class of ideas whose subjective correlative is reason, they are without sense and meaning for animals. Thus language, like every other manifestation which we ascribe to reason, and like everything which distinguishes man from animals, is to be explained by this one, simple factor as its source: concepts, abstract ideas which cannot be presented in perception, universal (not individual) in time and space. Only in specific cases do we pass from the concept to perception, do we construct images as *representatives of concepts* in perception, to which, however, they never do justice. [. . .]

Now, although concepts are fundamentally different from

ideas of perception, they stand in a necessary relation to them, without which they would be nothing. This relation therefore constitutes the whole nature and existence of concepts. Reflection is necessarily a copy, a repetition, of the original world of perception, albeit a special kind of copy in an entirely different material. Thus concepts may quite properly be called ideas of ideas. [. . .]

The Standpoint of Idealism

[...] 'The world is my idea' is, like the axioms of Euclid, a proposition which everyone must recognise as true as soon as he understands it, although it is not a proposition which everyone understands as soon as he hears it. To have brought this proposition to clear consciousness, and to have associated with it the problem of the relationship of the ideal to the real – *i.e.*, of the world in the head to the world outside the head – constitutes, along with the problem of moral freedom, the distinctive character of modern philosophy. For only after men had tried their hand for thousands of years at a mere philosophy of the object did they discover that, among the many things that make the world so puzzling and give us pause for thought, is first and foremost that, however immeasurable and massive this world may be, its existence hangs nonetheless by a single thread: that is, the actual consciousness in which it exists. The world's existence is irrevocably subject to this condition, and this brands it, in spite of all empirical reality, with the stamp of ideality, and therefore of mere phenomenal appearance. As a result, the world must be recognised, at least from this aspect, as akin to dreaming, and indeed as belonging to the same category. For the function of the brain which, during sleep, conjures up a completely objective, perceptible, and even palpable world, must have just as large a share in the presentation of the objective world of our waking hours. For both worlds, although different in their matter, are nonetheless made from the same mould. This mould is the intellect, the function of the brain.

Descartes was probably the first to attain to the degree of reflection which this fundamental truth demands, and consequently he made it the starting-point of his philosophy, though provisionally only in the form of sceptical doubt. By his taking the *cogito, ergo sum* ['I think, therefore I am'] as the only certainty, and by his provisionally regarding the existence of the world as problematical, the essential and only proper starting-point of all philosophy was found, and at the same time its true focus, which is essentially and inevitably the subjective, the individual consciousness. For only this is and remains immediate; everything else, whatever it may be, is mediated and conditioned by it, and is therefore dependent upon it. Hence Descartes is quite properly regarded as the founding father of modern philosophy. Not long afterwards, by travelling further along the same road, Berkeley arrived at idealism proper, *i.e.*, the knowledge that the world which is extended in space (that is, the objective, material world in general) exists as such simply and solely in our idea, and that it is false, and indeed absurd, to attribute to it, as such, an existence apart from all idea and independent of the knowing subject, thus to assume matter as something absolute and possessed of real being in itself. But this very accurate and profound insight really constitutes Berkeley's whole philosophy; he had given it all he had to give.

Thus true philosophy must always be idealistic; indeed, it must be so in order to be merely honest. For nothing is more certain than that no man ever stepped out of his own skin in order to identify himself directly with things which are different from him; but everything of which he has certain, and therefore immediate, knowledge, lies within his own consciousness. Beyond this consciousness, therefore, there can be no immediate certainty; but the first principles of a science must have such certainty. To the empirical standpoint of the other sciences it is quite appropriate to assume the objective world as something absolutely given; but it is not appropriate to the standpoint of philosophy, which by its nature has to go back to what is first and original. Only consciousness is immediately given; therefore the basis of philosophy is limited to facts of consciousness, *i.e.*, it is essentially idealistic.

Realism, which commends itself to the crude understanding by pretending to be factual, starts straight from an arbitrary assumption, and is therefore a figment, for it side-steps or falsifies the very first fact, namely that all we know lies within consciousness. For that the objective existence of things is conditioned by a subject whose ideas they are, and consequently that the objective world exists only as an idea, is no hypothesis, and still less a dogma, or even a paradox proposed for the sake of discussion. It is the most certain and the simplest truth; and its recognition is only made more difficult by its being too simple; and not everyone has sufficient power of reflection to return to the first elements of his consciousness of things. There can never be an absolute and independent existence; indeed such an existence is downright unthinkable. For the objective, as such, always and essentially has its existence in the consciousness of a subject, is thus the idea of this subject, and consequently is conditioned by it, and by the forms of ideation, moreover, which attach to the subject and do not belong to the object.

That the objective world would exist even if there were no conscious being, certainly seems at first sight unquestionable, because it can be thought in the abstract, without bringing to light its inner contradiction. But if we wish to realise this abstract thought, that is, to derive it from ideas of perception from which alone it (like everything abstract) can have content and truth, and if accordingly we try to imagine an objective world without a knowing subject, then we become aware that what we are now imagining is in fact the opposite of what we intended; is, in fact, nothing but the process in the intellect of the knowing subject who is perceiving an objective world, and so it is the very thing we had wanted to exclude. For this perceptible and real world is clearly a phenomenon of the brain; hence there is a contradiction in the assumption that as such it ought also to exist independently of all brains.

The principal objection to the inevitable and essential ideality of all objects, the objection which, distinctly or indistinctly, is voiced in everyone, is probably this: Even my own person is an object for someone else, and is thus his idea, and yet I know for certain that I would exist even if he were not forming an idea of me. But all other objects also stand in the same relation to his intellect as I do; consequently they also would exist without being perceived by him. The answer to this is: That other party, as whose object I now regard my person, is not simply the subject, but in the first instance a knowing individual. Therefore, even if he did not exist, and even, indeed, if there were not any other conscious being apart from myself, the subject (in whose idea alone all objects exist) would still not be thereby cancelled out. For I am myself this very subject, as every knowing conscious being is. Consequently, in the case we are considering, my person would certainly continue to exist, but in turn as idea – in my own knowledge, that is. For even by me it is always known only indirectly, never immediately; because to exist as idea is, always and in every instance, indirect. As object, *i.e.*, as extended, occupying space and acting, I know my body only in the perception of my brain. This is communicated by the senses and, upon data they supply, the percipient understanding performs its function of passing from effect to cause. So, by means of the eye's seeing the body or the hand's touching it, the understanding constructs that extended figure which in space presents itself as my body. But there is not given to me directly, either in some general feeling of bodily existence or in inner self-consciousness, any extension, form, or activity, which would match my own being in such a way that that being would, in order so to exist, require no other party in whose knowledge it presented itself. On the contrary, that general feeling of bodily existence exists directly (as does self-consciousness) only in relation to the will – that is, as agreeable or disagreeable – and as active in the acts of will, which for external perception present themselves as actions of the body. From this it follows that the existence of my person or body as something extended and acting always presupposes a knowing entity distinct from it, because it is essentially an existence in apprehension, in the idea, and hence an existence for some other entity. In fact, it is a phenomenon of brain, irrespective of whether the brain in which it exhibits itself is my own or belongs to another person. In the first case one's own person separates into the knowing and the known, into object and subject, which here as elsewhere stand contrasted one with the other, inseparably and irreconcilably. So if in order to exist as such, my own person always requires a knowing subject, this will hold true no less of all other objects, and to justify their existence independent of knowledge and of the subject of knowledge, was the purpose of the above objection.

However, it is evident that the existence which is conditioned through a knowing subject is only the existence in space, and therefore that of an extended and active being. Only this is always the existence known, and consequently an existence for another. On the other hand, every being that exists in this way may have in addition an existence for itself, for which it requires no subject. Yet this existence for itself cannot be extension and activity (together space-occupation), but is necessarily a being of another kind, that of a thing-in-itself, which, as such, can never be an object. This, then, would be the answer to the principal objection set out above, which accordingly does not refute the fundamental truth that the objectively given world can exist only as idea, and thus only for a subject.

Here we should note also that even Kant, at least in so far as he remained consistent, can have envisaged no objects among his things-in-themselves. For this follows from his proving that space is, like time, a mere form of our perception, which consequently does not belong to things-in-themselves. What is neither in space nor in time cannot be object, either; thus the being of things-in-themselves cannot be objective, but is of quite a different kind, a metaphysical being. Consequently that Kantian principle implies in turn a further principle: that the objective world exists only as idea.

Idealism is, in spite of all that one may say, more persistently and repeatedly misunderstood than anything else, in that it is interpreted as meaning that one is denying the empirical reality of the external world. Hence the recurrent appeal to common sense. This appears in many forms and guises, such as, for example, in the 'basic conviction' of the Scottish school, or in Jacobi's faith in the reality of the external world. By no means does the external world give itself, as Jacobi depicts it, merely on credit and is accepted by us in good faith: it gives itself as what it is, and immediately performs what it promises.

True idealism, on the contrary, is specifically not the empirical, but the transcendental. This leaves the empirical reality of the world untouched, but maintains that every object, in other words, the empirically real in general, is conditioned by the subject twice over; in the first place materially or as object generally, because an objective existence is conceivable only in relation to a subject and as that subject's idea; and in the second place formally, in that the mode or manner of the object's existence — its being perceived per space, time and causality — follows from the subject, and is predisposed in the subject. So the simple or Berkeleian idealism which concerns the object in general, is closely succeeded by the Kantian idealism, which concerns the specially given mode and manner of objective existence. This proves that the whole material world, with its bodies, which are extended in space and, by means of time, have causal relations to one another, and everything that depends upon this — that all this is not something which is given independently of our mind, but which has its basic premises in our brain-functions by means of which, and in which alone, such an objective arrangement of things is possible. For time, space, and causality, upon which all those real and objective events rest, are themselves nothing more than functions of the brain; hence the immutable order of things which supplies the criterion of, and the clue to, their empirical reality itself, proceeds only from the brain, and has its credentials from this alone. All this Kant has expounded fully and thoroughly, save that he talks not of the brain but of 'the faculty of knowledge'. [. . .] The Kantian doctrine [. . .] leads to the insight that things and the whole manner and mode of their existence are inseparably bound up with our consciousness of them. So anyone who has clearly grasped this is soon convinced that it is really absurd to assume that things also exist as such, apart from and independently of our consciousness. We are so deeply immersed in time, space, causality, and the whole regular routine of experience which rests upon them, and we (and indeed the animals) are so perfectly at home in it, and from the start know our way around. This would not be possible if our intellect were of one kind and things were of another kind, but can be explained only from the fact that the two constitute a whole, that the intellect itself creates that order, and exists only for things, while they, in turn, exist only for it.

The subjective and the objective do not form a continuum. That of which we are made immediately conscious is limited by our skin, or rather by the very tips of the nerves which emanate from the cerebral system. Beyond this lies a world of which we have no knowledge except through pictures in our head. Now the question is whether, and to what extent, a world independent of us corresponds to these pictures. Contact between the two could be made only via the law of causality; for only this law leads from what is given to something quite different from it. But this law itself has first of all to prove its validity. It must either be of objective or of subjective origin; but in either case it lies on one river-bank or the other, and therefore cannot serve as the bridge between them. If, as Locke and Hume assumed, it is *a posteriori*, and hence drawn from experience, it is of objective origin, and so itself belongs to the external world in question. Hence it cannot guarantee the reality of this world, for then, according to Locke's method, the law of causality would be proved from experience, and the reality of experience from causality. If, on the contrary, it is given *a priori*, as Kant has more correctly taught us, then it is of subjective origin, and in that case it is clear that accordingly we will always remain in the subjective sphere. For the only thing in perception that is actually given empirically is the accession of a sensation in the organ of sense; and the presupposition that this must have any cause at all is based on a law rooted in the form of our knowledge, *i.e.*, in the functions of our brain. The origin of this law is thus just as subjective as is the sensation itself. The cause of the given sensation – a cause assumed in consequence of this law – presents itself at once in perception as an object which has space and time as the form of its manifestation. But these forms themselves again are entirely of subjective origin; for they are the mode and method of our faculty of perception. That inference from the sensation to its cause which, as I have repeatedly pointed out, lies at the foundation of all sense-perception, is certainly sufficient to signal for us the empirical presence in space and time of an empirical object, and is therefore quite enough for the practical purposes of life; but it is by no means sufficient to afford us any conclusion as to the existence and real nature, or rather as to the intelligible substratum, of the phenomena which in this way arise for us. So, if occasioned by the accession of certain sensations in my sense-organs, there comes about in my mind a perception of things which are extended in space, permanent in time, and causally active, that by no means justifies my assumption that such things exist in themselves – that with these properties belonging simply to them, they exist independently and outside my head.

This is what the Kantian philosophy correctly establishes. Kant's conclusion is related to what Locke had – just as accurately, but more comprehensibly – concluded before him. For even if, as Locke's doctrine permits, external things are assumed to be simply the causes of sensation, there can still be no similarity between the sensation in which the effect consists and the objective character of the cause which occasions it. For the sensation, as an organic function, is primarily determined by the highly artificial and complicated nature of our sense-organs. It is thus merely stimulated by the external cause, but is then completed entirely in accordance with its own laws, and is thus wholly subjective. Locke's philosophy was the critique of the functions of sense; Kant has furnished us with the critique of the functions of the brain. But now to all this we have yet to submit the Berkeleian findings as I have renewed and reasserted them: the conclusion, that is, that every object, whatever its origin, is as object already conditioned by the subject, for it is in essence merely its idea. Realism aims precisely at the object without subject; but it is impossible even to envisage such an object distinctly.

This whole account shows clearly and certainly that the purpose of comprehending the inner nature of things is not to be achieved by the methods of mere knowledge and perception. For knowledge always comes to things from outside, and therefore must for ever remain outside. This purpose could be achieved only by our finding ourselves in the interior of things, which would thereby become known to us directly. Now, in how far this is actually the case is considered in my Second Book. But so long as we remain concerned, as in this First Book, with objective comprehension – that is, with knowledge – the world is, and remains, for us a mere idea, for here there cannot be a path to lead us beyond it.

To adhere to the idealistic viewpoint is, moreover, a necessary counterpoise to the materialistic. The controversy concerning the real and the ideal may also be regarded as a controversy concerning the existence of matter. For it is the reality or ideality of this that is ultimately in question. Does matter, as such, exist only in our idea, or does it also exist independently of it? In the latter case it would be the thing-in-itself; and anyone who takes matter to be self-existent must also, if he is consistent, be a materialist, *i.e.*, he must make matter the principle of explanation of all things. Anyone who, on the contrary, denies its existence as a thing-in-itself is by definition an idealist. Among the moderns only Locke has plainly and directly asserted the reality of matter; and hence his teaching has led, by way of Condillac, to the sensualism and materialism of the French. Only Berkeley has plainly and unreservedly denied matter. Taken to its logical development, the antithesis is thus that of idealism and materialism, represented at its extremes by Berkeley and by French materialists like Holbach. [. . .]

It is just as true that the knower is a product of matter, as that matter is merely an idea of the knower; but it is also just as one-sided. For materialism is the philosophy of the subject that forgets to take account of itself. For that very reason, against the assertion that I am a mere modification of matter, it must be asserted that all matter exists merely in my idea; and it is no less right. Some inkling of this state of affairs seems to have inspired Plato's dictum 'Matter is a lie, and yet true.' [. . .]

On the other hand, there is also something inadequate about the subjective starting-point and first principle 'the world is my idea', partly because it is one-sided, since the world is far more than that (namely the thing-in-itself, will), and indeed its existence as idea is to a certain extent only accidental to it; but partly also because it merely expresses the fact that the object is conditioned by the subject, without at the same time saying that the subject, as such, is also conditioned by the object. For the assertion, 'the subject would still remain a knowing being even if it had no object, i.e., if it had absolutely no idea', is just as false as the assertion of the crude understanding, 'the world, the object, would still exist, even if there were no subject'. A consciousness without an object is no consciousness. As its object, a thinking subject has concepts; a subject of sense-perception has objects with the qualities corresponding to its organisation. If we rob the subject of all its more precise characteristics and forms of its knowledge, all the properties of the object vanish also, and nothing remains but matter without form and quality, which can no more occur in experience than can a subject without the forms of its knowledge, but which stands opposite the naked subject as such, as its reflexion, which can disappear only as and when it does. Although materialism imagines that it is postulating nothing more than this matter – in the form, for instance, of atoms – it is nevertheless unconsciously adding to it not only the subject, but also space, time, and causality, which depend upon special properties of the subject.

The world as idea, the objective world, has thus, as it were, two poles: the knowing subject, simply without the forms of its knowledge, and then crude matter without form and quality. Both are completely unknowable: the subject because it is the knower, matter because without form and quality it cannot be perceived. Yet both are fundamental conditions of all empirical perception. Thus the knowing subject, merely as such, which is a presupposition of all experience, stands opposite, as its pure counterpart, to the crude, formless, and utterly dead (i.e., will-less) matter, which, though not given in any, is presupposed in every experience. This subject is not in time, for time is only the more definite form of all its ideation. The matter which stands over against it is, correspondingly, eternal and imperishable, endures through all time, but is, properly speaking, not even extended, for extension gives form, thus it has no spatial properties. Everything else is caught up in a constant process of coming into being and passing away, while these two represent the serenely motionless poles of the world as idea. The permanence of matter may thus be regarded as the reflexion of the timelessness of the pure subject construed simply as the condition of all object. Both belong to the phenomenon, not to the thing-in-itself, but they are the framework of the phenomenon. Both are discovered only by abstraction, and are not given immediately, pure and for themselves.

The fundamental error of all systems is the failure to recognise this truth, the truth that intellect and matter are correlatives, *i.e.*, that the one exists only for the other, both stand and fall together, the one is only the reflexion of the other, and indeed, they are really one and the same thing regarded from two opposite points of view; and this one thing, I am here anticipating, is the manifestation of the will, or the thing-in-itself. Consequently both are secondary, and therefore the origin of the world is not to be sought in either of the two. But because they fail to recognise this, all systems (with the exception, perhaps, of Spinoza's) have sought the origin of all things in one of those two. For some systems suppose an intelligence, νοῦς, as the absolutely First thing and δημιουργός. It follows that by so doing they are allowing an idea of things and of the world to precede their actual existence; thus they are quite mistakenly drawing a distinction between the real world and the world of idea. Hence matter now comes on the scene as the means of distinguishing the two, as the thing-in-itself. As a result they find themselves at a loss to procure this matter, the ὕλη, in order that when it attaches itself to the bare idea of the world, it may impart reality to it. That original intellect must now either find matter available and to hand, in which case matter is just as much an absolute First as that intellect itself, and we have then two absolute Firsts, the δημιουργός and the ὕλη; or the absolute intellect will produce this matter out of nothing, an assumption which our understanding resists, for it is capable of comprehending the changes which matter undergoes, but not its coming into or its passing out of existence: and at bottom this is precisely because matter is the essential correlative of the understanding.

The systems opposed to these, which make the other of the two correlatives – that is, matter – the absolutely First, posit a matter which would exist without being perceived; and, as emerges quite clearly from all that has been said above, this is a direct contradiction, for by the existence of matter we always mean simply its being perceived. But then these systems will find themselves at a loss to add to this matter (which is their sole absolute First) the intellect which is ultimately to find out about it. [...]

In my system, on the other hand, matter and intellect are inseparable correlatives which exist only for each other, and so exist only relatively. Matter is the idea which intellect forms, and only in the idea formed by intellect does matter exist. Together these two constitute the world as idea, which is the very same as Kant's phenomenon, and is, consequently, something secondary. The primary is what is manifest, the thing-in-itself, which later we shall identify as the will. This is in itself neither the perceiver nor the perceived, but is entirely different from the mode of its manifestation.

These reflections have been as important as they are difficult, and I will round them off by personifying these two abstractions, and presenting them in a dialogue.

THE SUBJECT: I am, and besides me there is nothing. For the world is my idea.

MATTER: What a crazy presumption! *I am*, and besides me there is nothing, for the world is my fleeting form. You are merely the sum of a part of this form, and entirely accidental.

THE SUBJECT: What foolish arrogance! Neither you nor your form would be there without *me*; you are conditioned by me. Anyone who thinks me out of existence, and then believes he can still think you there, is in the grips of a gross delusion, for your existence apart from my idea is a direct contradiction, a nonsense. *You are* simply means that you are perceived by me. My idea is the place where you exist; hence I am the first condition of your existence.

MATTER: Fortunately your impudent assertion will soon be refuted in a real way, and not by mere words. In a few more moments you will actually no longer be. With all your boasting, you will have lapsed into the void, will have drifted past like a ghost, and suffered the fate of all of my transient forms. But *I* will remain, unscathed and undiminished, from millennium to millennium, through infinite time, and without qualms I will observe the play of my changing forms.

THE SUBJECT: This infinite time through which you proudly claim to live, exists, like the infinite space you fill, only in my idea. Indeed, it is merely the form of my idea, the form I carry ready-made within me and in which you show yourself, which receives you, and by means of which you exist in the first place. But the annihilation with which you threaten me does not affect me, for if it did, then you would be annihilated along with me. Rather, it merely affects the individual which temporarily supports me and is, like everything else, my idea.

MATTER: And if I concede this, and go so far as to regard existence (inseparably linked as it is, after all, to that of these fleeting individuals) as something which has an independent life, it will still remain dependent upon mine. For you are a subject only in so far as you have an object; and I am this object. I am its kernel and its content, the permanent part of it, the bonds that bind it together, and without which it would be as incoherent, tenuous and insubstantial as the dreams and fantasies of your individuals; and even their ostensible content they have borrowed, in the last analysis, from me.

THE SUBJECT: You quite properly refrain from disputing my existence on the grounds that it is tied to individuals, for just as inseparably as I am linked to them, you are linked to your sister, form, and have never appeared without her. No eye has yet seen either you or me naked and isolated; for we are both mere abstractions. At bottom it is *one* being that perceives itself and is perceived by itself, but whose being-in-itself cannot consist either in perceiving or in being perceived, since these functions are apportioned separately between the two of us.

BOTH: So, then, we are inseparably joined together as parts of one whole which comprises both of us and exists by virtue of us. Only a misunderstanding can set us against each other and mislead one into disputing the other's existence – along with which his own existence stands or falls.

This totality that encompasses the two is the world as idea, or the phenomenon. Once this is taken away, there will remain only the purely metaphysical, the thing-in-itself, which in the Second Book we shall recognise as the will.

BOOK TWO

BOOK TWO

The World as Will

The objectification of the Will

It is us he inhabits, not the underworld, nor the stars in the sky.
The spirit who lives in us makes those.

[Agrippa von Nettesheim, *Epist.* V]

§ 17. In the first book we considered the idea only as such, that is, only according to its general form. It is true that as far as the abstract idea, the concept, is concerned, we obtained a knowledge of it in respect of its content also, in so far as it has all content and meaning only through its relation to perceptive ideation, without which it would be worthless and empty. So, relying wholly on perceptive ideation, we shall now endeavour to arrive at a knowledge of its content, its more exact definition, and the forms which it presents to us. We are concerned especially to gain insight into their real meaning, that meaning which is otherwise merely felt, but by virtue of which these images do not drift past us, entirely alien and meaningless, as they must otherwise do, but speak to us directly, are understood, and acquire an interest which involves our whole being.

We turn our attention to mathematics, natural science, and philosophy, each of which holds out the hope that it will give us a part of the insight we desire. Now, taking philosophy first, we find it to be a monster with many heads, each of which speaks a different language. It is true that they are not all at variance on the point we are considering here – the significance of the idea of perception. For, with the exception of the Sceptics and the Idealists, the others, for the most part, agree with one another in speaking of an *object* which constitutes the *basis* of the idea, and which, although different in its whole being and nature from the idea, is in all points as similar to it as one egg is to another. But this does not help us, for we do not know how to distinguish such an object from the idea, but find that they are one and the same, for every object always and for all time presupposes a subject, and therefore to the end remains idea. Likewise we recognised objectivity as belonging to the most universal form of the idea, which is just this – division into subject and object. As well as that, the principle of sufficient reason, which is cited in this context, is similarly for us only the form of the idea, the proper combination of one idea with another, but not the combination of the whole finite or infinite series of ideas with something which is not idea at all, and which therefore cannot be presented in perception. [. . .]

If we seek in mathematics the closer knowledge we want of the idea of perception (so far known to us only generally, merely in its form) we find that mathematics treats of these ideas only in so far as they fill time and space, that is, in so far as they are quantities. With the greatest accuracy it will state quantity and extent, but as this is always merely relative – that is to say, merely a comparison of one idea with others, and a comparison drawn only one-sidedly in respect of quantity – this also will not be the information we most seek.

Lastly, if we look at the wide province of natural science, which is divided into many fields, we may first distinguish two main parts. It is either the description of forms, which I call *Morphology*, or the explanation of alterations, which I call *Aetiology*. The first studies the permanent forms, the second studies the changing matter, according to the laws of its transition from one form to another. The first is the whole of the subject that we rather loosely call natural history. In botany and zoology, in particular, it teaches us about the various forms which (despite the ceaseless fluctuation of their individual parts) are themselves permanent, organised, and therefore definitely determined forms; and constitute a great part of the content of the idea of perception. In natural history they are classified, segregated, combined, arranged according to natural and artificial systems, and brought under categories which make possible a general view and knowledge of them all. Further, an infinitely subtle analogy both in the whole and in the parts of these forms, and running through them all (*unité de plan* [unity of plan]) is established, and thus they are similar to complex variations on a theme which is not openly stated. The transfusion of matter into these forms (that is to say, the origin of individuals) is not a main part of the study, for every individual is, as a result of procreation, born of his like – a process equally mysterious among all the species, and which has as yet evaded our clear comprehension. The little that is known on the subject is appropriately included in physiology, which belongs to that part of natural science I have called aetiology. Mineralogy, especially where it becomes geology, inclines towards aetiology, though in substance it belongs to morphology. Aetiology proper comprises all those branches of natural science which are concerned chiefly with the knowledge of cause and effect. The sciences teach how, according to an invariable rule, one condition of matter is necessarily followed by a second specific condition; how one change inevitably determines and produces a second specific change; the demonstration of this is called *explanation*. The principal sciences with this function are mechanics, physics, chemistry, and physiology.

If, however, we are attentive to its teaching, we soon become aware that aetiology can no more give us the information we seek than can morphology. This latter shows us countless infinitely complex forms which are nonetheless related and show an unmistakable family likeness. For us these are ideas, and when considered only in this way, they remain forever alien to us, and in our eyes they are like hieroglyphics which we do not understand. Aetiology, on the other hand, teaches us that, according to the law of cause and effect, this specific condition of matter brings about that second specific condition, and therewith science has explained material state and done its duty. However, it really is doing nothing more than to indicate the proper order according to which the states of matter appear in space and time, and generalising from this, show which phenomenon must necessarily occur at a particular time in a particular place. It thus determines the position of phenomena in time and space, according to a law whose specific content experience has dictated, but whose universal form and necessity is known to us independently of experience. But it gives us not the least inkling of the inner nature of any one of those phenomena: this is called a *force of nature*, and it lies outside the province of causal explanation, which calls the constant uniformity with which manifestations of such a force appear (whenever their known conditions are present) a *law of nature*. But this law of nature, these conditions, and this emergence in a particular place at a particular time, are all that it knows or ever can know. The force itself which manifests itself, the inner nature of the phenomena which occur in accordance with these laws, remains always a secret to it, something entirely strange and unknown in respect both of the simplest and of the most complex phenomena. For although as yet aetiology has most adequately achieved its goal in mechanics, and least adequately in physiology, still the force by virtue of which a stone falls to the ground, or one body repels another, is in essence no less strange and mysterious than that which produces the movement and growth of an animal. The science of mechanics presupposes matter, gravity, impenetrability, the communicability of motion by impact, inertia and so forth as ultimately inexplicable, calls them forces of nature, and their necessary and regular appearance under certain conditions it calls a law of nature. Only after this does its explanation begin, and it consists in indicating accurately and with mathematical exactness, how, where and when each force manifests itself, and in tracing to one of these forces every phenomenon it meets with. Physics, chemistry, and physiology proceed in the same way in their own field, only they presuppose much more and accomplish less. Consequently, the most complete aetiological explanation of the whole of nature can never be more than an inventory of forces which cannot be explained, and an authoritative statement of the rule according to which phenomena appear in time and space, follow on from and make way for one another. But the inner nature of the forces which thus appear would always have to remain unexplained by this aetiology, because the rule which it follows does not extend to that, and it could go no further than phenomena and their classification. In this respect it may be compared to a section of a piece of marble which shows many different veins side by side, but does not allow us to trace the course of the veins from the interior of the marble to its surface. Or, if I may use an absurd but more striking comparison, the philosophical investigator must always feel towards the complete aetiology of the whole of nature like a man who has somehow stumbled into a group of people whom he does not know at all, and in which each person in turn presents another to him as his friend and kinsman, and thereby makes them to some degree acquainted, and yet this man, while at each introduction he expresses pleasure, asks himself constantly: 'But how the devil do I come to be in this company?'

Thus about those phenomena which we know only as our ideas, aetiology can never give us the information that we want and which could carry us beyond this point. For, after all its explanations, they still remain quite strange to us, as mere ideas whose significance we do not understand. The causal connection merely gives us the rule and the relative order of their appearance in space and time, but gives us no further detail about the phenomenon which comes about in this way. Moreover, the law of causality itself has validity only for ideas, for objects of a definite class, and it has meaning only in so far as it presupposes them. Thus, like these objects themselves, it always exists only in relation to a subject, that is, conditionally; and so it is known just as well if we start from the subject, *i.e.*, *a priori*, as if we start from the object, *i.e.*, *a posteriori*, as Kant has taught us.

But what now spurs us on to investigate is precisely that we are *not* satisfied with knowing that we have ideas, that they are this idea or that idea, and that they are connected according to this law and that law which collectively we term the principle of sufficient reason. We want to know the significance of these ideas; we ask whether this world is nothing more than idea, in which case it could only pass by us like an insubstantial dream or a ghostly vision, not worth our notice; or whether it is also something else, something besides idea, and if so, what. This much is certain, that what we seek must be completely and by its whole nature radically different from the idea; that the forms and laws of the idea must therefore be completely foreign to it; further, that if we take the idea as our starting-point, we cannot reach our goal by way of the path marked by those laws which merely connect objects with ideas. This last is the function of the forms of the principle of sufficient reason.

Thus we see already that *from without* we can never arrive at the real nature of things. However much we investigate, we can never reach anything but images and names. We are like a man who goes round a castle, in vain seeking an entrance, and sometimes sketching the external walls. And yet this is the path taken by all the philosophers before me.

§ 18. In fact, the meaning we seek of that world which is present to us only as our idea, or the transition from the world as mere idea of the knowing subject to whatever it may be besides this, would never be found if the investigator himself were nothing more than the pure knowing subject (a winged cherub without a body). But he is himself rooted in that world; he finds himself in it as an *individual*, that is to say, his knowledge which is the necessary support of the whole world as idea, is nonetheless entirely communicated through the medium of a body whose affections are, as we have shown, the starting-point for the understanding in its perception of that world. His body is, for the pure knowing subject, an idea like every other idea, an object among objects. To that extent its movements and actions are only as familiar to him as the changes in all other perceived objects, and would be just as strange and incomprehensible to him if the riddle of their meaning were not resolved for him in an entirely different way. Otherwise he would see his actions follow upon given motives with the constancy of a law of nature, just as the fluctuation in other objects follows upon causes, stimuli, or motives. But he would not understand the influence of the motives any more than the connection between every other effect which he sees and its cause. The inner nature of these incomprehensible manifestations and actions of his body he would then call a force, a quality, or a character, as he pleased, but he would have no further insight into it. But all this is not what actually happens; instead, the subject of knowledge, in his phenomenal existence as an individual, is given the answer to the riddle, and the answer is *will*. This, and this alone, gives him the key to his phenomenal existence, reveals the meaning, shows him the inner working of his being, of his behaviour, of his movements.

The body is given in two entirely different ways to the subject of knowledge, who becomes an individual through his identity with it. It is given as an idea in intelligent perception, as an object among objects and beholden to the laws of objects. And it is also given in quite a different way, as that which is immediately known to everyone, and is signified by the word *will*. Every true act of will is also at once and without exception a movement of the body: he cannot really will the act without being at the same time aware that it manifests itself as a movement of his body. The act of will and the movement of the body are not two different things objectively known, which the bond of causality unites; they do not stand in the relation of cause and effect; but they are one and the same, although given in two entirely different ways – immediately, and again in perception for the understanding. The action of the body is nothing but the act of the will objectified, *i.e.*, passed into perception. It will be shown later that this is true of every movement of the body, not merely those which follow upon motives, but also involuntary movements which follow upon mere stimuli, and, indeed, that the whole body is nothing but objectified will, *i.e.*, will become idea. All this will be proved and will become clear in the course of this work. In one respect, therefore, I shall call the body the *objectivity of will*; as in the previous book, and in the essay *On the Principle of Sufficient Reason*, in accordance with the one-sided point of view intentionally adopted there (that of the idea), I called it the *immediate object*. Thus in a certain sense we may also say that will is the knowledge *a priori* of the body, and the body is the knowledge *a posteriori* of the will. Resolutions of the will which relate to the future are merely deliberations of the reason about what we shall will at a particular time, and are not actual acts of will. Only the carrying out of the resolve stamps it as will, for till then it is never more than an intention that may be changed, and that exists only in the reason *in abstracto*. It is only in reflection that to will and to act are different; in reality they are one. Every true, genuine, immediate act of will is also, at once and immediately, a visible act of the body. And, corresponding to this, every impression upon the body is also, on the other hand, at once and immediately an impression upon the will. As such it is called pain when it is opposed to the will; gratification or pleasure when it is in accordance with it. The gradations of the two are widely different. It is quite wrong, however, to call pain and pleasure ideas, for they are by no means ideas, but immediate affections of the will in its manifestation, the body: they are a willing or not-willing, unsought and momentary, of the impression which the body endures.

Only a few quite specific impressions made on the body do not excite the will, and it is through these alone that the body is an immediate object of knowledge, for, as perceived by the understanding, the body is already an indirect object like all others. These impressions are to be treated directly as mere ideas, and are therefore to be seen as an exception to what we have just said. We mean the affections of the purely objective senses of sight, hearing, and touch, though only in so far as the relevant sense-organs are affected in the manner characteristic, specific and natural to them. This is so extremely weak a stimulation of the heightened and specifically modified sensibility of these parts of the body that it does not affect the will, but only supplies the understanding with the data from which the perception is born, undisturbed by any excitement of the will. But every affection of these sense-organs which is stronger than that, or alien, is painful (that is to say, averse to the will) and thus they also belong to its objectivity. Nervous debility is indicated where impressions which ought to be just strong enough to make them data for the understanding reach the higher degree at which they move the will, that is to say, excite pain or pleasure (though more often pain, albeit to some extent dull and undefined) so that it not only makes sounds and strong light painful to us, but causes a generally unhealthy and hypochondriacal disposition. The cause is not clearly recognised. The identity of the body and the will shows itself also in, among other things, the way in which every vehement and immoderate movement of the will, *i.e.*, every emotion, brings immediate shock to the body and its inner workings, and disturbs the course of its vital functions. This is shown in detail in my *Will in Nature*.

Lastly, the knowledge which I have of my will, though it is immediate, cannot be separated from the knowledge that I have of my body. I know my will not as a whole, not as a unity, not completely according to its nature, but I know it only in its individual acts, thus in time, which is the form of the phenomenal aspect of my body as it is of every object. So the body is a condition of the knowledge of my will. Accordingly, I cannot really imagine this will apart from my body. In the essay on the principle of sufficient reason, the will, or rather the subject which wills, is treated as a special class of ideas or objects. But even there we saw this object become one with the subject; that is, we saw it cease to be an object. We there called this union the miracle κατ᾽ ἐξοχήν [*par excellence*] and the whole of the present work is to a certain extent an explanation of this. In so far as I know my will actually as object, I know it as body. But then I am back again to the first class of ideas drawn up in that essay, *i.e.*, real objects. As we pursue this topic we will appreciate that that first class of ideas is illuminated and clarified only by those of the fourth class as set out in the essay, which could no longer be properly opposed to the subject as object, and that accordingly we must learn to understand the inner nature of the law of causality which is valid in the first class, and of what happens in accordance with this law, from the law of motivation which governs the fourth class.

The identity of the will and the body, which we have now set out provisionally, can be proved only as it has been done here for the first time, and as it is to be done again and again in the course of our inquiry. By 'proved' we mean raised from the immediate consciousness, from knowledge in the concrete to knowledge of the reason, or transferred into abstract knowledge. On the other hand, by its very nature it can never be demonstrated, that is, deduced as indirect knowledge from some other knowledge more direct, since it is itself the most direct knowledge; and if we do not grasp it and retain it as such, we shall in vain expect to receive it again in some indirect way as derivative knowledge. It is knowledge of quite a special kind, whose truth for that very reason cannot properly be brought under any of the four rubrics under which I have classified all truth in the essay *On the Principle of Sufficient Reason*, §29 – the logical, the empirical, the transcendental, and the metalogical – for it is not, like all these, the relevance of an abstract idea to another idea, or to the necessary form of perceptive or of abstract ideation, but it is the relevance of a judgement to the relationship which an idea of perception, the body, has to that which is not an idea at all, but something *toto genere* different: that is, will. I should like therefore to distinguish this from all other truth, and call it κατ' ἐξοχήν [*philosophical truth*]. We can turn the formulation of this truth in different ways and say: My body and my will are one; or, What as an idea of perception I call my body, I call my will, in so far as I am conscious of it in an entirely different way which cannot be compared to any other; or, My body is the *objectivity* of my will; or Apart from its being my idea, my body is still my will, and so forth.

§ 19. In the first book we were reluctantly driven to explain our own body as merely idea of the subject which knows it, like all the other objects of this world of perception. But it has now become clear that what enables each one of us consciously to distinguish the idea of our own body from all other ideas which in other respects are similar to this idea, is that our body appears in consciousness in quite another way *toto genere* different from idea, and this we denote by the word *will*; and that it is just this double knowledge which we have of our own body that gives us information about it, about its activity and its response to motives, and also about what it suffers as a result of outside intervention; in a word, about what it is, not as idea, but over and above that, what it is *in itself*. We have not such direct information about the character, activity and tolerance of all the other real objects.

It is precisely by way of this special relationship to one body that the knowing subject is an individual; and viewed apart from this relationship, his body is to him only an idea like all other ideas. But the relationship by virtue of which the knowing subject is an *individual*, is for that very reason a relationship which exists only between him and a single one of all his ideas, and so he is conscious of this one not merely as an idea, but at the same time in quite a different way, as a will. If, however, he abstracts from that special relationship, from that twofold and completely heterogeneous knowledge of what is one and the same thing, then that *one*, the body, is an idea like all other ideas. Therefore, in order to understand the matter, the individual who knows must either assume that what distinguishes that one idea from others is merely that his knowledge stands in this double relationship to it alone; that only into this one object of perception is he allowed insight in two modes simultaneously, and that this is to be explained not by the difference of this object from all others, but only by the difference between the relationship of his knowledge to this one object, and its relationship to all other objects. Or else he must assume that this object is essentially different from all others; that it alone of all objects is at once both will and idea, while the rest are only ideas, *i.e.*, only phantoms. Thus he must assume that his body is the only real individual in the world, *i.e.*, the only phenomenon of will and the only immediate object of the subject. That other objects, considered merely as *ideas*, are like his body – that is that they, as it does, fill space (which itself can be present only as idea), and also, like it, are causally active in space – is indeed demonstrably certain from the law of causality which is *a priori* valid for ideas, and which admits of no effect without a cause; but apart from the fact that from an effect we may infer some cause or other, but not specifically a like cause, we are still in the realm of mere ideas, in which alone the law of causality is valid, and beyond which realm the law can never take us.

But whether the objects known to the individual only as ideas are, like his own body, nonetheless manifestations of a will, is, as was said in the First Book, the real meaning of the question as to the reality of the external world. To deny this is the purport of *theoretical egoism*, which as a consequence holds all phenomena, excepting its own individual self, to be phantoms, exactly as practical egoism does in respect of practical matters – a man regards and treats only his own person as a real person, and all others as mere phantoms. While theoretical egoism can never be proved false, in philosophy it has never been used other than as a sceptical sophism, *i.e.* only for show. As a serious conviction, on the other hand, it could be found only in a madhouse, and as such it would need not so much a refutation as a cure. So we will concern ourselves with it no further, but regard it as merely the last bastion of scepticism, which is always polemical. Now, our knowledge, which is always bound to individuality and is thereby limited, implies that each of us can only *be one*, while on the other hand, he can *know all*; and it is precisely this limitation that creates the need for philosophy. So we who for this very reason are through philosophy striving to extend the limits of our knowledge, will treat the sceptical argument of theoretical egoism which obstructs our path as a small frontier-post. While the fortress can never be taken, neither can the garrison ever sally forth from it, so that we may pass it, and without danger leave it in our rear.

The double knowledge given in two completely different ways, which each of us has of the character and functioning of his own body, has now been clearly brought out. We shall accordingly make further use of it as a key to the character of every phenomenon in nature, and shall judge all objects which are not our own bodies (and are consequently not given to our consciousness in the double mode, but only as ideas) according to the analogy of our own bodies, and shall hence assume that as on one hand they are idea, just like our bodies, and in this are of the same kind, so on the other hand, what remains of objects when we set aside their existence as idea of the subject, must in its inner nature be the same as that in us which we call *will*. For what other kind of existence or reality should we attribute to the rest of the material world? Where should we obtain the elements from which to put together such a world? Besides will and idea nothing is known to us, or is even conceivable. If we wish to attribute the greatest known reality to the material world which exists immediately only in our idea, we give it the reality which our own body has for each of us; for that is for everyone the most real thing. But if we now analyse the reality of this body and its actions, apart from its being our idea, we find nothing in it but the will; with that even its reality is exhausted. So nowhere can we find another kind of reality to attribute to the material world. Thus if the material world is to be something more than merely our idea, we must say that besides being idea (that is, in itself and according to its inmost nature) it is what we find immediately in ourselves as *will*. I say according to its inmost nature; but we must first get to know more closely the will's essential character so that we can distinguish from it what belongs not to the will itself, but to its eventual manifestation, which has many grades. Such, for example, is its being accompanied by knowledge and, conditional upon this, its being determined by motives. As we shall see farther on, this does not belong to the essential nature of will, but merely to its most distinct manifestation as animal or human being. So if I say that the force which attracts a stone to the ground is according to its nature, in itself, and apart from all idea, will, no one will foolishly interpret this statement as meaning that the stone moves in accordance with a known motive, just because in man the will manifests itself in this way. But let us now more clearly and in detail demonstrate, offer reasons for, and develop to its full extent, what till now has been presented only provisionally and generally.

§ 20. The will, as we have said, proclaims itself primarily in the voluntary movements of our own body, as this body's nature in itself, as what it is besides being object of perception, idea. For these voluntary movements are nothing but the visible aspect of the individual acts of will, with which they are directly coincident and identical, and from which they are distinguished only by the form of the knowable into which they have passed, that is, the form of idea.

But these acts of will have always a ground or reason outside themselves, in motives. Yet these motives never determine more than what I will at *this* time, in *this* place, and under *these* circumstances, not *that* I will in general, or *what* I will in general, that is, the maxim which characterises all my volition. So the character of my volition cannot be explained from the motives, which merely determine its manifestation at a given point in time: they are merely the occasion of my will's showing itself. But the will itself lies outside the jurisdiction of the law of motivation, which determines nothing but its appearing at each point in time. Only given my empirical character is the motive a sufficient ground of explanation for my action. But if I abstract from my character and then ask why I should ever will this and not that, no answer is possible, because it is only the *manifestation* of the will that is subordinate to the principle of sufficient reason, and not the will itself, which in this respect is to be called *groundless*. At this point I am taking for granted Kant's doctrine of the empirical and intelligible character, and also my own treatment of the subject in *The Fundamental Problems of Ethics*. I shall also have to speak more fully on the question in the Fourth Book. For the present, I have only to point out that the establishing of one phenomenon by means of another, as the deed is established here by means of the motive, does not at all conflict with the phenomenon's real nature as will which itself has no *ground*; for as the principle of sufficient reason in its every embodiment is merely the form of knowledge, its validity extends only to the idea, to the phenomenon, to the visibility of the will, but not to the will itself that is becoming visible.

If now every action of my body is the manifestation of an act of will in which, under given motives, my will as a whole, and hence my character, expresses itself again, then manifestation of the will must be the indispensable condition and presupposition for that action. For the will's becoming manifest cannot depend upon something which does not exist directly and only through it, which consequently is for it merely accidental, and through which its manifestation itself would be merely accidental: *that* condition is the whole body itself. So the body itself must be manifestation of the will, and it must be related to my will as a whole (that is, to my intelligible character, whose phenomenal appearance in time is my empirical character) as the individual action of the body is related to the individual act of the will. The whole body, then, must be simply my will become visible, must be my will itself, so far as this is object of perception, an idea of the first class. To support this I have already stated that every impression made upon my body also affects my will at once and immediately, and in this respect is called pain or pleasure, or, in its lower degrees, agreeable or disagreeable sensation; and also, conversely, that every violent movement of the will, every emotion or passion, shocks the body and disturbs the course of its functions. Indeed we can also give an aetiological account, albeit very incomplete, of my body's origin, and a somewhat better account of its development and continuing existence; and this is the substance of physiology. But physiology explains its theme only in precisely the same way as motives explain action. Thus the physiological explanation of bodily functions no more detracts from the philosophical truth – that this body's whole existence and all its functions are merely the objectification of that very will which appears in the same body's outward actions in accordance with motives – than does the grounding of the individual action in the motive, and the necessary consequence of the action upon the motive, conflict with the fact that any action is, of its nature, only the manifestation of a will which is itself groundless. If, however, physiology tries to trace even these outward actions, the directly voluntary movements, to causes in the organism – for example, if it explains the movement of the muscles as resulting from the accession of fluids ('like the contraction of a cord which becomes wet', says Reil in his *Archiv für Physiologie*, vi, 153) – even supposing that one really could furnish a thorough explanation of this kind, this would still never invalidate the immediately certain truth that every voluntary motion (*functiones animales*) is the manifestation of an act of will. And it is just as implausible that the physiological explanation of vegetative life (*functiones naturales vitales*), however far it may advance, could ever invalidate the truth that the whole of this evolving animal life is the manifestation of will. In general, then, as we have discussed above, no aetiological explanation can ever tell us more than the necessarily determined position in time and space of a particular manifestation, its necessary emergence then and there, according to a fixed law; but the inner nature of every phenomenon cannot ever be fathomed in this way, and is presupposed by every aetiological explanation, and merely designated by the terms 'force', or 'law of nature', or, if we are speaking of action, 'character' or 'will'. So although when character and motive are given, every action follows of necessity; and although growth, nourishment, and all the changes of the animal body occur in accordance with causes which act of necessity (stimuli), yet the whole series of actions, and consequently every individual act, and likewise also its condition, (that is, the whole body itself which accomplishes it, and consequently also the process through which and in which the body exists) are nothing but the manifestation of the will, the becoming visible, *the objectification of the will*. This is the basis for the perfect conformity overall of the human and animal body to the human and animal will, a conformity resembling, though far surpassing, that between a purpose-made tool and the will of its maker, and on this account appearing as appropriateness, *i.e.*, the assumption that the body can be interpreted teleologically. So the parts of the body must perfectly correspond to the principal desires through which the will manifests itself; they must be the visible expression of these desires. Teeth, throat, and intestines are objectified hunger; the genitals are objectified sexual desire; the grasping hands, the swift feet, correspond to the strivings of the will which they represent at a grade later and more indirect. As the human form generally corresponds to the human will generally, so the individual physique corresponds to the individually modified will – the character of the individual – and hence it is entirely and in every detail indicative and expressive of the individual character. [. . .]

§ 21. By way of these reflections the reader may have gained a knowledge also *in abstracto*, and therefore clearly and certainly, of what everyone knows directly *in concreto*, *i.e.*, as feeling. This is the knowledge that this will is the real inner nature of his own phenomenal being which manifests itself to him as idea both in his actions and in the permanent substratum of these, his body. This will comprises what is most immediate in his consciousness, though it has not as such completely passed into the form of idea in which object and subject stand over against each other, but makes itself known in a direct manner, in which one does not quite clearly distinguish subject and object, yet to the individual himself it becomes recognisable not in its entirety, but only in his separate acts. The reader who with me may have gained this conviction will find that it will automatically become for him the key to the knowledge of the inmost being of the whole of nature; for he now applies it to all those phenomena which are given to him, not like his own phenomenal existence in direct knowledge as well as in indirect, but only in the latter, and so merely one-sidedly as *idea* alone.

This will of which we are speaking he will recognise as the inmost nature not only in those phenomena which are closely similar to his own, in men and animals, but further reflection will lead him also to recognise the force which stirs and vegetates in the plant, and indeed the force by which the crystal is formed, that by which the magnet turns to the North Pole, the force whose shock he experiences from the contact between different metals, the force which appears in the elective affinities of matter as repulsion and attraction, separation and combination, and, lastly, even gravitation, which pulls so powerfully through all matter, draws the stone to the earth and the earth to the sun – all these he will recognise as different only in their phenomenal existence, but in their inner nature as identical, as what is directly known to him so intimately and so much better than anything else, and which, in its most distinct manifestation, is called *will*. Only this use of reflection forbids us to stop at the phenomenon, and instead leads us beyond it to the *thing-in-itself*. Phenomenon means idea, and nothing more. All idea, of whatever kind it may be, all *object*, is *phenomenon*, but the *will* alone is *thing-in-itself*. As such it is emphatically not idea, but *toto genere* different from it; it is that of which all idea, all object, is the phenomenal appearance, the visibility, the objectification. It is the inmost nature, the kernel, of every individual thing, and also of the whole. It is manifest in every force of nature that operates blindly, and it is manifest, too, in the deliberate action of man; and the great difference between these two is a matter only of degree of the manifestation, not in the nature of what is made manifest.

§ 22. Now, if we are to think as an object this thing-in-itself (we will keep the Kantian term as a standing phrase) – which, as such will never be object, because all object has in its turn already become its mere manifestation, and is no longer itself – we must borrow for it the name and concept of an object, of something in some way objectively given, consequently of one of its own manifestations. But if this is to facilitate understanding, then it must be none other than the most complete of all its manifestations, *i.e.*, the most distinct, the most developed, and directly enlightened by knowledge. The human *will* satisfies this requirement exactly. But it is important to note that here we are, of course, only making use of a *denominatio a potiori*, through which, for that very reason, the concept of will is given greater scope than it has hitherto had. To recognise the identical in different phenomena, and difference in similar phenomena, is, as Plato so often remarks, a *sine qua non* of philosophy. But till now it was not recognised that every force in nature which is in any way striving and active is essentially identical with will, and hence the myriad phenomena which are only different species of the same genus were not seen as such, but were considered heterogeneous. Consequently there could be no word to denote the concept of this genus. And so I name the genus after its most important species, the more easily accessible direct knowledge of which guides us to the indirect knowledge of all other species. But anyone who is incapable of extending the concept as required here, will be under a misapprehension: for by the word *will* he would persist in understanding only that one species of it which till now has been exclusively designated – the will which is guided by knowledge, and only in accordance with motives, and indeed only abstract motives, in short, the will as it shows itself when directed by reason – which, as we have said, is only the most obvious manifestation of will. The inmost essence of this manifestation, which is known to us directly, we must now distinctly separate in thought and then transfer it to all the weaker, less obvious manifestations of the same nature, and thus we accomplish the required extension of the concept of will. From the opposite point of view I should be equally misunderstood by anyone who might think that it is all the same in the end whether we designate this inner nature of all phenomena as *will* or call it by any other name. This would be the case if that thing-in-itself were something whose existence we merely *inferred*, and thus knew only indirectly and only in the *abstract*. Then, indeed, we might call it what we pleased; the name would stand merely as the symbol of an unknown quantity. But the word *will*, which, like a magic spell, is to reveal to us the essence of everything in nature, by no means designates an unknown quantity, something arrived at only by inference, but rather something that is in every way immediately recognised and so familiar to us that we know and understand what will is far better than anything else. The concept of *will* has hitherto commonly been subordinated to that of *force*, but I do the very opposite, and desire that every force in nature should be thought of as will. It should not be supposed that this is merely quibbling, or of no consequence; rather, it is of the greatest significance and importance. For the concept of *force* is, like all other concepts, based ultimately on perceptive knowledge of the objective world, that is to say, the phenomenon, the idea; and from this the concept is drawn. It is an abstraction from the realm in which cause and effect reign, *i.e.*, from ideas of perception, and means the causal nature of causes at the point at which this causal nature can be explained no further aetiologically, but is the necessary presupposition of all aetiological explanation. The concept *will*, on the other hand, is of all possible concepts the only one which has its source *not* in the phenomenal, *not* in the mere perceptive ideation, but comes from within, and arises in the most immediate consciousness of each of us. In this each of us knows his own individuality, knows it according to its essential nature, knows it immediately, apart from all form, even that of subject and object: knows it and at the same time *is* this individuality, for here the knowing subject and the object become one and the same. If, therefore, we derive the concept of *force* from that of *will*, we have in fact derived the less known from what is infinitely better known; indeed, from the one thing that is really immediately and fully known to us, and have very greatly extended our knowledge. If, on the contrary, we subsume the concept of *will* under that of *force*, as has till now been done, we are renouncing the only immediate knowledge of the inner nature of the world that we have, in allowing it to be engulfed in a concept which is abstracted from the phenomenon, and with which we can therefore never transcend the phenomenon.

§ 23. The *will* as a thing in itself is totally different from its phenomenon, and entirely free from all the forms of the phenomenal. Since the will enters into these forms only at the very moment when it manifests itself, they have to do only with its *objectivity*, and are alien to the will itself. Even the most universal form of all idea, that of being object for a subject, is irrelevant to it; still less the forms which are subordinate to this and which collectively have their common expression in the principle of sufficient reason. To these, we know, time and space belong, and consequently plurality also, which exists and has become possible only through these. In regard to this last I shall call time and space the *principium individuationis*, borrowing a term from the old scholastic philosophy proper, and I ask my readers to note this, once and for all. For only through the medium of time and space does that which is one and the same, both by its nature and in its concept, appear as different, as a plurality of co-existent and successive phenomena. Time and space are in consequence the *principium individuationis*, the subject so much pondered and disputed among the schoolmen whose arguments Suarez has collected and recorded (*Disp.* 5, Sect. 3). The will as a thing-in-itself lies (as follows from what I have said above) outside the province of the principle of sufficient reason in all its forms, and hence is completely groundless, although each one of its manifestations is wholly subordinated to the principle of sufficient reason. It is, in addition, free from all *plurality* although its manifestations in time and space are countless. It is itself one, though not in the sense in which an object is one, for the unity of an object can be known only by contrast with a possible plurality; nor yet in the sense in which a concept is one, for the unity of a concept originates only by way of abstraction from a plurality; but it is one as that which lies outside time and space, the *principium individuationis*, *i.e.*, the potential for plurality. Only when all this has become quite clear to us through the subsequent examination of the will's phenomena and different manifestations, can we fully understand the meaning of the Kantian doctrine that time, space and causality do not belong to the thing-in-itself, but are only forms of knowing.

The will's groundlessness has, indeed, been recognised where as man's will it manifests itself most conspicuously, and this has been called free, independent. But the groundlessness of the will itself has obscured the necessity to which it is subject wherever it is manifest. So man's actions have been interpreted as free, which they are not, for every individual action follows with strict necessity from the impact of motive on character. All necessity is, as we have already said, the relationship of the consequent to the reason, and strictly no more. The principle of sufficient reason is the universal form of all phenomenon, and man in his action must, like every other phenomenon, be subject to this. But because in self-consciousness the will is known directly and in itself, in this consciousness lies also the consciousness of freedom. But we fail to see that the individual, the person, is not will as a thing-in-itself, but is a *phenomenon* of will, and as such is already determined and has entered into the form of the phenomenal, the principle of sufficient reason.

Hence the strange fact that everyone regards himself as *a priori* perfectly free, even in his individual actions, and believes that at any moment he could embark upon a different path in life, which would mean his becoming a different person. But *a posteriori*, through experience, he finds to his astonishment that he is not free, but subject to necessity; that in spite of all his resolutions and reflections he does not alter his conduct, and that from the beginning of his life to the end of it, he must continue to play the very role which he himself condemns, and, as it were, play to the end the part he has undertaken. I cannot pursue these thoughts further here, for they belong, being ethical, to another part of this work. In the meantime I wish only to point out that the *phenomenon* of the will, which in itself is groundless, is as such subordinated nonetheless to the law of necessity (that is, the principle of sufficient reason). I say this so that the necessity with which natural phenomena occur should not be a stumbling block to our recognising them as manifestations of will.

Only those changes which have no ground other than a motive, *i.e.*, an idea, have been regarded as manifestations of will. Hence in nature a will has been attributed only to man, or, at a pinch, to animals; for only the attaining of knowledge, the perceiving of ideas, is of course, as I have said elsewhere, the authentic and exclusive characteristic of animal life. But that the will is active even where no knowledge directs it, we see at once in the instinct and the mechanical skill of animals. There is no question here of their having ideas and knowledge, for the goal towards which they are working just as if it were a motive they recognised, is unknown to them. Thus their action takes place here without motive, is not directed by the idea, and shows us before all else and most distinctly how without any knowledge the will may be active. The bird of a year old has no idea of the eggs for which it builds a nest; the young spider has no idea of the prey for which it spins a web; nor has the ant-lion any idea of the ant [his prey] for which he digs a pit for the first time. In the timber in which it is to await its metamorphosis the larva of the stag-beetle makes the hole twice as big if it is going to be a male beetle as it does if it is going to be a female, so that if it is a male there may be room for the horns, of which, however, it has still no inkling. In such activity the will is clearly operative, as it is in the other actions of these creatures, but this is blind activity which, while accompanied by knowledge, is not guided by it. Once we have understood that idea as motive is not a necessary and essential condition of the activity of the will, we shall more easily recognise the activity of will in cases where it is less apparent. For example, we shall no more attribute the snail's shell to a will foreign to the snail but directed by knowledge, than we shall think that the house which we ourselves build comes into being through will other than our own; but we shall recognise both houses as the work of a will which objectifies itself in both phenomena – a will which in us works according to motives, but in the snail still works only blindly as creative instinct which is directed outwards. In us, too, the same will operates blindly in many ways: in all our bodily functions which are not directed by knowledge, in all its vital and vegetative processes, digestion, circulation, secretion, growth, reproduction. Not only the body's actions, but the body itself in its entirety is, as we have shown above, phenomenon of the will, objectified will, concrete will. All that happens in it must therefore happen through will, although here this will is not directed by knowledge, does not decide in accordance with motives, but operates blindly according to causes, which in this case are called *stimuli*.

I call a *cause*, in the narrowest sense of the word, that state of matter which, while it is necessarily producing a second state, itself suffers a change just as great as the change it is causing; this sequence is expressed in the rule, 'action and reaction are equal'. Further, in the case of what is properly speaking a cause, the effect increases exactly in proportion to the cause, and in its turn therefore also the reaction. So that, once the mode of operation is known, the degree of the effect may be measured and calculated from the degree of the intensity of the cause; and conversely the degree of the intensity of the cause may be calculated from the degree of the effect. Such causes, properly so called, operate in all the phenomena of mechanics, chemistry, and so forth; in short, in all the changes in inorganic bodies. On the other hand I give the name *stimulus* to a cause that sustains no reaction proportional to its effect, and the intensity of which does not vary directly in proportion to the intensity of its effect, with the result that the effect cannot be measured by it. On the contrary, a small increase in the stimulus may cause a very great increase in the effect, or conversely, it may neutralise the previous effect altogether, and so on. All effects upon organic bodies as such are of this kind: thus all properly organic and vegetative changes in the animal body follow from stimuli, not from mere causes. But the stimulus, like any cause, and motive, never determines anything beyond the point of time and space at which the manifestation of each force is to emerge, and does not determine the inner nature of the force itself which is becoming manifest. The inner nature we know from our previous argument to be will, and hence we attribute to it both the unconscious and the conscious changes of the body. The stimulus mediates, makes the transition between the motive – which is causality that has passed through knowledge – and the cause in the narrowest sense. In individual instances it is sometimes nearer a motive, sometimes nearer a cause, but it can still be distinguished from each of these. Thus, for example, the rising of the sap in a plant occurs as a response to stimulus and cannot be explained from mere causes, according to the laws of hydraulics or capillary attraction; yet it is certainly assisted by these, and by and large it is very close to a purely causal change. On the other hand, the movements of the [honeysuckle-like] *Hedysarum gyrans* and the *Mimosa pudica* [whose leaves fold when touched], although still resulting from mere stimuli, are very like movements which result from motives, and seem almost to want to make the transition. The contraction of the pupils of the eyes as the light increases is due to stimuli, but it passes into movement which is due to motive; for it occurs because light too strong would painfully affect the retina, and to avoid that we contract the pupils. The occasion of an erection is a motive, because it is an idea, yet it operates with the necessity of a stimulus: that is to say, it cannot be resisted, but we must banish the idea in order to render it ineffective. This is also the case with nauseating things which make us want to vomit.

We have just treated the instinct of animals as an actual mediating link, of quite a different kind, between movement following upon stimuli and action following upon a known motive. Now we might be tempted to regard breathing as another connecting link of this kind, for whether it belongs to the voluntary or to the involuntary movements has been debated, that is to say, whether it results from motive or stimulus, and perhaps it may be explained accordingly as something which lies midway between the two. [. . .] However, in the end we must count it among the expressions of will which result from motives. For other motives, *i.e.*, mere ideas, can determine the will to restrict it or accelerate it, and like every other voluntary action, it gives the impression that we could discontinue, stop – and, of our own choice, suffocate. And in fact we could do so if any other motive influenced the will powerfully enough to outweigh the pressing need for air. According to some accounts Diogenes actually put an end to his life in this way (Diog. Laert. VI. 76). This would be a compelling example of the influence of abstract motives, *i.e.*, of the predominance of properly rational over merely animal will. That breathing is at least partially determined by cerebral activity is shown by the fact that prussic acid kills by first of all paralysing the brain, and so by indirectly stopping the breathing; but if the breathing be artificially maintained till the numbing of the brain has passed, death will not ensue. At the same time, by the way, breathing offers us the most striking example of the fact that motives act with just as much necessity as stimuli, or as causes in the narrowest sense of the word; and that similarly they can be put out of action only by contrary motives, as pressure is neutralised by counter-pressure. For, in the case of breathing, the illusion that we can stop when we like is incomparably weaker than in the case of other movements which result from motives; because in breathing the motive is very urgent, very imminent, and to gratify it is very easy, for the muscles which accomplish it are never tired, nothing, as a rule, prevents it, and the whole process is upheld by the person's most inveterate habit.

And yet all motives act with the same necessity. The recognition that necessity is common both to movements following upon motives and those following upon stimuli, makes it easier for us to understand that even what takes place in our bodily organism in response to stimuli and quite routinely, is nonetheless essentially will, which in all its manifestations, though never in itself, is subordinated to the principle of sufficient reason, that is, to necessity. Accordingly, we shall not stop at recognising animals in their actions as much as in their whole existence, physique and organisation, as manifestations of will, but shall extend to plants, too, this immediate knowledge of the essential nature of things that is given to us alone. All the movements of plants follow from stimuli; for the absence of knowledge, and the movement following from motives which is conditioned by knowledge, constitutes the only essential difference between animals and plants. Therefore, what for the idea manifests itself as plant life, as mere vegetation, as blind energy of growth, we shall claim, in accordance with its inner nature, for will, and recognise it as just the same as constitutes the basis of our own phenomenal being, as it expresses itself in our actions, and even in the whole existence of our body itself, too.

It remains only for us to take the final step, and to extend our thesis to all those forces which in nature act in accordance with universal, immutable laws under which all those bodies move which, being wholly without organs, are not susceptible to stimuli, and cannot perceive motive. The key to the understanding of the inner nature of things (which only the immediate knowledge of our own existence was able to give us) we must use now to unlock those phenomena of the inorganic world which are most remote from us. When we scrutinise them closely, we observe the tremendous, irresistible force with which rivers hurry down to the sea, the persistence with which the magnet turns again and again to the North Pole, the readiness with which iron flies to the magnet, the eagerness with which in electricity opposite poles strive to be re-united, and which, just like human desire, is the more intense for being thwarted: when we see the crystal swiftly and suddenly form with such symmetry (plainly only a striving, quite decisive and precisely determined, in different directions, which is arrested and captured by torpidity) when we observe the process of selection by which bodies repel and attract each other, combine and separate, when they are set free in a fluid state, and liberated from the bonds of rigidity; lastly, quite immediately, when we feel how a burden which hampers our body by its gravitation towards the earth, insistently presses and weighs upon it in pursuit of its own tendency; when we observe all this, it will cost us no great effort of the imagination, even at so great a distance, to recognise our own nature. What in us pursues its purposes by the light of knowledge, here, in the weakest of its manifestations, strives only blindly, dumbly, partially and immutably, yet because wherever it is, it is one and the same, both of these must bear the name *will*, just as the first dim dawn shares the name *sunlight* with the rays at noon. For the name *will* denotes the being-in-itself of everything in the world, and the sole kernel of every phenomenon.

Yet the discrepancy indeed, the apparently total difference, between the phenomena of inorganic nature and the will which we perceive as the core of our own being, arises chiefly from the contrast between the wholly determined conformity to law of the one species of phenomena, and the apparently lawless arbitrariness of the other. For individuality is a dominant feature of mankind. Every person has a character of his own; hence the same motive has not the same influence on everyone, and a thousand small details which occupy the ample scope of one man's ken, while they are unknown to other people, modify its effect. For this reason a deed cannot be predicted on the basis of the motive alone, for the other factor is wanting: the close knowledge of the individual character, and of the discernment which goes with it. On the other hand, the manifestations of natural energies mark the opposite extreme in this respect. They act according to universal laws, without deviation, without individuality, in circumstances which are open to view, subject to the most exact predetermination; and the same natural energy appears in its million phenomena in precisely the same way. To throw light on this point and to demonstrate the identity of the *one* indivisible will in all its very different phenomena, in the weakest as much as in the strongest, we must first of all consider the relation of the will as thing-in-itself to its phenomenon, that is, the relation of the world as will to the world as idea. This paves the way for us towards a more profound exploration of the whole topic treated in this Second Book.

§ 24. We have learnt from the great Kant that time, space, and causality, with the system they impose, and with the potential for all their modes, are present in our consciousness quite independently of the objects which appear in them and which constitute their content; or, in other words, whether our starting-point is the subject or the object, they are equally accessible. Thus it is as correct to call them forms of intuition or perception of the subject as it is to call them qualities of the object *in so far as it is object* (in Kant's term, phenomenon), that is, *idea*. We can also regard these forms as the irreducible boundary between object and subject: hence, while all objects must be manifest in them, the subject, too, independently of the object thus manifest, has them totally in its possession and in its sight. But if the objects manifest in these forms are not to be empty phantoms, but are to have a meaning, they must refer to something, must be the expression of something which is not in its turn, like themselves, object, idea, an existence merely relative (that is, for a subject), but which exists without such dependence upon something which stands over against it as a condition of its being, and independent of the forms of such a thing, *i.e.*, is specifically *not idea*, but a *thing-in-itself*. Accordingly, it could at least be asked: Are these ideas, these objects, anything else in addition to and apart from their being ideas, objects of the subject? And what would they then be in this sense? What is that other aspect of them which is *toto genere* different from idea? What is the thing-in-itself? The *will*, we have answered; yet for the time being I hold that answer in reserve.

Whatever the thing-in-itself may be, Kant was right in his conclusion that time, space and causality (which we have later recognised as forms of the principle of sufficient reason, which is itself the general expression of the forms of the phenomenon) could not be its properties, but could accede to it only after, and in so far as, it had become idea: that is to say, they belonged only to its phenomenal existence, not to itself. For since the subject perceives and constructs them entirely out of itself, independently of all object, they must appertain to *existence qua idea*, not to what becomes idea. They must be the form of the idea as such, but not qualities of what has assumed this form. They must be implicit (not in concept but in actuality) in the fundamental polarity of subject and object, and consequently they must be only the more specific condition of any form of knowledge, of which the universal condition is that polarity itself. Now, what in the phenomenon, in the object, is in its turn conditioned by time, space and causality (in that it can become idea only by means of these): namely, *plurality*, through co-existence and succession, *change* and *permanence* through the law of causality, *matter* which can become idea only under the presupposition of causality, and lastly, all that becomes idea only by means of these – all this is not essentially the property of what is here manifest, what has passed into the form of idea, but belongs merely to this form itself. And conversely, what in the phenomenon is *not* conditioned by time, space and causality, and cannot be related to them nor explained in accordance with them, is precisely that in which the thing being manifest, the thing-in-itself, directly reveals itself. Accordingly, what is proper to knowledge *as such*, and hence to the *form* of knowledge, is necessarily most completely knowable, that is to say, clearest, most distinct and amenable to the most exhaustive investigation; but not what in itself is *not* idea, *not* object, but which has become knowable only through entering these forms, in other words, has become idea, object. So only what depends solely upon being known, upon existing *qua* idea (not upon that which *becomes* known, and has only *become* idea), and hence which belongs equally to everything that is known and which for that very reason is to be found just as well when our starting-point is the subject as when we start from the object – only this can unstintingly provide knowledge which is satisfying and exhaustive, a knowledge crystal-clear even where it runs deep. But this source of knowledge flows only from those forms of all phenomena of which we are conscious *a priori*, and which may be expressed collectively as the principle of sufficient reason. The forms of this principle which relate to perceptive knowledge – our sole concern here – are time, space, and causality. The whole of pure mathematics and pure natural science *a priori* is based on these alone. Hence it is only in these sciences that knowledge finds no obscurity, does not stumble upon the inexplicable (the groundless, *i.e.*, the will), on what cannot be further teased out. In this respect Kant wanted, as we have said, to give the name 'science' specially, and even exclusively, to these branches of knowledge, as well as to logic. But, on the other hand, these branches of knowledge show us nothing more than mere connections, relevance of one idea to another, form devoid of all content. All content which they receive, every phenomenon which fills these forms, contains something which is no longer completely knowable in its whole nature, something which can no longer be entirely explained through something else, something, then, which is groundless, through which knowledge instantly loses its persuasive clarity and forfeits its perfect transparency. But what eludes investigation here is precisely the thing-in-itself, is that which is essentially not idea, not object of knowledge, but has become knowable only by entering that form. The form is originally alien to it, and the thing-in-itself can never become entirely one with it, can never be derived from mere form, and, since this form is the principle of sufficient reason, can never be completely *understood*. Hence, even if all mathematics gives us exhaustive knowledge of what in phenomena is quantity, position, number, in a word, spatial and temporal relations; even if all aetiology gives us a complete account of the regular conditions under which phenomena, with all their determinations, become manifest in time and space, but teaches us nothing more, for all that, than why in every instance each and every phenomenon must appear precisely here and now; even with their help we will never penetrate to the inner nature of things. There will always remain something which no explanation is allowed to challenge, but which, on the contrary, it always takes for granted: the forces of nature, the set way in which things behave, the quality and character of every phenomenon, that which is without ground, that which does not depend upon the form of the phenomenal, does not depend on the principle of sufficient reason, and is something to which this form in itself is foreign, but is something which has entered this form, and now appears according to its law. But the law determines only the process of becoming manifest, not *what* becomes manifest; it determines only the manner, not the substance of the phenomenon; it determines only the form, not the content. Mechanics, physics, and chemistry teach us the rules and laws according to which the forces of impenetrability, gravitation, rigidity, fluidity, cohesion, elasticity, heat, light, affinity, magnetism, electricity, and so forth, operate; that is to say, the law, the rule which these forces observe in respect of every instance of their entering time and space. For all our pretence, the forces themselves remain *qualitates occultae*. For it is no less than the thing-in-itself, which through its becoming manifest, exhibits these phenomena. Yet it is itself entirely different from them. Although in its manifestation it is completely subordinated to the principle of sufficient reason as the form of the idea, it can never itself be derived from this form, and so cannot be fully explained aetiologically, can never be fully and finally accounted for. Although it is perfectly comprehensible in so far as it has assumed that form, that is, in so far as it is phenomenon, its inner nature is not in the least explained by its being so comprehensible. The more probable the proposition, and the more it contains of what cannot by any other means be thought or presented in perception (like spatial relations, for example), the clearer and more satisfactory it is as a result. Correspondingly, the less purely objective content it has, or the less reality, properly speaking, is given in it. And conversely, the more there is in it which must be understood as pure chance, and the more it strikes us as given merely empirically, the more proper objectivity and true reality is there in such a proposition, and at the same time, the more that is inexplicable, that is, that cannot be deduced from anything else beyond that.

In every age some aetiology or other has mistakenly tried to reduce all organic life to chemistry or to electricity, and in turn to reduce all chemistry (that is to say, quality) to mechanism (activity determined by the shape of the atoms), and to reduce this, in turn, partly to the subject of phoronomy (*i.e.*, time and space so brought into association that movement is possible), sometimes to the subject of mere geometry (*i.e.*, position in space) much in the same way as by methods that are purely geometrical we, rightly, deduce the diminution of an effect from the square of the distance, and work out the theory of the lever. In the last analysis, geometry can merge with arithmetic, which because of its one dimension, is the most intelligible, the clearest and most thoroughly comprehensible form of the principle of sufficient reason. The atoms of Democritus, the vortex of Descartes, are specific instances of the method which I am characterising more generally here. [. . .] Finally, the crude materialism which at this very moment, in the middle of the nineteenth century, presents itself refurbished, unaware that it is not original, is of the same type. Obdurately denying vital force, it tries first to explain the phenomena of life from physical and chemical forces, and to attribute those in turn to the mechanical effects of the matter, position, form, and motion of imagined atoms; and in this way it would like to trace all the forces of nature back to thrust and counter-thrust as its thing-in-itself. Accordingly even light is said to be the mechanical vibration, or perhaps even undulation, of an imaginary ether, postulated for this end. This ether, if it reaches the eye, beats rapidly upon the retina, and gives us the knowledge of colour. So, for example, a rate of four hundred and eighty-three billion beats per second produces red, and seven hundred and twenty-seven billion beats in a second produces violet, and so on. (People who are colour-blind would then be those who cannot count the beats, we must suppose!). [. . .] Aetiology will have achieved its purpose once it has identified and classified as such all the original forces of nature, and established their mode of operation, *i.e.*, the law according to which, under the sway of causality, their phenomena become manifest in time and space, and determine their position with regard to one another. But certain original forces will always remain unaccounted for; there will always remain as an insoluble residue a content of phenomena which cannot be attributed to their form, and thus cannot be explained from something else in accordance with the principle of sufficient reason.

For in everything in nature there is something for which no ground can ever be cited, of which no explanation is possible, and no ulterior cause is to be sought. This is the specific nature of its activity, *i.e.*, the nature of its existence, its being. It is true that of a thing's each and every effect a cause may be demonstrated, a cause from which it follows that the thing had to act at precisely this time and precisely in this place; but no cause can ever be found from which it follows that the thing should act in *some* way and act precisely in *this* way. Even if it has no other qualities, if it is merely a mote in a sunbeam, it will still exhibit this unfathomable something, if only as weight and impenetrability. But this, I say, is to the mote what his *will* is to a man; and like man's will it is by its nature not subject to explanation; indeed, it is in itself identical with this will. A motive can probably be cited for the will's every manifestation, for the will's every act, at a particular time and in a particular place; and in consequence of this motive, and given the person's character, this act must inevitably take place. But no reason can ever be claimed for the person's having this character, or for his willing anything at all, or for its being, among several motives, precisely this one and no other, that moves his will; or indeed, for there being any motive at all which can move it. What in man is the unfathomable character that is taken for granted in every explanation of his actions from motives is, in every inorganic body, its definitive quality – the mode of its action, the manifestations of which are elicited by impressions from without, while it is itself, on the other hand, determined by nothing extraneous, and thus is also inexplicable. Its particular manifestations, through which alone it becomes visible, are subordinated to the principle of sufficient reason; it is itself groundless. The kernel of this was accurately perceived by the schoolmen, who called it *forma substantialis* (Suarez, *Disputationes Metaphysicae* xv 1).

It is an error great as it is common that the most frequent, most universal and simplest phenomena are those that we best understand; but these are only the ones to which we have grown most accustomed – accustomed, that is, both to seeing them and to our own ignorance in relation to them. It is just as inexplicable to us that a stone should fall to the ground as that an animal should move. It has been supposed, as we have remarked above, that, starting from the most universal forces of nature (gravitation, cohesion, impenetrability), one might explain from them the rarer forces, which operate only under a combination of circumstances (for example, chemical quality, electricity, magnetism); and that from these one might finally understand the organism and the life of animals, and even the nature of human knowing and willing. Men quietly resigned themselves to starting from mere *qualitates occultae* which they had given up trying to elucidate because they intended to build on them, not to excavate beneath them. That sort of thing cannot, as we have said, succeed. But apart from that, a building so built would never stand on firm foundations. Of what use are explanations which only lead us back in the end to something just as puzzling as the problem from which we started? Do we in the end understand more about the inner nature of these universal natural forces than about the inner nature of an animal? Is not the one as much a closed book to us as the other? – unfathomable because it is without ground, because it is the content, the substance of the phenomenon, which can never be derived from the form, from the manner, from the principle of sufficient reason. But we, whose purpose here is to practise not aetiology but philosophy (that is, not relative but absolute knowledge of the real nature of the world) take the opposite course, and start what we know immediately and most completely, from what is fully and entirely familiar to us, from what is closest to us, in order to understand what we know only remotely and partially and indirectly. From the most powerful, most significant, and most distinct phenomenon we want to gain an understanding of the phenomenon that is weaker and less complete. Of everything except my own body I know one aspect only – that of the idea: the inner nature of everything else is inscrutable and a deep secret, even if I know all the causes which bring about change in these things. Only by comparison with what happens in me if my body performs an action when I am influenced by a motive – only by comparison with the inner nature of my own changes determined by external reasons – can I gain insight into the way in which these lifeless bodies are changed under the influence of causes, and so understand what their inner nature is: my knowing the cause of its becoming manifest will tell me merely the rule of its appearing in time and space, and nothing more than that. I can make this comparison because my body is the only object of which I know not merely the *one* aspect, that of the idea, but also the other aspect which is called *will*. Thus, instead of believing that I would better understand my own organic nature, and thereafter my own knowing and willing and my being moved by motives, if only I could attribute them to my being moved by causes *via* electricity, chemistry and mechanics, I must, in so far as I am pursuing philosophy and not aetiology, learn on the contrary to understand, first and foremost from being myself moved by motives, the inner nature of the simplest and commonest movements of the inorganic body which I see as following from causes. I must recognise the inscrutable forces which manifest themselves in all natural bodies as identical in kind with what in me is the will, and as differing from it only in degree. That is to say, the fourth class of ideas set out in the essay *On the Principle of Sufficient Reason* must become for me the key to knowledge of the inner nature of the first class, and by means of the law of motivation I must come to understand the inner meaning of the law of causality.

Spinoza (*Epist*. 62) says that if a stone which has been catapulted through the air had consciousness, it would think that it was flying of its own will. I add only that the stone would be right. That catapulting is for the stone what the motive is for me, and what in the case of the stone, in the condition it has assumed, appears as cohesion, gravitation, rigidity, is essentially the same as what I recognise in myself as will, and what the stone also, if it were granted the insight, would recognise as will. In this passage Spinoza focuses on the necessity with which the stone flies, and he wants, quite rightly, to extend this necessity to that of a person's particular act of will. I have in mind, on the other hand, the inner nature which is vital as its *sine qua non* to imparting meaning and validity to all real necessity (*i.e.*, effect following upon a cause). In people this is called character, while in a stone it is called quality, but it is the same in each.

When it is known immediately, it is called *will*. In the stone it is visible, is object, in the weakest degree, while in man it is in the strongest degree visible and object. [. . .]

§ 25. We know that *plurality* is necessarily conditioned by space and time, and is conceivable only in them; and in this context we call them the *principium individuationis*. But we recognised time and space to be forms of the principle of sufficient reason, the principle in which all our knowledge *a priori* is expressed. However, as we have argued above, this *a priori* knowledge, as such, applies only to the knowableness of things, not to the things themselves, *i.e.*, it is only our form of knowledge, it is not a property of the thing-in-itself. The thing-in-itself is, as such, free from all forms of knowledge, even the most universal, that of being an object for the subject; in other words, the thing-in-itself is something altogether different from the idea. If, now, this thing-in-itself is *the will*, as I believe I have amply and convincingly proved it to be, then, regarded as such and apart from its manifestation, it lies outside time and space, and thus knows no plurality, and is consequently *one*. Yet, as I have said, it is one not in the sense in which an individual or a concept is one, but as something to which the potential for plurality, the *principium individuationis*, is an alien condition. The plurality of things in space and time, which collectively constitute the *objectification* of will, does not, for that reason, affect the will itself, which, despite it, remains indivisible. It is not that there is somehow a smaller part of will in the stone and a larger part in the human being, for the relationship of part and whole belongs exclusively to space, and loses its meaning as soon as we turn aside from this form of intuition or perception. 'More' and 'less' are applicable only to the *phenomenon* of will, that is, its visibility, its objectification. There is a higher degree of this in the plant than in the stone; in turn, a higher degree in the animal than in the plant: indeed, the emergence of will into visibility, its objectification, has gradations as innumerable as there are between the dimmest twilight and the brightest sunlight, between the loudest note and its faintest echo. We shall return later to consider these grades of visibility that belong to the will's objectification, to the mirroring of its inner character. But just as the gradations of its objectification do not directly affect the will itself, even less is it affected by the plurality of phenomena at each of these stages, that is, by the number of individuals of each form, or by the number of separate manifestations of each energy. For this plurality is directly conditioned by time and space, in which the will itself never engages. The will reveals itself just as completely and as much in *one* oak as in millions: their number and multiplication in space and time has no significance for the will itself, but only for the plurality of individuals who in space and time have knowledge and are even multiplied and dispersed. Yet the multiplicity of these individuals relates not to the will itself, but only to its manifestation. Hence we might even argue that if, *per impossible*, a single creature, even the most insignificant, were to be entirely annihilated, the whole world would necessarily perish with it. The great mystic Angelus Silesius expresses this conviction:

> God cannot live, I know, one moment without me,
> As soon as my life ends, He, too, must cease to be.

Thinkers have tried by one means or another to make the immeasurable universe more comprehensible for the individual, and have then made that the occasion for moralising on, for instance, the relative smallness of the earth, and even of man; then again, on the contrary, they have moralised on the greatness of mind in this little man − a mind that can guess at, grasp, and even measure the greatness of the universe, and such like. This is all very well; but to me, when I consider the vastness of the world, the most important factor is that this existence-in-itself, of which the world is the manifestation, cannot, whatever it may be, have its true self spread out and dispersed in this fashion in boundless space, but that this endless extension belongs solely to its manifestation, while existence-in-itself, on the contrary, is present entire and undivided in everything in nature and in everything that lives. Hence we lose nothing if we linger in contemplation over only one of its phenomena, and we gain true wisdom not by measuring the boundless world, nor (more to the purpose) by travelling personally through endless space, but by investigating some one individual phenomenon in its entirety in an attempt fully to know and to understand its true and specific nature.

Accordingly, the subject to be studied in detail in our next book, as every student of Plato will already have guessed, is that these different grades of the will's objectification which are manifest in innumerable individuals, exist as their unattained models or as the eternal forms of things, not themselves emerging into time and space (which are the medium of individual phenomena), but remaining fixed, not subject to any change, always being, never having finally become, while the particular things arise and pass away are, always becoming and never are. These *grades of the will's objectification* are nothing other than *Plato's Ideas*. I touch on this now so that later I can use the word Idea in this sense [on the distinction between 'Idea' and 'idea', see Editorial Introduction VI]. So in my work the word is always to be understood in the genuine and original meaning given to it by Plato, and is not in any way to be associated with those abstract productions of dogmatising scholastic reason which Kant has characterised by using inappropriately and unjustly the word Plato had already adopted and used most fittingly. By *Idea*, then, I understand every definite and fixed *grade of the will's objectification* in so far as it is thing-in-itself and thus remote from plurality. These grades are, of course, related to individual things as their eternal forms or prototypes. Diogenes Laertius (III. 12) expresses this famous Platonic doctrine most briefly and pithily:

> Plato has said that the Ideas in nature exist, so to speak, as patterns; and that everything else only resembles them and exists as their copies.

§ 26. The most universal forces of nature present themselves as the lowest grade of the will's objectification. Some of these forces appear in all matter without exception, functioning as gravity and impenetrability, whereas others have dispersed through the available matter in such a way that certain of them dominate one species of matter while others dominate another species (thereby constituting its specific difference), functioning as rigidity, fluidity, elasticity, electricity, magnetism, chemical properties and qualities of every kind. They are in themselves immediate manifestations of will, just as human activity is, and as such they are groundless, like human character; only their particular phenomena are subject to the principle of sufficient reason, like the particular acts of men. They can never, on the other hand, themselves be called either effect or cause, but are the prior and presupposed conditions of all causes and effects through which their own nature unfolds and is revealed. For this reason it is silly to seek the cause of gravity or of electricity, for they are original forces. They *do*, of course, undeniably manifest themselves in accordance with the law of cause and effect, so that their each and every separate manifestation has a cause which is itself, in turn, a similar separate manifestation which determines that this force must express itself here, must here emerge into space and time; yet the force itself is by no means the effect of a cause, nor is it the cause of an effect. Hence, to say 'gravity is causing the stone to fall' is also incorrect, for the cause here is, rather, proximity to the earth, in that it is attracting the stone. Move the earth away and the stone will not fall, although gravity is still where it had been. The force itself lies quite outside the chain of causes and effects which presupposes time in that this chain has meaning only in relation to time; the force, however, lies outside time. The individual change is always caused by, in turn, another change just as individual, rather than by the force of which it is the manifestation. For what always confers its effectiveness on a cause, however often it may operate, is a force of nature, and as such, it is groundless, *i.e.*, it lies outside the chain of causes and outside the province of the principle of sufficient reason altogether. It is known in philosophy as the immediate objectivity of the will that is the 'in-itself' of the whole of nature; but in aetiology, in this context physics, it is presented as an original force, *i.e.*, a *qualitas occulta*.

At the higher grades of the will's objectivity, and especially in man, we see individuality assume prominence. It shows itself through the wide variety of individual character, *i.e.*, through the personality in its entirety, expressed outwardly through a strongly marked individual physiognomy, and involving the whole physique. No animal has this individuality to a degree that approaches this, though the higher animals have a trace of it; but the character of the species completely predominates over it, and for this reason they have little individual physiognomy. The lower the species, the more every trace of the individual character merges with the common character of the species, and only the physiognomy of the species remains. We know the psychological character of the species, and from that we know exactly what is to be expected of the individual. In the human species, on the other hand, every individual requires to be studied and fathomed separately, and because of the potential for dissimulation which first emerges only with the faculty of reason, it is extremely difficult to predict how he will behave. It is probably relevant to this difference between the human species and all the others that the furrows and convolutions of the brain, which are not yet present to any degree in birds and are still only very faint in rodents, are even in the higher animals far more symmetrical on both sides, and more constantly the same in each individual, than they are in man. Additionally, we should consider it a phenomenon of this peculiar individual character which distinguishes men from all the lower animals that in the animals the sexual instinct seeks its satisfaction without picking and choosing, while in man this choice is pursued in an instinctive way that is independent of all reflection, so that it surges to become a violent passion. So while every man is to be regarded as a specially determined and characterised phenomenon of will, and indeed to a certain extent as a special Idea, in the animals this individual character is wholly absent, in that only the species has characteristic significance. The more remote these animals are from man, the fainter the trace of this individual character, so that, ultimately, plants have only those individual characteristics that can be attributed entirely to the favourable or unfavourable external influences of soil, and of climate, or to other chance circumstance. So, at the last, in the inorganic kingdom of nature all individuality disappears utterly. Only the crystal is to be regarded as to a certain extent an individual: movement in definite directions is arrested by crystallisation in such a way that the path of this movement is made permanent. The crystal is, at the same time, a cumulative repetition of its nuclear form, bound into unity by an Idea, just as the tree is an aggregate of the single growing fibre which is displayed in the leaf's every rib, in every leaf, in every branch. This repeats itself, and to some extent makes each of these appear to be a separate growth which feeds parasitically on the bigger growth, so that the tree is, like the crystal, a systematic aggregate of small plants, albeit nothing short of the sum total can represent an indivisible Idea – that is, this particular grade of the will's objectification. But between the individuals of the same species of crystal there can be only such a difference as is produced by external contingency: we can even induce the formation, in any species, of big crystals or of small crystals, as we choose.

But the individual as such (that is, with traces of an individual character) is not to be found at all in inorganic nature as we have found it in organic nature. All the phenomena of inorganic nature are manifestations of universal natural forces, *i.e.*, of those grades of the will's objectification which do not objectify themselves (as in organic nature) through the variety of individualities which, piecemeal, express the whole of the Idea; on the contrary they show themselves only in the species, and in each separate phenomenon they present the species in its entirety and without deviation. Because time, space, plurality, and the state of being conditioned by causes do not belong to the will or to the Idea (the grade of the will's objectification) but only to their particular phenomena, a force of nature like, for example, gravity or electricity, must show itself as such in precisely the same way in all its millions of phenomena, and only external circumstances can modify the phenomenon. This unity of character in all its phenomena, the unalterable constancy of their occurrence as soon as, initiated by causality, conditions are right, is called a *law of nature.* Once this law has become familiar to us through our own experience, we can accurately predict and calculate the manifestation of the force of nature which the law makes explicit and establishes. But it is just this regularity of the phenomena of the lower grades of the will's objectification which makes them appear so different from the phenomena of the same will in the higher (that is to say, the more distinct) grades of its objectification. In animals and in people, and in their activity, individuality is evinced more or less strongly or weakly, as is the susceptibility to motives which, because they are embedded in the faculty of knowledge, often remain hidden from the observer. Hence the identity of the inner nature of the two kinds of phenomena has till now gone entirely unrecognised.

If we start from the knowledge of the particular, and not from that of the Idea, the infallibility of the laws of nature may surprise us, and even, at times, make us shudder with awe. It might astonish us that nature never once forgets her laws; that if, for example, it has once been according to a law of nature that where certain substances come together under given conditions, a chemical combination will take place, or gas will form, or they will combust: if these conditions are fulfilled, whether through our doing or just by chance (and in this case the promptness is the more astonishing, because unexpected), today just as well as a thousand years ago, the phenomenon occurs at once and without delay. We feel the wonder of this most keenly with phenomena which are rare, and occur only in very complex circumstances, but which, given those conditions, have been predicted. For example, when certain metals touch, alternating between like metal and an acidified moisture, the silver leaf placed between the extremities of this sequence will suddenly burst into a green flame; likewise, under certain conditions, a hard diamond will change into carbonic acid. It is the ghostly omnipresence of the forces of nature that takes us by surprise then, and we notice here what in everyday phenomena no longer strikes us: how the connection between cause and effect is really as mysterious as that in fiction between a magic formula and the genie that unfailingly appears when conjured up by it. On the other hand, if we have thoroughly grasped the philosophical insight that a force of nature is a definite grade of the will's objectification, that is to say, a definite grade of what we, too, recognise as our own inmost nature, and that this will, in itself and distinct from its phenomena and their forms, lies outside time and space, and hence that plurality (which is conditioned by time and space) is a property not of the will, nor directly of the grade of its objectification, *i.e.*, the Idea, but only of the phenomena of the Idea; and if we remember that the law of causality is meaningful only in relation to time and space, in that there it determines the position of the teeming phenomena of the different Ideas in which the will reveals itself, governing the order in which they are to become manifest; if, I say, with this insight the deeper meaning of Kant's great doctrine has dawned on us – the doctrine that time, space, and causality do not belong to the thing-in-itself, but merely to the phenomenon, that they are only the forms of our knowledge, not qualities of things in themselves – then we shall understand that astonishment at the regularity and the prompt operation of a force of nature, astonishment at the perfect parity of all its millions of phenomena and their unfailingly regular occurrence, is really like that of a child or a savage who, when for the first time he looks through a many-facetted glass at a flower, marvels that the countless flowers he sees are absolutely identical, and counts the petals of each of them, one by one.

So every universal, original force of nature is in essence only the objectification of will at a low grade, and we call every such grade an eternal *Idea*, in Plato's sense of the word. But the *law of nature* is the application of the Idea to the form in which it is manifest. This form is time, space, and causality, which are necessarily and inseparably connected and related to one another. Through time and space the Idea reproduces itself in countless phenomena; but the order in which time and space enter those forms of its proliferation is firmly determined by the law of causality; this law is, as it were, the standard which sets the limits of these phenomena of different Ideas, in accordance with which time, space, and matter are divided up between them. Hence this standard necessarily applies to the identity of the total available matter which is the substratum common to all those different phenomena. If all these had not been assigned to that common matter in whose domain they must disperse, there would be no need for such a law to decide their claims: they might all, simultaneously and side by side, occupy boundless space and endless time. So, only because all these manifestations of eternal Ideas are assigned to one and the same matter, there must be a rule for their entrances and exits, for otherwise the one would not leave room for the other. In this way the law of causality is essentially linked to the law of the persistence of substance; each derives significance only from the other, reciprocally. Time and space, in turn, are related to them in the same way. For time is merely the potential for conflicting states of the same matter, and space is merely the potential for the endurance of the same matter under all conflicting states. For this reason, in the last Book we explained matter as the union of space and time, and this union shows itself as variability of accidents despite the permanence of the substance, which is made possible precisely by causality or becoming. For that reason, too, we said that matter is causality through and through. We explained the understanding as the subjective correlative of causality, and said that matter (and thus the whole world as idea) exists only for the understanding; the understanding is its condition, its supporter as its necessary correlative. I mention all this in passing merely to remind us of what I have argued more fully in the First Book. We must pay attention, if we wish to understand them completely, to the fundamental unity of the two Books: for what in the real world is joined inseparably – its two aspects, will and idea – has been in these two Books torn asunder, for the clearer recognition of each in isolation. [. . .]

§ 27. If the foregoing reflections on the forces of nature and their phenomena have made plain to us how far an explanation from causes can go, and where it must stop short if it is not to degenerate into the foolish attempt to attribute the content of all phenomena to their mere form (in which case there would, in the end, be nothing left but form), we shall now be able to determine what, in general, is to be expected of any aetiology. Its task is to find out the causes of nature's phenomena, to discover the circumstances under which they invariably appear. Then, in those phenomena whose form varies with their different circumstances, aetiology should trace back to original forces of nature the element that operates in every phenomenon and is presupposed in the cause. It should correctly distinguish whether a variation in the phenomenon arises from a variation in the force, or results merely from a difference in the circumstances under which the force is manifesting itself; and it should be as wary of taking the manifestation of one and the same force under different circumstances for the manifestations of different forces, and conversely, of taking for manifestations of one and the same force what in origin belongs to different forces. For this, judgement is necessary, and that is why so few people are capable of increasing their *insight* into physics, while everyone can broaden his practical knowledge of it. In our indolence and ignorance we tend prematurely to look to original forces for an answer. This shows, with an exaggeration that comes close to satire, in the entities and quiddities of the scholastics: to have helped to reintroduce them is the last thing I want. It is no more permissible to appeal to the objectification of will, instead of offering an explanation from physics, than it is to appeal to the creative energy of God. For physics demands causes, whereas the will is never a cause: its relation to the phenomenon is not at all in accordance with the principle of sufficient reason. But what in itself is will exists in another aspect as idea; that is to say, is phenomenon. As such, it obeys the laws which constitute the form of the phenomenon. So, for example, every movement, although always a manifestation of will, must, nonetheless, have a cause from which it is to be explained in relation to a particular time and space; that is, not theoretically, according to its inner nature, but as a *particular* phenomenon. With a stone, the cause is mechanical; in a person's movement, it is a motive; but it can never be absent. On the other hand, the universal common nature of all phenomena of one particular kind, without which the explanation from causes would have neither sense nor meaning, is the universal force of nature, which must in physics remain a *qualitas occulta*, because there the etiological explanation ends and the metaphysical begins. But the chain of causes and effects is never broken by an original force upon which one is obliged to rely for support. It cannot be retraced to such a force as though that had been its first link; on the contrary, the nearest link in the chain draws upon the original energy as much as does the farthest, and could otherwise explain nothing. A series of causes and effects can be the manifestation of the most heterogeneous forces, whose successive emergence into visibility is conducted through it. But the heterogeneity of these original forces – which cannot be derived from one another – by no means breaks the unity of that chain of causes, and the connection between all its links.

The aetiology of nature and the philosophy of nature never detract from each other, but go hand in hand, studying the same object from different points of view. Aetiology gives an account of the causes which inevitably produced the particular phenomenon which it seeks now to explain. As the basis for all its explanations, it shows up the universal forces which are active in all these causes and effects. It accurately determines these forces, their number, their differences, and then indicates all the different effects in which each force appears with variation proportionate to the variation in circumstance, always in accordance with its own specific character which it develops in obedience to an unerring rule called *a law of nature*. As soon as physics has accomplished this in every particular, it will have attained the pinnacle of its achievement. There will then be no more unknown forces in inorganic nature, and no effect which has not been proved to be the manifestation of one of these forces under definite circumstances, in accordance with a law of nature. Yet a law of nature is nothing more than the rule we have seen operate in nature, by which she invariably proceeds as soon as certain circumstances arise. Hence a law of nature may be defined at least as a fact expressed as though it were universally valid – *un fait généralisé* – so that a full statement of all the laws of nature would in the end be only a long list of facts.

After that, *morphology* completes the study of nature as a whole. It enumerates, compares, and classifies all the enduring forms of organic nature. About the cause of the emergence of individual creatures it has little to say, since for all of them that is procreation (the theory of which is quite another matter), and in rare cases it is the *generatio aequivoca*. But to this last belongs, strictly speaking, also the manner in which all the low grades of the will's objectification, that is to say, physical and chemical phenomena, emerge individually, and it is precisely the task of aetiology to specify the conditions for this emergence. Philosophy, on the other hand, considers only the universal, in nature as everywhere else. The original forces themselves are the focus of its interest here, and it recognises in them the different grades of the will's objectivity, which is the inner nature, the 'in-itself' of this world; the world, considered apart from this, philosophy declares to be merely the idea of the subject.

But if aetiology, instead of preparing the way for philosophy, and giving its doctrines some practical application by citing instances, supposes rather that its aim is to deny the existence of all original forces save perhaps *one*, the most universal, for example, impenetrability, which it fancies it thoroughly understands and to which accordingly it tries forcibly to relate all the others – then it deserts its own fundamental position and can give us only error instead of truth. The content of nature is supplanted now by its form; everything is attributed to outward circumstances, and nothing to the inner nature of things. Now, if success really lay on this path, a simple sum, as we said earlier, would ultimately solve the riddle of the universe. But this is the path taken in order to attribute (as I have already mentioned) all physiological effects to form and combination, maybe to electricity, and this in turn to chemistry, and then chemistry to mechanics. Here Descartes, for example, and all the Atomists, were in error, in that they attributed the motion of the heavenly bodies to the impact of a fluid, and the qualities to the interconnection and form of the atoms; and they endeavoured to explain all the phenomena of nature as merely manifestations of impenetrability and cohesion. Although we have abandoned this, in our own day the electrical, chemical and mechanical physiologists are doing the same thing in trying obstinately to explain the whole of life and all the functions of the organism from the 'form and combination' of its constituent parts. [. . .]

On close examination these views are seen to be based ultimately on the assumption that the organism is merely an aggregate of phenomena of physical, chemical, and mechanical forces which, meeting here by chance, produced the organism as a freak of nature without further significance. Accordingly, the organism of an animal or of a human being would be, if considered philosophically, not the demonstration of an Idea specific to itself – that is, not itself immediate objectivity of the will at a definite higher grade – but in it would appear only those Ideas which objectify the will in electricity, in chemistry and in mechanics. So from the meeting of these forces the organism would have formed as haphazardly as do the shapes of people or of animals in clouds or in stalactites, and in that case it would be of no further interest for its own sake. However, we shall see immediately in how far it may be, nonetheless, within certain limits permissible and useful to apply physical and chemical modes of explanation to the organism; for I shall argue that the vital force certainly avails itself of, and uses, the forces of inorganic nature; yet the vital force no more consists of these forces than does a blacksmith consist of hammer and anvil. For this reason, even the very simplest example of plant life can never be explained from these forces by, for example, the theory of capillary attraction or of endosmosis; and animal life is even less amenable to such explanation. The following thoughts will pave the way for this rather difficult discussion.

It follows from all we have said that the sciences are mistaken in wanting to derive the higher grades of the will's objectification from lower grades; for failing to recognise and denying original and autonomous forces of nature is just as much a mistake as it is without grounds to assume specific and characteristic forces, when what is taking place is only a particular kind of manifestation of forces already familiar. Hence Kant is right when he says that it is absurd to hope for the Newton of a blade of grass, meaning, for the man who would reduce the blade of grass to the manifestation of physical and chemical forces, of which it would be the chance product and therefore a mere freak of nature in which no special Idea appeared – *i.e.*, the will did not directly reveal itself in it in a higher and specific grade, but just as in the phenomena of inorganic nature, and by chance in this form. The scholastics who would not have allowed any such thing, would rightly have said that it was a total denial of the *forma substantialis*, and a degradation of it to the mere *forma accidentalis*. For Aristotle's *forma substantialis* denotes exactly what I call the grade of the will's objectification in a thing. On the other hand, we should not overlook that in all Ideas, that is, in all forces of inorganic and all forms of organic nature, it is *one and the same will* that reveals itself, that is to say, which enters the form of the idea and passes into *objectivity*. Hence its unity must also be recognisable through an inner relationship between all its phenomena. Now this reveals itself in the higher grades of the will's objectification, where the whole phenomenon is more distinct. So in the vegetable and animal kingdoms its unity reveals itself through the pervasive analogy of all forms, through the fundamental type which recurs in all phenomena. [. . .] Indeed, since all things in the world are the objectification of one and the same will, and are consequently in their inner nature identical, there must be between them not only that unmistakable analogy, and in everything more imperfect there must be seen the trace, outline, and plan of the more perfect thing that lies next to it, but also because all these forms belong, after all, only to the world as *idea*, it is even to be supposed that in the most universal forms of the idea, in what is properly the framework of the phenomenal world – that is, in space and time – it may be possible to discern and to trace the fundamental type, outline and plan of what fills the forms. [. . .]

If several of the phenomena of will in the lower grades of its objectification – that is, in inorganic nature – come into conflict in that each of them, as causality disposes, wants to gain control over the available matter, there emerges from the conflict the phenomenon of a higher Idea which overwhelms all the less perfect phenomena which had existed previously, yet in such a way that it allows their essential nature to survive in a subordinate mode by absorbing an analogue of it. Only the identity of the will manifest in all the Ideas, and its striving after ever higher objectification, allows us to grasp this process. So we see in the hardening of the bones, for example, an unmistakable analogy to crystallisation as the force which originally governed the calcium, although ossification can never be attributed to crystallisation. This analogy shows less distinctly in the firming of the flesh. So, too, the combination of humours in the animal body is, together with secretion, analogous to chemical combination and separation, and here, indeed, the laws of chemistry still operate, albeit they are subordinated, much modified, and overpowered by a higher Idea. For this reason mere chemical forces outside the organism will never produce such humours; but, on the contrary,

> Nature's knack, as chemistry calls it,
> Deprecating, yet ignorant.

> Goethe [*Faust*, 1940–1]

The more complete Idea resulting from this victory over several lower Ideas or objectifications of will, gains an entirely new character by absorbing, from every Idea vanquished, a more potent analogue. The will objectifies itself in a new, more distinct way: vital humour, vegetable, animal, and man arise originally by way of *generatio aequivoca,* and thereafter by assimilation to the germ already there. Thus from the strife of lower phenomena the higher phenomenon emerges, swallowing them all, and yet in the higher grade realising the ambition of them all. So even at this early stage the law applies: *Serpens nisi serpentem comederit non fit draco* [the serpent does not become a dragon save by first eating the serpent.]

I wish that by a clear exposition it had been possible for me to dispel the obscurity which clings to the subject of these thoughts; but I see very well that the reader's own reflection on the matter must come to my aid if I am ever to be fully and correctly understood. According to the view I have expressed, we will indeed be able to point out in the organism the traces of chemical and physical processes, although these can never explain the organism because it is simply not a phenomenon produced by the concerted action of such forces; and produced, in consequence, by chance; it is, rather, a higher Idea which has conquered these lower ideas by *dominating assimilation.* For the *one* will (which objectifies itself in all Ideas) in striving for the highest possible objectification at this point, after a struggle: surrenders the lower grades of its manifestation in order to appear the more powerfully at a higher grade. No victory without a struggle: since the higher Idea, or objectification of will, can emerge only by conquering the lower, it experiences resistance from these lower Ideas, which, although forced into submission, nonetheless strive still to attain to the independent and complete expression of their being. The magnet that has lifted a piece of iron keeps up a continuing conflict with gravitation, which, as the lowest objectification of will, has a prior right to the matter of that iron; and in this constant battle the magnet even grows stronger; for the resistance stimulates it, as it were, to greater effort. In the same way every manifestation of the will, including that which expresses itself in the human organism, wages a constant war against the many physical and chemical forces which, as lower Ideas, have a prior right to that matter. Hence the arm falls which, by defeating gravity, we have for a while held up. Hence the comfortable sensation of health which proclaims the victory won by the Idea of the self-conscious organism over the physical and chemical laws which originally governed the humours of the body: but this comfortable sensation is so often interrupted by, and is always accompanied by, major or minor discomfort arising from the resistance of those forces. In this way the vegetative part of our life is constantly associated with mild suffering. Thus, too, digestion depresses all the animal functions because it harnesses all our vitality in order to overcome the chemical forces of nature by assimilating them. Hence the burden of physical life in general, the inevitability of sleep, and, finally, of death; for after long subjugation these forces of nature at last regain, from an organism wearied by its own constant victory, the matter it had wrested from them, and now they attain to an uninhibited expression of their being. For that reason we can also say that every organism expresses the Idea it mirrors only according to the deduction of the portion of its energy expended in subduing the lower Ideas that contest its claim on matter. This seems to be what Jakob Boehme had in mind when he says somewhere that all the bodies of men and animals, and all plants, too, are really half dead. The more or less successfully the organism subordinates the forces of nature which express the lower grades of the will's objectification, the more or less completely it attains to the expression of its Idea, or, in other words, the more or less closely it approximates to the *ideal* of beauty in its species.

So everywhere in nature we see strife, conflict, and the fickleness of victory, and in that we shall recognise more clearly the discord which is essential to the will. Every grade of the will's objectification competes with the others for matter, space, and time. Permanent matter must constantly change its form; for, as causality ordains, mechanical, physical, chemical and organic phenomena, jostling in their eagerness to emerge, wrest the matter from each other, for each desires to reveal its own Idea. This strife may be seen to pervade the whole of nature; indeed nature, in its turn, exists only through it: 'For, as Empedocles says, if there were no strife in things, everything would be one and the same.' (Aristotle, *Metaph.*, B.5). This very strife is, after all, only the revelation of that discord which is essential to the will. The universal conflict becomes most clearly visible in the animal kingdom. For animals have the whole of the vegetable kingdom to feed on, and, in turn, within the animal kingdom itself every beast is the prey and the food of another; that is, the matter in which its Idea would express itself every animal must relinquish for the expression of another Idea, for each animal can sustain its life only by the ceaseless destruction of another's life. So the will to live invariably preys upon itself, and in different forms is its own nourishment, till finally the human race, because it conquers all the others, regards nature as made for its use. But the human race, too, as we shall see in the Fourth Book, reveals in itself with most terrible clarity this conflict, this discord of the will, with the result *homo homini lupus* [man preys on his fellow man].

Meanwhile we recognise this same strife, this same subjugation, just as well in the lower grades of the will's objectification. Many insects, and especially ichneumon-flies, lay their eggs on the skin, and even in the body, of the larvae of other insects, which the newly-hatched brood at once slowly destroys. The young hydra, which grows as a branch out of the old one, and afterwards separates itself from it, fights while it is still joined to the old one for the prey that offers itself, so that the one snatches it out of the mouth of the other. But the bulldog-ant of Australia affords us the most startling example of this type in that, if it is cut in two, a battle begins between the head and the tail. The head seizes the tail with its teeth, and the tail defends itself bravely by stinging the head: the battle usually lasts for half an hour, until they die or are dragged away by other ants. This is the way it happens on every occasion. (From a letter by Howitt in the *W. Journal*, reprinted in *Galignani's Messenger*, 17 November 1855.) On the banks of the Missouri one sometimes sees a mighty oak-tree of which the trunk and branches are so entwined, bound and tied by a gigantic wild vine, that it can only wither as if choked. The same thing shows itself in the lowest grades; for example, when by organic assimilation water and carbon are changed into vegetable sap, vegetables or bread into blood, and so wherever, along with the restriction of chemical forces to a subordinate mode of activity, animal secretion takes place. This occurs also in inorganic nature, when, for example, crystals in process of formation meet, cross and so impinge on one another that they are unable to assume the pure, fully evolved crystalline form, so that almost every cluster of crystals is an image of such a conflict of will at this low grade of its objectification; or again, when a magnet imposes its magnetism upon iron, in order to express its Idea in this, too. [. . .] On a large scale it shows itself in the relation between the central body and the planet, for although the planet is in clear dependence, yet it always resists, just like the chemical forces in the organism; hence arises the constant tension between centripetal and centrifugal force which keeps the globe in motion, and is itself an expression of that universal conflict essential to the manifestation of will, which we are now considering. [. . .]

So here at the lowest grade we see the will express itself as blind desire, an obscure, dull impulse, outside the range of the immediately knowable. It is the simplest and the weakest mode of its objectification. And it appears as this blind desire and ignorant striving throughout inorganic nature. Physics and chemistry work to discover the primal forces and to study their laws, each of which reveals itself to us in millions of phenomena which are homogeneous and regular, and show no trace of individual character, but are merely reproduced through space and time, *i.e.*, by way of the *principium individuationis*, as a picture is reproduced through the facets of a glass, or polyoptron.

Although it is to objectify itself more distinctly with each successive grade, in the vegetable kingdom the will acts as an obscure impelling force, still entirely without insight. By this stage, the bond of its phenomena is no longer actual causes, but stimuli; and, finally, even in the vegetative part of the animal phenomenon, in the generation and maturing of every animal, and in sustaining its inner economy, the manifestation of will is still always determined by mere stimuli. Successively higher grades of the will's objectivity bring us finally to the point at which the individual who represents the Idea could no longer receive food for his assimilation merely through movement that follows upon stimuli. For such a stimulus must be waited for, but in this instance the food is more precisely specialised and with the ever-increasing number and variety of the phenomena, the hustle and bustle has become so great that they obstruct one another, and the chance upon which the individual who is moved merely by stimuli depends for his food would be too slender. From the point, therefore, at which the animal has freed itself from the egg or the womb in which it had vegetated without consciousness, its food must be sought and selected. Thus movement following upon motives, and for its sake, consciousness, become necessary; and so it enters upon the scene as a mechanical aid, μηχανή, needed at this stage of the will's objectification for the preservation of the individual and the propagation of the species. It emerges, represented by the brain or a large ganglion, just as every other endeavour or purpose of the self-objectifying will is represented by an organ, that is to say, manifests itself for the idea as an organ.

But with this mechanical aid, this μηχανή, the *world as idea* comes into existence at a stroke, with all its forms, object and subject, time, space, plurality, and causality. The world now shows its second aspect. Hitherto *mere will*, it is now at the same time *idea*, object of the knowing subject. The will, which hitherto has been following its desire in the dark, confidently and unerring, has at this stage struck a light in order to offset the disadvantage which would result from the jostling crowd and the complex character of its manifestations, and which would affect precisely the most advanced. The unerring confidence and regularity with which it worked till now in inorganic and merely vegetative nature, depended upon its being active exclusively in its original being, as blind impulse, will, without support, but also without interference from a second and entirely different world, the world as idea, which although only the image of its own inner being, is of quite another nature, and now meddles in the sequence of its phenomena. As a result, its unerring certainty comes to an end. Animals are already exposed to illusion, to deception. They have, however, merely perceptive ideation, no concepts, no reflection, and hence they are bound to the present; they cannot consider the future.

It seems as if this knowledge without reason had not in all

cases been adequate to its purpose, and at times required, as it were, some assistance. For we are presented with a very remarkable spectacle whereby the blind activity of the will and the activity enlightened by knowledge encroach quite astonishingly on each other's spheres in two kinds of phenomena. So in the one case we find, in the very midst of animal behaviour which is governed by perceptive knowledge and its motives, one act performed without these – an act carried out, that is, under compulsion from the will which acts blindly. I have in mind the mechanical skills which, directed by no motive, nor by knowledge, nonetheless have the appearance of operating from motives that are even abstract and rational. Our second instance, the opposite of this first, is that in which, on the contrary, the light of knowledge penetrates the workshop of the blindly active will, and illuminates the vegetative functions of the human organism: I have in mind clairvoyance.

Finally, when the will has reached the highest grade of its objectification, that knowledge of the understanding that has dawned on the animals – the understanding for which the senses furnish the data, and from which results merely perception tied to the present – is no longer enough. That complicated, many-sided, malleable being, man, who has many needs and is exposed to countless injuries, had to, for his own survival, be illuminated by a double knowledge. Perceptual knowledge to a higher power, as it were, had to be added to such perception as is in animals restricted to the present; while reflection had to be added to the understanding such as had evolved in the animals, and which now in man becomes reason, the faculty for framing abstract concepts. With this reason came self-conscious reflectiveness which ranges over the future and the past, and, as a consequence, deliberation, careful concern, the capacity for premeditated action independent of the present, and finally, the altogether distinct consciousness of one's own decisions as such. Suppose that, at that earlier stage, along with mere perceptual knowledge there emerged the possibility of illusion and deception, which superseded that immunity to error previously enjoyed by the will while it acted without knowledge, so that mechanical skills and other instincts, as expressions of the will without knowledge, had to come to its aid alongside those manifestations of the will which are directed by knowledge: then with the emergence of reason, that confidence and unerring certainty of the will's manifestations (which, at the other extreme, in inorganic nature, appears as strict regularity) is almost entirely lost; instinct recedes altogether; deliberation, which is supposed to compensate for the loss of everything else, produces vacillation and diffidence; then error becomes possible, and in many cases prevents the will from objectifying itself appropriately through actions. For although in the character the will has already taken its definite and unalterable course, and consistent with this, volition, which is itself unerring, arises as motives elicit it, nonetheless error can adulterate the will's manifestations in that illusory motives can infiltrate in the same way as do real ones, and cancel these out. So it is, for example, when superstition puts forward fictitious motives which compel a person to act in a manner directly opposed to that in which, in the given circumstances, his will would otherwise express itself. Agamemnon slays his daughter; a miser gives alms out of pure egotism in the hope that in return he may some day receive a hundred-fold; and so on.

So any knowledge, rational as well as merely perceptual, proceeds originally from the will itself, belongs essentially to the higher grades of its objectification as a mere μηχανή, a means of supporting the individual and the species, just as much as any organ of the body. Originally intended to serve the will, to implement its aims, knowledge remains in nearly everything wholly subservient to it: so it is in all animals and in almost all people. Yet we shall see in the Third Book how in individual people knowledge can elude this servitude, throw off its yoke, and free from all the will's purposes, exist purely for itself, simply as a clear mirror of the world, which is the source of art. Finally, in the Fourth Book, we shall see how, if this kind of knowledge reacts on the will, it can bring about self-denial, *i.e.* resignation, which is the final goal, and, indeed, lies at the heart of all virtue and sanctity, and is redemption from the world.

§ 28. We have considered the great variety and diversity of the phenomena in which the will objectifies itself, and we have seen their endless and implacable strife with one another. Yet, as we have been saying throughout our exposition hitherto, the will itself, as thing-in-itself, is by no means involved in that plurality and fluctuation. The diversity of the (Platonic) Ideas, *i.e.*, grades of objectification, the sheer number of individuals in which each of these grades manifests itself, the way in which the forms strive for matter – none of this affects the will itself, but is only the mode of its objectification, and only through that role does this bear an indirect relation to the will, and by virtue of that relation it belongs to the expression of the will's nature for the idea. Just as a magic lantern shows many different pictures, but it is only one and the same flame which makes them all visible, so in all the different phenomena which side by side fill the world's space, or in sequence, supplant one another as events, only *one will* manifests itself, of which everything is the visibility, the objectivity, and which remains unmoved, in the midst of that fluctuation; it alone is thing-in-itself; but all that is object is manifestation, or, to speak Kant's language, phenomenon.

Although in man, as (Platonic) Idea, the will finds its clearest and most complete objectification, this objectification was unable on its own to express his nature. In order to appear with fitting importance, the Idea of man had to be manifest not alone and isolated from everything else, but accompanied by the whole series of grades, down through all the forms of animals, through the vegetable kingdom to inorganic nature. For the complete objectification of will, *all* of these are required to complement one another; they are presupposed by the Idea of man in the same way as the blossoms of a tree presuppose leaves, branches, trunk and root; they form a pyramid of which man is the apex. If we enjoy comparisons, we can also say that their manifestations accompany that of man as inseparably as the full light is accompanied by all the gradations of the penumbra through which, little by little, it merges with darkness; or one might call them the resonance of man, and say that animal and plant are the descending fifth and third of man, and that the inorganic kingdom is the lower octave. However, the full truth of this last simile will become clear to us only when in the next book we try to fathom the deep significance of music. There it will be shown to us how the melody which surges forwards on coherent high, nimble notes, may be regarded as in some sense expressing man's life and endeavour, to which his capacity for reflection lends coherence, whereas, on the other hand, the unconnected complemental notes and the ponderous bass, which provide the harmony necessary to complete the music, represent the rest of the animal kingdom and the whole of nature that is without knowledge. But we will speak of this in its own place, where it will no longer sound so paradoxical.

But we also find that the *inner necessity* in the graded sequence of the will's manifestations, which is inseparable from the will's adequate objectification, is expressed by an *outer necessity*, overall, among these manifestations themselves. Hence man needs the animals for his sustenance, and the animals, down through their grades, need one another; then they, too, need plants, which in their turn need soil, water, chemical elements and their combinations, the planet, the sun, rotation and orbit round the sun, the angle of the ecliptic, and so forth. Fundamentally this is the result of the will's having to consume itself, for besides the will there is nothing else, and it is a hungry will. Hence the chase, the apprehension, the grieving.

It is only our recognising the unity of will as thing-in-itself, the endless diversity and variety of the phenomena, that throws light on that wonderful, unmistakable analogy between all of nature's products, that family likeness that induces us to see them as variations on the same theme, a theme, albeit, not yet divulged. So in like measure, through our clearly recognising and profoundly comprehending that harmony, that essential connectedness between all of the world's separate parts, that necessity for their gradation which we have just been considering, we will gain true and satisfying insight into the inner nature and meaning of the undeniable aptness of all nature's organic products, an aptness we presuppose even *a priori* when we are considering and appraising them.

This aptness is twofold: at times it is *internal*, that is, a harmony of all the parts of a particular organism so arranged that the survival of the individual and the species results from it, and thus it presents itself as the purpose of that arrangement. Sometimes, however, the aptness is *external*, a relation of inorganic to organic nature generally, or of particular parts of organic nature to one another, which makes possible the survival of the whole of organic nature, or of individual animal species; and so to us, as observers, it seems to be made for this purpose.

Inner aptness comes into the context of our study as follows. If, as we have said, all variations of forms in nature, and all plurality of individuals, belong not to the will itself, but merely to its objectivity and the form of this objectivity, it necessarily follows that the will is indivisible and is present in its entirety in every manifestation, although the grades of its objectification, the (Platonic) Ideas, are very different from one another. To make this easier to grasp, we may think of these different Ideas as individual and in themselves simple acts of will, in which its character expresses itself to some degree. Individuals, however, are in turn manifestations of the Ideas, and thereby of these acts of will, in time, space, and multiplicity.

Now, in the lowest grades of objectivity such an act (or an Idea) retains its unity in the manifestation, while, in order to appear in higher grades, it needs a whole series of conditions and developments in time which only when combined complete the expression of its character. So, for example, the Idea that reveals itself in any general force of nature has always just one single expression, although it presents itself differently according to external circumstances, for otherwise its identity could not be demonstrated as it is by separating from it the variation that results merely from external circumstance. In the same way the crystal has only one manifestation of life, its crystallisation, which is thereafter most appropriately and comprehensively expressed in the crystalline form, the cadaver of that momentary life. But slightly higher up the scale, the plant expresses the Idea whose phenomenon it is, not all at once and through a single manifestation, but through time, through the development of its organs in succession. The animal not only develops its organism in the same way, in a succession of forms which are often very different (which is what we term metamorphosis), but this animal form itself, although it is already objectivity of will at this grade, is not adequate to express its Idea in its entirety. This expression must be supplemented through the animal's activity. In this the empirical character common to the whole species manifests itself, and is essential to the full revelation of the Idea, a revelation which presupposes the particular organism as its first condition. In human life the empirical character in every individual is a specific personal character (indeed, as we shall see in the Fourth Book, even to the extent of supplanting the character of the species, that is, through the elective denial of all volition). What is known as the empirical character – marked by the necessary development in time and the division into separate actions that time imposes – is, when we abstract from this temporal form of the manifestation, the *intelligible character*, in Kant's term. In establishing this distinction and explaining the relationship between freedom and necessity, *i.e.*, between the will as thing-in-itself and its manifestation in time,[1] Kant has done magnificent and lasting service. Thus the intelligible character coincides with the Idea, or, more accurately, with the original act of will which reveals itself in it. To that extent, then, the empirical character not only of every person, but also of every species of animal, of every plant, and even of every original force in inorganic nature, is to be regarded as the manifestation of an intelligible character, that is, of a timeless, indivisible act of will.

I should like here in passing to draw attention to the naivety with which every plant expresses and lays open its whole character in its mere form, revealing its whole being and willing. This is why the physiognomy of plants is so interesting. But an animal, if we wish to know it in its Idea, requires us to observe it in action, and man requires to be exhaustively investigated and tested, for the faculty of reason makes him capable of a high degree of dissimulation. Just as the animal is more naive than the man, so, by the same margin, the plant is more naive than the animal. In the animal we see the will to life more naked, as it were, than in the man, in whom it is clad in so much knowledge and, in addition, so cloaked by his capacity for dissimulation that the will's true character shows through almost only by chance and only here and there. In the plant it shows itself quite naked, but also much weaker, as mere blind striving for existence without aim or purpose. For the plant reveals its whole being to our first glance. In its complete innocence it is unembarrassed by its carrying its reproductive parts uppermost and exposed to view, whereas in all animals the genitals have been positioned where they are most hidden. The plant's innocence is based on its lack of knowledge: for guilt lies not in willing, but in willing with knowledge. Every plant speaks to us first of all of its habitat, the climate and the soil-type from which it has originated. Hence even with only a very little experience we can easily tell whether an exotic plant belongs to the tropical or the temperate zone, and whether it grows in water, in bog, on mountains or on moorland. But as

---

[1] Cf. *Critique of Pure Reason*. 'Solution of the Cosmological Ideas of the Totality of the Deduction of the Events in the Universe' and *Critique of Practical Reason*. Cf. my essay on the *Principle of Sufficient Reason*, § 43.

well as that, every plant articulates the special will of its species, and says something that cannot be expressed in any other language. [. . .]

§ 29. Here I conclude the second main part of my exposition in the hope that, so far as is possible in communicating for the very first time a new-born thought which cannot be quite free from traces of the individuality in which it was first conceived, I have succeeded in conveying to the reader the clear certainty that this world in which we live and have our being is in its whole nature through and through *will*, and at the same time through and through *idea*: that this idea as such presupposes a form, namely object and subject, and is therefore relative; and if we ask what is left if we take away this form, and all those forms which are subordinate to it and expressed by the principle of sufficient reason, the answer is that, as something *toto genere* different from idea, this can only be *will*, which is thus properly the *thing-in-itself*. Everyone finds himself to be the will in which the real nature of the world consists, and he also finds himself to be the knowing subject whose idea the whole world is, the world which exists only in relation to his consciousness, as its indispensable support. So everyone is, doubly, the whole world itself, the microcosm; he finds both aspects whole and complete in himself. And what he recognises as his own being also exhausts the being of the whole world, the macrocosm; thus the world, like man, is through and through *will*, and through and through *idea*, and beyond that there is nothing else. So we see the philosophy of Thales, which concerned the macrocosm, coincide at this point with that of Socrates, which dealt with the microcosm, in that the object of these two proves to be the same. But all the insight imparted in the two first books will be completed and confirmed in the next two, and questions (whether more or less explicit) that may have arisen in the course of our study will, I hope, be satisfactorily answered.

In the meantime one such question may be discussed on its own here, for, properly speaking, it can be asked only as long as one has not fully penetrated the meaning of the exposition, and to that extent it may serve to clarify it. That one question is the following. Granted that every will is a will to something, has an object, a purpose in its willing, we ask, then, of that will which is presented to us as the being-in-itself of the world: what is its ultimate desire, the goal of its ambition? This question rests, like so many others, on the confusion of the thing-in-itself with the manifestation. The principle of sufficient reason, of which the law of motivation is also a form, extends only to manifestation, not to the thing-in-itself. It is only of phenomena, of individual things, that a ground can be given, never of the will itself, nor of the Idea in which it adequately objectifies itself. So, then, for every single movement or change of any kind in nature, we may seek a cause (that is, a condition that of necessity produced this movement or change) but never for the natural force itself which is revealed in this phenomenon and in countless others of the same sort. Hence it is a genuine misunderstanding, due to thoughtlessness, to ask for a cause of gravity, electricity, and so on. Only if one had somehow shown that gravity and electricity were not original forces peculiar to nature, but only the phenomenal modes of a more general force already known, might one seek the cause that is here making this force produce the phenomena of gravity or of electricity. All this has already been fully explained. Likewise, the knowing individual's every act of will – and the individual is only the will's manifestation as the thing-in-itself – had necessarily a motive without which that act would never occur; but just as the material cause merely determines that at this time, in this place, and in this matter, this or that natural force must be made manifest, so the motive determines only the knowing creature's act of will at this time, in this place, and under these circumstances, as something specific and singular, but by no means determines that this creature wills in principle, or wills after this fashion: this is the expression of his intelligible character, which, as will itself, the thing-in-itself, is groundless, for it lies outside the province of the principle of sufficient reason. Therefore every person has constant aims and motives in accordance with which he directs his conduct, and he can always account for his individual actions; but if he were asked why he wills at all, or why he wills to exist at all, he would have no answer. Rather, the question would seem to him absurd; and this response would reflect his awareness that he himself is nothing but will, and that his willing is self-evident and needs to be more precisely determined by motives only in its individual acts, in each instance.

Indeed, the absence of any goal and of any limits is essential to the will, for it is an endless striving. [...] This also shows itself in its simplest form at the lowest grade of the will's objectification, namely in gravitation which, as we see, is constantly striving even though an ultimate objective is plainly not possible. For if, as gravitation wills it, all existing matter were combined in one mass, then within this mass gravity, in striving towards the centre, would still be struggling with impenetrability in the form of rigidity or elasticity. Thus the striving of matter can always only be checked, but never fulfilled or satisfied. And this is precisely the case with all the striving of all the will's phenomena. Every goal attained is the starting-point of a new lap in the race, and so on *ad infinitum*. From the seed, by way of the stem and leaf, the plant advances its phenomenal existence to the point of blossom and fruit, which is again only the beginning of a new seed, a new individual that runs through the old cycle, and so on through time without end. The course of an animal's life is similar; its peak is procreation, and once it has reached this peak, the life of the first individual will sooner or later wane, while a new life guarantees the preservation of the species in nature and repeats the same phenomenon. Indeed, that the matter of every organism is perpetually renewed we should see as merely manifesting this continual pressure and change. Physiologists are now ceasing to hold that it is the necessary replacement of the substance consumed in movement, for the possible wear and tear on the machine certainly cannot be equivalent to what it is constantly gaining by way of food. Eternal becoming, endless flux, is essential to the revealing of the will's nature. We see the same thing in human aspirations and desires; the fulfilment of these masquerades as the ultimate objective of our willing, but once we have attained them, they no longer look the same, so that soon, forgotten and out of date, they are almost always set aside (even if we do not admit it) as vanished illusions. We consider ourselves fairly fortunate if there is still something to wish for, and to strive after, to keep up the game whereby desire constantly passes into satisfaction, and satisfaction into new desire – if the pace of this is swift, it is called happiness, and if it is slow, sorrow – and does not falter and come to the standstill that shows in dreadful, stultifying boredom, in lifeless yearning without a definite object, a deadening languor.

It is consistent with all this that the will, when it is enlightened by knowledge, always knows what it wills here and now, but never what it wills more generally. Every individual act of will has its aim, its objective, but the act of willing in its entirety has none; just as every individual phenomenon of nature is determined by a sufficient cause in respect of its occurrence in this place, at this time, but the force which manifests itself in it has no general cause, for it is a stage in the manifestation of the thing-in-itself, the groundless will. But the sole self-knowledge of the will as a whole is the idea as a whole, the perceptible world in its entirety. That is the will's objectification, its revelation, its mirror. What it tells us in this capacity will be the subject of further reflection for us.

On the Primacy of the Will in Self-Consciousness

The will, as the thing in itself, constitutes the inner, true, and indestructible nature of man; yet in itself it is unconscious. For consciousness is conditioned by the intellect, and the intellect is a mere accident of our being, for it is a function of the brain which, together with the associated nerves and spinal cord, is merely a fruit, a product, of the rest of the organism, and even its parasite in so far as it does not directly engage with its inner mechanism but merely serves the purpose of self-preservation by regulating the relations of the organism with the external world. The organism itself, on the other hand, is the visibility and objectivity of the individual will, the will's image as it presents itself in that very brain (which in the First Book we learned to recognise as the condition of the objective world in general) and hence is communicated by the same brain's forms of knowledge – space, time, and causality – and consequently presents itself as extended, successively acting, and material, *i.e.*, as something operative or efficient. Only in the brain are the parts of the body both directly felt and also perceived by means of the senses. In consequence one may say that the intellect is the secondary phenomenon, the organism the primary phenomenon, that is, the immediate manifestation of the will; that the will is metaphysical, the intellect physical; that the intellect, like its objects, is merely phenomenal appearance; that the will alone is the thing-in-itself. Then, in a more and more *figurative* sense, speaking metaphorically: that the will is the substance of man, the intellect the accident; that the will is the matter, the intellect is the form; that the will is warmth, the intellect is light.

We shall now first of all document and elucidate this thesis by means of the following facts relating to the inner life of man; and this may well yield more knowledge of the inner man than is to be found in many systematic psychologies.

1. Not only the consciousness of other things, *i.e.*, the apprehension of the external world, but also *self-consciousness*,

implies, as we have mentioned above, a knower and a known; otherwise it would not be *consciousness*. For *consciousness* consists in knowing; but knowing requires a knower and a known; hence self-consciousness could not come about if there were not in it also an element which vis-à-vis the knower is both known and distinctly different. For as there can be no object without a subject, so also there can be no subject without an object, *i.e.*, no knowing subject without something different from it which is known. Hence a consciousness which would be, completely and utterly, pure intelligence cannot possibly exist. The intelligence is like the sun, which does not illuminate space if there is no object from which its rays are reflected. The knower himself cannot, as such, be known; otherwise he would be the known of another knower. But, as the *known* in self-consciousness we identify the *will*, and nothing else. For not merely willing and resolving in the narrowest sense, but also all striving, wishing, shunning, hoping, fearing, loving, hating – in short, all that directly constitutes our own weal and woe, pleasure and displeasure – is clearly only affection of the will, is a stirring, a modification of willing and not-willing, is precisely what reveals itself, in operating outwardly, as an act of will proper. In all knowledge, however, the known is first and essential, not the knower; for the former is the πρωτότυπς [prototype] the latter the ἔκτυπς [copy]. Hence in self-consciousness, too, the known (that is, the will) must be first and original; the knower, on the other hand, only secondary, the accessory, the mirror. [. . .]

2. But in order not merely to describe consciousness figuratively, but to know it thoroughly, we have first of all to search for what is present in the same way in every consciousness; for this, as the common and constant element, will also be the essential. Then we shall consider what distinguishes *one* consciousness from another, and this accordingly will be the non-essential and secondary element.

Consciousness is, in any event, known to us only as a property of animal nature; therefore we may not, and cannot, think of it as anything but *animal consciousness*, so that this very expression is tautological. Now, what in *every* animal consciousness, even the most imperfect and the weakest, is ever present and ever fundamental to it, is, in widely varying degrees, the immediate awareness of *craving*, and of its alternate satisfaction and non-satisfaction. This we know to a certain extent *a priori*. For marvellously varied as the countless species of animals may be, and however oddly a form which we have never seen before, may strike us, we confidently anticipate its inmost nature as though it were well known and entirely familiar to us. For we know that the animal *wills*, and even also *what* it wills – namely, existence, well-being, life, and reproduction – and in confidently assuming that this animal is in this identical to ourselves, without demur we attribute to it unmodified all the affections of will which we know from ourselves, and speak without hesitation of its desire, aversion, fear, anger, hatred, love, joy, sorrow, longing, etc. On the other hand, as soon as phenomena of mere knowledge come up for discussion, this confidence deserts us. We do not dare to say that the animal understands, thinks, judges, knows: we confidently give it credit only for having any ideas at all because without them its *will* could not fall into the emotional states we have cited. But with regard to the mode of perception specific to animals, and its precise limits in a given species, we have only a vague idea and rely on guesswork. Hence it is often difficult for us to make ourselves understood, and we can establish an understanding with animals only by contriving it, and by dint of experience and practice. Here, then, lie differences between one consciousness and another. On the other hand, a craving, desiring, wishing, or a detesting, shunning, and not wishing, is a feature of every consciousness: man has it in common with the polyp. This is, accordingly, the essential element in and the basis of every consciousness. Variation in its manifestation in the various species of animal beings depends upon the varying extent of their sphere of knowledge, in which the motives for those manifestations lie. From our own nature we understand directly all the actions and behaviour of animals which express the stirring of the will; thus we sympathise with them in many ways. On the other hand, the gulf between us and them results simply and solely from the difference of intellect. [. . .] For in man not only does the faculty of ideas of *perception*, which had till now been the only one, reach the highest degree of perfection, but the *abstract* idea, thought, *i.e.*, the faculty of *reason*, and with it reflection, is added. Thus significantly enhanced, the intellect (which is the secondary part of consciousness) now outweighs the primary part in so far as it becomes from now on the predominantly active part. While in the animal the immediate awareness of its satisfied or unsatisfied desire constitutes by far the most important feature of its consciousness (and the more so, indeed, the lower the grade of the animal, so that the lowest animals are distinguished from plants only by the addition of a dull idea), in man the opposite is the case. Vehement as are his desires, even more vehement than those of any animal, and rising to the level of passions, yet his consciousness remains continuously and predominantly occupied and filled with ideas and thoughts. Without doubt this, more than anything else, has been the occasion of that fundamental error of all philosophers whereby they designate thinking as that which is essential and primary in the so-called soul (*i.e.*, in the inner or spiritual life of man), always putting it first, whereas willing, as a mere product of thinking, they allow to follow afterwards in a secondary role and as a consequence of willing. But if willing merely proceeds from knowing, how could the animals, even the lower grades of them, with so very little knowledge, often show such an indomitable and vehement will? Because that fundamental error of the philosophers makes the accident, as it were, into the substance, it leads them into sidetracks from which, later, it is impossible to steer clear. Now this relative predominance, as it occurs in man, of the *knowing* consciousness over the *desiring*, and thus of the secondary part over the primary, may, in particular, exceptionally favoured individuals, go so far that at its most intense moments the secondary or knowing part of consciousness detaches itself altogether from the willing part, and on its own it passes into free activity; that is, not activated by the will, and consequently no longer serving it. By this means it becomes purely objective, and the clear mirror of the world, and from it the conceptions of *genius* then arise, which are the subject of our third book.

3. [...] The fundamentally different nature of the will and the intellect, the essential simplicity and originality of the former in contrast to the complicated and secondary character of the latter, becomes even clearer to us when we observe their curious interplay within us, and now consider in detail how the images and thoughts which arise in the intellect set the will in motion, and how utterly separated and different are the roles which the two play. True, we notice this even in real events which vividly excite the will, while primarily and in themselves they are merely objects of the intellect. Yet, on the one hand, it is not so obvious

that this reality as such is present primarily only in the intellect; and, on the other hand, the change does not usually occur as quickly as it must if the thing is to be taken in at a glance and thus be readily comprehensible. Both of these conditions, however, are fulfilled if it is merely thoughts and fantasies which we allow to act on the will. If, for example, alone with ourselves, we think over our personal affairs, and now perhaps vividly imagine the threat presented by a danger actually present and the possibility of an unhappy outcome, anxiety at once constricts the heart, and the blood flows sluggishly. But if the intellect then shifts to the possibility of an opposite outcome, and allows the imagination to elaborate upon the happiness long hoped for and thereby attained, all the pulses quicken at once with joy and the heart feels light as a feather, till the intellect awakes from its dream. After that, suppose that some incident should reawaken the memory of an insult or injury suffered long ago, at once anger and bitterness invade the breast that was tranquil till this moment. But then arises, invoked by chance, the image of a beloved woman long lost, and with this image the whole romance and its scenes of enchantment are associated; then that anger will at once yield to profound longing and melancholy. Finally, if we are overtaken by the memory of some humiliating incident, we flinch, we would like to disappear into the ground, we blush with shame, and often try forcibly to distract and divert our thoughts by some loud exclamation, as if to dispel these evil spirits.

Obviously the intellect calls the tune, and the will must dance to it. Indeed the intellect makes the will play the part of a child who, by the tales his nursemaid tells of things by turns glad and sad, is transported at her will from one mood to another. The basis for this is the will's being of itself without knowledge, while the understanding, which is joined to it as its partner, is without will. Hence the will behaves like a body which is moved, while the understanding behaves like the causes which set it in motion, for it is the medium of motives. But for all that, the primacy of the will becomes clear again when this will (which, as we have shown, becomes the play-thing of the intellect as soon as it allows the intellect to rule) as a last resort makes its supremacy felt by prohibiting the intellect from entertaining certain ideas, by suppressing certain trains of thought, because it knows (*i.e.*, learns from that self-same intellect) that they would plunge it into some one of the emotions described above. It now bridles the intellect, and compels it to direct itself to other things. Hard as this often may be, it must nonetheless succeed as soon as the will is in earnest about it, for the resistance here comes not from the intellect, which typically remains indifferent, but from the will itself, which in one respect is well disposed towards an idea that, in another respect, it abhors. For this idea is in itself interesting to the will precisely because it excites it, but at the same time abstract knowledge tells the will that this idea will gratuitously deal it a blow which will be both painful and humiliating: it now decides in accordance with this insight, and forces the intellect to obey. This is called 'being master of oneself'. Clearly the master here is the will, the servant the intellect, for in the last instance the will always keeps the upper hand, and therefore constitutes the true core, the inner being, of man. In this respect the title Ἡγεμοιχόνυ would befit the *will*; yet it seems, on the other hand, to apply to the *intellect* in so far as it is the director and guide, like the cicerone who precedes the visitor in an unfamiliar place. In truth, however, the most appropriate metaphor for the relationship of this pair is that of the strong man who is blind supporting on his shoulders the lame man who can see.

The relation of the will to the intellect as described here can be recognised again, too, in the fact that the intellect is originally a stranger to the will's decisions. It supplies the motives to the will, but only later does it learn, entirely *a posteriori*, what effect they have had, just as someone who makes a chemical experiment brings together the reagents and awaits the result. Indeed the intellect remains so totally excluded from the real decisions and secret resolutions of its own will that sometimes it can find out about them only as it would about those of a third party, by eavesdropping on them and surprising them, and must catch the will in the act of expressing itself in order to get to the bottom of its real intentions. For example, I have proposed a scheme, but I myself have still some scruple against it, and on the other hand its implementation is, from the point of view of its feasibility, altogether uncertain, for it depends upon external and still undecided circumstances. Hence it would in any case be unneccesary to come to a decision about it yet, and so for the present I let the matter rest. Now I often do not know how firmly I am in secret already committed to that plan, and how much, in spite of the scruple, I desire its implementation: that is to say, my intellect does not know. But just let me hear of conditions favourable to the implementing of my scheme and, at once a jubilant, irresistible joy wells up in me, suffusing my whole being, and taking permanent possession of it, to my own astonishment. For only now my intellect learns how firmly my will had embraced that scheme, and how perfectly the scheme suited it, while the intellect had regarded it as quite problematic and barely able to counter that scruple. To take another instance: I have entered eagerly into a contract which I believed to be very much in accordance with my wishes. But as the matter progresses, the disadvantages and burdens of it make themselves felt, and I begin to suspect that I even regret what I had so eagerly initiated; yet I purge myself of this suspicion by assuring myself that even if I were not bound by my contract I would continue on the same course. But now, the contract is unexpectedly dissolved by the other party and I note with astonishment that this is to my great satisfaction and relief.

Often we don't know what we wish or what we fear. We may cherish a wish for years without even confessing it to ourselves, or even allowing it to come to clear consciousness, for the intellect is to know nothing about it because the good opinion which we have of ourselves might thereby suffer. But if our wish is fulfilled we learn from our joy (and not without shame) that we have wished this; it may be, for example, the death of a near relation from whom we are to inherit. And sometimes we do not know what we really fear, because we lack the courage to bring it to distinct consciousness. Indeed, we are often mistaken as to our real motive in doing or not doing something, till some chance in the end reveals our secret to us, and we recognise that what we had taken to be the motive was not that one but another which we had not wanted to admit to ourselves, because it is not at all compatible with the good opinion we hold of ourselves. For example, we refrain from doing something on purely moral grounds, as we believe, but later we learn that we were restrained only by fear, for as soon as all danger is removed, we do it. In some instances this may go so far that a person does not even guess the actual motive of his action, and moreover, he does not believe himself capable of being influenced by such a motive; and yet it is the actual motive for his action. [...] If now, on the contrary, as all philosophers might imagine, the intellect constituted our actual nature and the will's resolutions were merely the sum-total arrived at through knowledge, then only the motive from which we *imagined* we were acting would be decisive for our moral worth, in just the same way as the intention, not the outcome, is critical in this matter. But in practice the distinction between imagined and true motive would then be impossible. All the instances I have described – and in addition to these, any perceptive person can observe parallels in his experience – show us how the intellect is so alien to the will that it is sometimes even mystified by it: for while it does indeed provide motives for it, it does not penetrate the secret workshop of its decisions. Certainly the intellect is on a familiar footing with the will, but it will not be privy to all its business. This is also further confirmed by the fact – which almost everyone will at some time have occasion to observe in himself – that sometimes the intellect does not quite trust the will. If, for instance, we have made a bold decision – which is, after all, really only a promise made by the will to the intellect – we often feel, deep down, though we do not admit it, a faint lingering doubt as to whether this promise is seriously intended, and whether in carrying it out we will not waver or yield, but will have enough firmness and persistence to fulfil it. Only the *fait accompli* can convince us of the good faith behind our own resolve. All these facts are evidence of the difference between the will and the intellect, and they bear witness, too, to the primacy of the former and the subordinate position of the latter. [. . .]

BOOK THREE

The World as Idea

The idea independent of the principle of sufficient reason: the Platonic Idea: The object of art

What is that which always is, and has no becoming? And what is that which is always becoming, and never is?

Plato, *Timaeus*

§ 30. In the First Book the world was shown to be mere *idea*, object for a subject. In the Second Book we considered it from its other aspect, and found that this is *will*, which proved to be simply what this world is *besides* being idea. In accordance with this insight we called the world as idea, both as a whole and in its parts, the *objectification of will*, which accordingly means the will become object, *i.e.*, idea. We remember, too, that this objectification of will was found to have many but definite grades, in which, with gradually increasing distinctness and completeness, the nature of will emerged in the idea, that is to say, presented itself as object. In these grades we recognised the Platonic Ideas, in so far as these grades are the same as the definite species, or the original unchanging forms and qualities of all natural bodies, both organic and inorganic, and also the universal forces which reveal themselves according to natural laws. These Ideas, then, express themselves, one and all, in innumerable individuals and entities, and are related to these as are archetypes to their copies. The plurality of such individuals is conceivable only through time and space, since their appearing and disappearing is attributable to causality, and in all these forms we recognise merely the different modes of the principle of sufficient reason, which is the ultimate principle of all that is finite, of all individual existence, and the universal form of the idea as it comes to the knowledge of the individual as such. The Platonic Idea, on the other hand, does not come under this principle, and for this reason it has neither plurality nor change.

While the individuals in which it expresses itself are innumerable, and unceasingly come into being and pass away, it remains unchanged as one and the same, and the principle of sufficient reason has no relevance for it. However, since this is the form under which all knowledge of the subject comes, in so far as the subject knows as an *individual*, the Ideas will lie quite outside the sphere of its knowledge. Thus the Ideas can become objects of knowledge only on condition that the individuality of the knowing subject is suspended. The more exact and detailed explanation of this is what will now claim our attention.

§ 31. First, however, the following very essential remark. I hope that in the preceding book I have convincingly shown that what in the Kantian philosophy is called the *thing-in-itself*, and appears there as so important and yet so obscure and paradoxical a doctrine, and (especially as a result of the way Kant introduced it: as an inference from the caused to the cause) was considered a stumbling block, and the weak aspect of his philosophy – I hope to have shown that this, if it is reached by the entirely different route by which we have arrived at it, is nothing but the *will*, when the sphere of that concept is extended and defined in the way I have shown. I hope, further, that after what has been said there will be no hesitation in recognising the definite grades of the objectification of the will, which is the inner reality of the world, to be what Plato called the *eternal Ideas* or unchangeable forms (εἴδη); a doctrine which is regarded as the principal, but at the same time the most obscure and paradoxical, dogma of his system, and has been the subject of reflection, of controversy, of ridicule and of reverence, to so many and such different minds down the centuries. [. . .]

§ 32. [. . .]The Idea is for us rather the immediate, and therefore adequate, objectivity of the thing-in-itself, which is, however, itself the *will* – the will as not yet objectified, not yet become idea. For the thing-in-itself must, according to Kant himself, be free from all the forms attendant on knowing as such; and it is merely an error on his part that he did not count among these forms, before all others, that of being object for a subject, for this one is the first and most universal form of all phenomena, *i.e.*, of all idea. Hence he should have explicitly denied objective existence to his thing-in-itself; and this would have saved him from a great inconsistency that was soon detected. The Platonic Idea, on the other hand, is necessarily object, something known, an idea, and is thereby, and only thereby, different from the thing-in-itself. It has merely laid aside the subordinate forms of the phenomenon, all of which we include in the principle of sufficient reason; or rather, it has not yet assumed them. But it has retained the first and most universal form, that of the idea in principle, the form of being object for a subject. It is the forms which are subordinate to this (whose general expression is the principle of sufficient reason) that reproduce and replicate the Idea in particular transitory individuals, whose number is a matter of complete indifference to the Idea.

The principle of sufficient reason is thus again the form into which the Idea enters when it comes to the knowledge of the subject as individual. The particular thing that manifests itself in accordance with the principle of sufficient reason is thus only an indirect objectification of the thing-in-itself (which is the will), for between it and the thing-in-itself stands the Idea as the only direct objectivity of the will, in that it has assumed no form peculiar to knowledge as such but that of the idea in general, *i.e.*, the form of being object for a subject. Thus it alone is the most *adequate objectivity* possible of the will or thing-in-itself; indeed it is the whole thing-in-itself, only under the form of the idea. This is the basis for the great agreement between Plato and Kant, although, in strict accuracy, they are not talking about the same thing. But individually things are not a completely adequate objectivisation of the will, for in them its objectivity is obscured by those forms whose collective expression is the principle of sufficient reason, but which are conditions of the knowledge accessible to the individual as such.

We may draw conclusions from an impossible presupposition, we would, in fact, no longer comprehend particular things, nor events, nor change, nor plurality, but would comprehend only Ideas – only the stages in the objectification of that one will, of the thing-in-itself, in pure unclouded knowledge. Consequently our world would be a *nunc stans*, if it were not that, as knowing subjects, we were also individuals, *i.e.*, if our perceptions were not conveyed through the medium of a body from whose affections that perception begins. This body is itself only concrete willing, objectivity of the will, and thus is an object among objects, and as such comes into the knowing consciousness in the only way in which an object can, through the forms of the principle of sufficient reason. Consequently it presupposes, and therefore introduces time, and all other forms which that principle expresses. Time is only the fragmented and piecemeal view which the individual being has of the Ideas, which are outside time and consequently *eternal*. Thus Plato says 'time is the moving picture of eternity' [in *Timaeus* 37 D].

§ 33. As individuals we have no other knowledge but that which is subject to the principle of sufficient reason, and this form excludes knowledge of the Ideas. So it is certain that if we can possibly raise ourselves from the knowledge of particular things to that of the Ideas, this can happen only by an alteration taking place in the subject. This change is analogous to, and corresponds to, the great change of the whole nature of the object; and by virtue of it the subject, in so far as it knows an Idea, is no longer an individual.

We will remember from the preceding book that any knowledge belongs to the objectification of will at its higher grades; and sensibility, nerves, and brain, just like other parts of organic life, are the expression of the will at this stage of its objectivity. Thus the idea which arises through them is likewise intended for the will's service as a means to attaining its now complicated aims, and to sustain a being of many different needs. So both in origin and by its nature, knowledge is completely subject to the will; and, like the immediate object, which by the application of the law of causality becomes the starting-point of knowledge, it is only objectified will. Thus all knowledge which follows the principle of sufficient reason remains in a relationship to the will which is more or less close or remote. For the individual finds his body as an object among objects, to all of which it is related and connected according to the principle of sufficient reason. Thus all investigations of these relations and connections lead back, whether by a shorter or a longer route, to his body, and consequently to his will. Since it is the principle of sufficient reason which places the objects in this relation to the body, and, through it, to the will, the one endeavour of the knowledge which is subject to this principle will be to find out the relations in which objects are placed to each other through this principle, and thus to trace their innumerable connections in space, time, and causality. For only through these is the object *interesting* to the individual, *i.e.*, related to the will. Therefore the knowledge which is subject to the will knows nothing more about objects than their relations, knows the objects only so far as they exist at this time, in this place, under these circumstances, from these causes, and with these effects – in a word, as particular things; and if all these relations were to be suspended, for knowledge the objects would also have disappeared, just because, apart from this, it knew nothing about them.

We must not disguise the fact that what the sciences consider in things is also essentially nothing more than this – namely their relations, the circumstances of time and space, the causes of natural changes, the resemblance of forms, the motives for events – nothing but relations. What distinguishes science from ordinary knowledge is merely the form, the systematic, the facilitating of knowledge by the inclusion of all particulars in the universal (by means of the subordination of concepts) and the completeness of knowledge gained in this way. [. . .]

Now knowledge remains as a rule subordinate to the service of the will, as indeed it originated for this service, and grew, so to speak, out of the will as the head grew from the body. In the case of the animals this subjection of knowledge to the will can never be reversed. In the case of people it can be reversed only in exceptional cases, which we shall presently consider more closely. This distinction between man and animal is outwardly expressed by the difference in the relationship of the head to the body. In the lower animals head and body are joined together as one: in all animals the head is directed towards the ground, where the objects of its will lie; even in the higher species the head and the body are still far more one than in the case of man, whose head seems freely set upon his body as if only carried by, rather than serving, it. Man's superiority in this respect is shown in the highest degree by the Apollo of Belvedere; the head of the god of the Muses, with eyes ranging over the far distance, stands so freely on his shoulders that it seems wholly disengaged from the body and no longer subject to concern for it.

§ 34. The transition which we have referred to as possible, but to be regarded as only exceptional, from the common knowledge of particular things to the knowledge of the Idea, takes place suddenly; for knowledge breaks free from the service of the will, by the subject's ceasing to be merely individual and now becoming the pure will-less subject of knowledge. It no longer traces relations in accordance with the principle of sufficient reason, but rests in fixed contemplation of the object presented to it, seeing it apart from its connection with all others, and is absorbed by it.

A full explanation is necessary to make this clear, and the reader must suspend his surprise until we have summarised the thought which is to be communicated in this work, and then it will vanish of itself.

Raised by the power of the mind, a person relinquishes the usual way of looking at things, stops tracing, as the forms of the principle of sufficient reason prompt him to do, only their interrelatedness, the final goal of which is always a relation to his own will. He ceases to consider the where, the when, the why, and the whither of things, and looks simply and solely at the *what*. He does not allow abstract thought, the concepts of the reason, to take possession of his consciousness, but, instead, gives the whole power of his mind to perception, immerses himself entirely in this, and lets his whole consciousness be filled with the quiet contemplation of the natural object actually present, whether a landscape, a tree, a crag, a building, or whatever it may be. He *loses* himself in this object (to use a pregnant German idiom), *i.e.*, he forgets his very individuality, his will, and continues to exist only as the pure subject, the clear mirror of the object, so that it is as if the object alone were there without anyone to perceive it, and he can no longer separate the perceiver from the perception, but the two have become one, because the whole consciousness is filled and taken up with one single sensuous picture. If the object has to such an extent passed out of all relation to something outside it, and the subject out of all relation to the will, then what is known is no longer the individual thing as such, but the *Idea*, the eternal form, the immediate objectivity of the will at this grade. The person rapt in this perception is thereby no longer individual (for in such perception the individual has lost himself), but he is a pure, willess, painless, timeless *subject of knowledge*.

This, which in itself is so remarkable (which I well know confirms the saying that originated with Thomas Paine, 'It is only a short step from the sublime to the ridiculous'), will by degrees become clearer and less surprising from what follows. It was this that was in Spinoza's mind when he wrote: 'The mind is eternal in so far as it understands under the aspect of eternity'. (*Eth.* V. 31, note) In such contemplation the particular thing becomes at a stroke the Idea of its species, and the perceiving individual becomes *pure subject of knowing*. The individual, as such, knows only particular things; the pure subject of knowing knows only Ideas. For the individual is the subject of knowing in its relation to a definite particular manifestation of will, and in subjection to this. This particular manifestation of will is, as such, subordinated to the principle of sufficient reason in all its forms; therefore, all knowledge which relates to it also follows the principle of sufficient reason, and no other kind of knowledge is fitted to be of use to the will but this, which always consists merely of relations to the object. The knowing individual as such, and the particular thing known by him, are always in some place, at some time, and are links in the chain of causes and effects. The pure subject of knowledge and his correlative, the Idea, have passed out of all these forms of the principle of sufficient reason: time, place, the individual that knows, and the individual that is known, have for them no meaning.

When an individual knower has raised himself in the manner described to be pure subject of knowledge, and at the same time has raised the observed object to the Platonic Idea, *the world as idea* comes into being, entire, complete and pure, and the full objectification of the will takes place, for the Platonic Idea alone is its *adequate objectivity*. The Idea includes object and subject in like manner in itself, for they are its sole form; but in it they are perfectly balanced; for as the object here, too, is simply the idea of the subject, the subject, which is absorbed entirely into the perceived object has thus become this object itself, for the whole consciousness is nothing but its most distinct image. Now it is precisely this consciousness that constitutes the whole *world as idea*, for one imagines the whole of the Platonic Ideas, or grades of the will's objectivity, one after the other, passing through it. The particular things of all time and space are nothing but Ideas multiplied through the principle of sufficient reason (the form of the knowledge of individuals as such), and thus obscured as regards their pure objectivity. When the Platonic Idea is manifest, in it subject and object are no longer to be distinguished, for the Platonic Idea, the adequate objectivity of will, the true world as idea, arises only when the subject and object reciprocally fill and penetrate each other completely; and in the same way the knowing and the known individuals, as things in themselves, are not to be distinguished. For if we disregard that actual *world as idea*, there remains nothing but the *world as will*. The will is the 'in-itself' of the Platonic Idea, which perfectly objectifies it; it is also the 'in-itself' of the particular thing and of the individual that knows it, which objectify it incompletely. As will, outside the idea and all its forms, it is one and the same in the object contemplated and in the individual who, soaring aloft in this contemplation, becomes conscious of himself as pure subject. These two are, therefore, in themselves not different, for in themselves they are will which here knows itself; and plurality and variety exists only as the means whereby this knowledge comes to the will, *i.e.*, only in the phenomenon, by virtue of its form, the principle of sufficient reason.

Just as without the object, without the idea, I am not the knowing subject, but merely blind will, so without me as subject of knowing, the known thing is not object, but mere will, blind passion. This will is in itself, *i.e.*, outside the idea, one and the same with mine: only in the world as idea, whose form is always at least that of subject and object, we become distinct as the known *and* the knowing individual. As soon as knowledge, the world as idea, is suspended, there remains nothing but mere will, blind impulse. That it should receive objectivity, become idea, supposes at once both subject and object; but that this should be pure, complete, and adequate objectivity of the will, supposes the object as Platonic Idea, free from the forms of the principle of sufficient reason, and the subject as the pure subject of knowledge, free from individuality and subjection to the will.

Anyone who immerses himself in the contemplation of nature so that he continues to exist only as the pure knowing subject, becomes directly conscious that, as such, he is the condition, that is, the one who bears the burden of the world and all objective existence; for this now shows itself to be dependent upon his existence. Thus he draws nature into himself so that he sees it to be merely an accident of his own being. In this sense Byron says –

> Are not the mountains, waves, and skies, a part
> Of me and of my soul, as I of them?

> [*Childe Harold's Pilgrimage*, III]

But how shall he who feels this, regard himself as absolutely transitory, in contrast to imperishable nature? Rather, he will be seized by an awareness of what the Upanishad of the Veda expresses: 'I am all these creatures, and besides me there is no other being' (*Oupnek'hat*, i. 122).

§ 35. In order to gain a deeper insight into the nature of the world, it is absolutely necessary that we should learn to distinguish the will as thing-in-itself from its adequate objectivity, and to distinguish also the different grades in which this appears more and more distinctly and fully (*i.e.*, the Ideas themselves) from the merely phenomenal existence of these Ideas in the forms of the principle of sufficient reason, the individual's partial knowledge. We shall then agree with Plato when he attributes actual being only to the Ideas, and allows on the other hand only an illusive, dream-like existence to things in space and time, which for the individual comprise the real world. Then we shall understand how one and the same Idea reveals itself in so many phenomena, and to knowing individuals presents its nature only bit by bit, one side after another. Then we shall also distinguish the Idea itself from the way in which its manifestation occurs in the observation of the individual, and recognise the former as essential and the latter as inessential.

Let us consider this on the level of minutiae as well as on the grand scale. When the clouds move, the shapes which they form are not essential, but accidental to them; but that these clouds are made of vapour that expands and contracts, that they are compressed by the wind, driven along, spread out, or torn apart: this is their nature, the essence of the forces which objectify themselves in them, this is the Idea; their transient shapes are only for the individual observer. To the brook that flows over stones, the eddies, the waves, the foam-flakes which it forms are indifferent and inessential; but that it follows the pull of gravity, and behaves as inelastic, perfectly malleable, formless, transparent liquid: this is its nature; this, *if known through perception*, is its Idea; these accidental forms are only for us as long as we know as individuals. The ice on the window-pane forms into crystals according to the laws of crystallisation that reveal the essence of the natural force that is operating here, and exhibiting the Idea; but the trees and flowers which the ice forms on the pane are inessential, and exist only for us. What appears in the clouds, the brook, and the crystal is the weakest echo of that will which appears more fully in the plant, more fully still in the animal, and most fully in man. But only the essential in all these grades of the will's objectification constitutes the Idea; on the other hand, the unfolding or development of the idea, its being dispersed in the forms of the principle of sufficient reason into complex many-sided phenomena, is inessential to it and lies merely in the individual's mode of knowing and has reality only for this individual. The same thing necessarily holds good for the unfolding of that Idea which is the most complete objectivity of will. Therefore, the history of the human race, the throng of events, successive epochs, the many different forms of human life in different lands and centuries, all this is only fortuitously the form in which the Idea is manifest, belongs not to the Idea itself, in which alone lies the adequate objectivity of the will, but belongs only to the phenomenon which falls within the range of an individual's knowing, and is just as foreign, inessential, and indifferent to the Idea itself as the shapes which they assume are to the clouds, the form of its eddies and foam-flakes to the brook, or its trees and flowers to the ice.

Anyone who has thoroughly grasped this, and can distinguish between the will and the Idea, and between the Idea and its manifestation, will think the events of the world significant not in themselves but only in so far as they are the alphabet through which we may read the Idea of man. He will not believe, like ordinary folk, that time may produce something actually new and significant; that through it, or in it, something that is simply real may attain to existence, or indeed that time itself as a whole may have beginning and end, plan and development, and may even have as its ultimate aim the highest perfection (according to their notions) of the latest generation that lives a brief thirty years. Consequently he will no more, like Homer, people a whole Olympus with gods to direct those events than he will, like Ossian, regard the shapes of the clouds as individual beings; for, as we have said, both have just as much meaning as regards the Idea which appears in them. In the manifold forms of human life and in the unceasing flux of events he will consider permanent and essential only the idea in which the will to life has its fullest objectivity, and which shows its different aspects in the capacities, the passions, the errors and the excellences of the human race: in self-interest, hatred, love, fear, boldness, frivolity, stupidity, slyness, wit, genius, and so forth. All of these, converging and combining in thousands of forms (individuals), continually present the history of the great and the little world;

and it is all the same whether these worlds are set in motion by nuts or by crowns. In the end he will find that in this world it is the same as in the dramas of Gozzi, in all of which the same characters appear with like intention and with like fate; the motives and incidents are certainly different in each play, but the spirit of the incidents is the same; the characters in one play know nothing of the events of another, although they played a part in it themselves; so after all they have experienced and learned in the earlier plays, Pantaloon has become no more agile or generous, Tartaglia no more conscientious, Brighella no more courageous, and Columbine no more chaste.

Suppose we were allowed, for once, a clear glance into the kingdom of the possible, and over all the chains of causes and effects; if the earth-spirit appeared and showed us in a tableau all the greatest men, enlighteners of the world, and heroes whom chance destroyed before they were ripe for their work; then showed us the great events that would have changed the history of the world and brought in periods of the highest culture and enlightenment, but which the blindest chance, the most insignificant accident, hindered at the outset; lastly, the splendid powers of great individuals, that would have enriched whole epochs, but which, misled either by error or passion, or compelled by necessity, they squandered on unworthy or unfruitful objects, or even wasted in play. If we saw all this, we would shudder and lament at the thought of the lost treasures of whole periods of history. But the earth-spirit would smile and say, 'The source from which the individuals and their powers proceed is as inexhaustible and boundless as time and space; for, like these forms of all phenomena, they too are only phenomena, visibility of the will. No finite measure can exhaust that infinite source; therefore undiminished eternity is still open for the recurrence of any event or work that was nipped in the bud. In this world of phenomena true loss is only as possible as true gain. The will alone is; it is the thing in-itself, and the source of all those phenomena. Its self-knowledge, and the affirmation or denial chosen as a consequence, is the only event in itself.'

§ 36. History follows the thread of events; it is pragmatic in so far as it retraces them in accordance with the law of motivation, a law that determines the self-manifesting will wherever it is illuminated by knowledge. At the lower grades of its objectivity, where the will still acts without knowledge, natural science, in the form of aetiology, studies the laws governing the changes in its phenomena, and, in the form of morphology, it studies what is permanent in them. This almost endless task the natural sciences make easier by means of abstractions, drawing together what is general in order to separate what is particular. Lastly, mathematics considers the mere forms – time and space – in which the Ideas, stretched out into plurality, are made manifest to the knowledge of the subject as individual. All these, of which the collective name is science, proceed according to the principle of sufficient reason in its different forms, and their theme is always the phenomenon, its laws, its context and the resulting relations.

But what kind of knowledge is concerned with what is outside and independent of all relations, the only thing really essential to the world, the true content of its phenomena, that which is not subject to the flux of time and is thus known with equal truth for all time – in a word, the *Ideas*, which are the direct and adequate objectivity of the thing in-itself, of the will? It is *Art*, the work of genius. It repeats or reproduces the eternal Ideas grasped through pure contemplation, the essential and abiding element in all the phenomena of the world; and according to the material in which it reproduces, it is sculpture, painting, poetry or music. Its one source is the knowledge of Ideas; its one aim the communication of this knowledge. While science, following the ceaseless and inconstant stream of the fourfold forms of reason and consequence, is with each goal it attains bidden to go further and can never reach a final goal, nor attain full satisfaction, any more than by running we can reach the place where the clouds touch the horizon; art, on the contrary, is everywhere at its goal. For it plucks the object of its contemplation out of the stream of the world's course, and holds it isolated before it. And this particular thing, which in that stream was a minute part, becomes for art a representative of the whole, an equivalent of the endless multitude in space and time. So art pauses at this particular thing; it stops the wheel of time, for art the relations vanish; only the essential, the Idea, is its object.

We may, therefore, accurately define it as the *way of viewing things independent of the principle of sufficient reason*, in opposition to the way of viewing them which proceeds in accordance with that principle, and which is the method of experience and of science. This latter method of considering things may be compared to a line infinitely extended in a horizontal direction, and the former to a vertical line which cuts it at any point. The method of viewing things which proceeds in accordance with the principle of sufficient reason is the rational method, and it alone is valid and of use in practical life and in science. The method which turns away from the content of this principle is the method of genius, which is valid and of use only in art. The first is the method of Aristotle; the second is, on the whole, that of Plato. The first is like the mighty storm that rushes along without beginning and without end, bending, agitating, and carrying away everything before it; the second is like the ray of sun that calmly pierces the storm and is not deflected by it. The first is like the innumerable, violently agitated drops of the waterfall, constantly changing, never for an instant at rest; the second is like the rainbow, silently resting on this raging torrent.

Only through the pure contemplation described above, which is absorbed entirely in the object, are Ideas comprehended; and the nature of *genius* consists in pre-eminent capacity for such contemplation. Now, as this requires that a man should be oblivious of the self and the relations in which he stands, *genius* is simply the most complete *objectivity*, *i.e.*, the objective tendency of the mind, as opposed to the subjective which is directed to one's own self – in other words, to the will. Thus genius is the capacity to maintain oneself in the state of pure perception, to lose oneself in perception, and to withdraw from the service of the will the knowledge which originally existed only for that service; that is to say, genius is the power of leaving one's own interests, wishes, and aims entirely out of sight, thus of entirely divesting oneself of one's own personality for a time so as to remain *pure knowing subject*, clear eye of the world; and this is not merely at moments, but for long enough, and with consciousness enough, to enable one to reproduce by deliberate art what has thus been apprehended, and 'to fix in lasting thoughts the hovering images that float before the mind' [Goethe, *Faust*]. It is as if, for genius to appear in an individual, a far larger measure of the power of intellect has to have fallen to his lot than is necessary for the service of an individual will; and this available superfluity of knowledge now becomes subject purified of will, a clear mirror of the essence of the world. This explains the vitality, which borders on restlessness, in men of genius, for the present can seldom satisfy them, because it does not engross their consciousness. This gives them that restless ambition, that ceaseless desire for new things and for the contemplation of ennobling things; and also that longing, seldom satisfied, for people of like mind with whom they might communicate, whilst the common person, entirely engrossed and satisfied by the present, is taken up with it, and finding companions everywhere, enjoys in everyday life a complacency that is denied to genius.

Imagination has rightly been recognised as an essential element of genius; indeed it has sometimes even been regarded as identical with it; but the latter is a mistake. The objects of genius as such are the eternal Ideas – the permanent, essential forms of the world and all its phenomena – whereas the knowledge of the Idea is necessarily knowledge through perception, and is not abstract. Therefore the intellect of the genius would be limited to the Ideas of the objects actually present to him personally, and dependent upon the chain of circumstances that brought these objects to him, if his imagination did not extend his horizon far beyond the limits of his actual personal experience, and thus enable him to construct the rest of the picture out of the little that comes into his own actual apperception, and so to let almost all the possible scenes of life pass before him in his own consciousness. Further, the actual objects are almost always very imperfect copies of the Idea which shows itself in them; therefore the man of genius requires imagination in order to see in things not what Nature has actually fashioned, but what she tried to fashion but could not because of the conflict of her forms with one another, which we referred to in the previous Book. We shall return to this later in considering sculpture. The imagination then extends, both in quality and quantity, the intellectual horizon of the man of genius beyond the objects which actually present themselves to him.

In this way an unusually strong imagination accompanies genius, and is indeed its prerequisite. But the converse does not hold, for strength of imagination does not indicate genius; on the contrary, men who have no touch of genius may have much imagination. For, just as it is possible to consider a real object in two opposite ways – purely objectively, by grasping, as genius would, its Idea; or in the banal way, merely in the relations in which, in accordance with the principle of sufficient reason, it stands to other objects and to one's own will – so it is possible also to perceive the product of imagination in both of these ways. Regarded in the first way, it is a means of bringing to our knowledge the Idea, which the work of art communicates; in the second case, the product of the imagination is used to build castles in the air, such as are consistent with self-interest and personal whim, and which for the moment delude and gratify; and in this case only the relations of the associated fantasies are brought to our knowledge. The person who plays this game is fantasising; he will easily jumble up with reality those images that delight his solitude, and so unfit himself for real life. Perhaps he will write down these figments of his imagination, whereupon they will give rise to ordinary novels of every type. These will entertain people of disposition similar to this author, and, indeed, the general public, for the readers imagine themselves in the hero's situation, and then find the scenes he paints to be just what they like.

The ordinary person, this mass-product which Nature daily manufactures by the thousand, is not, as we have said, capable – at least, not continuously capable – of considering things in a way that is in every sense wholly disinterested, as real contemplation is. He can turn his attention to things only in so far as they have some relation to his will, however indirect it may be. Since for this, which never demands anything but the knowledge of relations, the abstract conception of the thing is sufficient, and for the most part even more useful, the ordinary man does not linger long over the mere perception, does not fix his attention long on one object, but in all that is presented to him looks quickly, as the lazy man looks for a chair, merely for the concept under which it is to be brought, and then it interests him no further. This is why he is so soon done with everything, with works of art, objects of natural beauty, and with life's spectacle from one scene to the next, truly meaningful as this always is. He does not linger; he seeks only his own way in life, or anything that might at any time become his way. Thus he makes topographical observations in the widest sense, but over the consideration of life itself as such he wastes no time. The man of genius, on the other hand, whose intellect can by its preponderance elude the service of will for some of the time, dwells on the consideration of life itself, strives to grasp the Idea of each thing, not its relation to other things; and in doing this he often neglects to consider his own path in life, and therefore for the most part pursues it rather clumsily. While to the ordinary man his faculty of knowledge is a lamp to lighten his path, to the man of genius it is the sun which reveals the world.

This great difference in their way of looking at life soon becomes visible in the outward appearance of the two. The man in whom genius lives and works is easily distinguished by his eyes, which are both vivacious and steady, and bear the stamp of thoughtfulness, contemplation. This can be seen from the portraits of the few men of genius whom Nature has produced here and there among countless millions. On the other hand, in the eyes of the ordinary man the very opposite can easily be seen, if indeed they are not dull or vacant, as they generally are. Accordingly 'the expression of genius' in a face consists in the visible predominance of knowledge over will, and consequently there also shows itself in it a knowledge that is entirely without relation to will, *i.e.*, *pure knowing*. On the contrary, in ordinary countenances the expression of will is predominant; and we see that knowledge becomes active only under the impulse of will, and thus is directed merely at motives.

Since the knowledge that pertains to genius, or the knowledge of the Idea, is that knowledge which does not follow the principle of sufficient reason, and, on the other hand, the knowledge which *does* follow that principle is that which gives us prudence and rationality in life, and which produces the sciences, men of genius are beset by the defects which follow from the neglect of this latter kind of knowledge. Yet what I say in this regard applies only in so far as, and while, they are actually engaged in that kind of knowledge which is peculiar to genius; and this is by no means at every moment of their lives, for the great (though spontaneous) exertion needed for the comprehension - which is free of will - of the Ideas must necessarily relax, and there are long intervals during which men of genius are placed in very much the same position as ordinary mortals, as regards both their merits and their deficiencies. Hence the operation of genius has always been regarded as an inspiration, or indeed, as the name indicates, the activity of a superhuman being distinct from the individual himself, and which takes possession of him only periodically.

The disinclination of men of genius to direct their attention to the content of the principle of sufficient reason will first show itself in regard to the ground of being, as dislike of mathematics; for the study of maths is directed to the most universal forms of the phenomenon, space and time, which are themselves merely modes of the principle of sufficient reason, and is consequently the very opposite of that method of thought which, disregarding all relations, seeks merely the *content* of the phenomenon, the Idea which expresses itself in it. Furthermore, the logical method of mathematics is repugnant to genius, for it does not satisfy, but obstructs true insight. Instead, by presenting merely a chain of conclusions in accordance with the principle of the ground of knowing, mathematics involves the memory more than other mental faculties, for it is necessary to keep in mind all the earlier propositions upon which the calculation is based. Experience has also proved that people of great artistic genius have no aptitude for mathematics; no-one was ever very distinguished for both. From the same cause may be explained the equally well-known fact that, conversely, excellent mathematicians have very little susceptibility for works of fine art. This is very naively expressed in the well-known anecdote about the French mathematician who, after having read Racine's *Iphigénie*, shrugged his shoulders and asked, '*Qu'est-ce que cela prouve?*'

Since, moreover, an acute understanding of relations in accordance with the laws of causality and motivation is what specially constitutes cleverness, whereas the knowledge which characterises genius is not directed to relations, a clever man as such will not be a genius, and a man of genius, as such, will not be a clever man. Lastly, perceptive knowledge generally, in the province of which the Idea always lies, is directly opposed to rational or abstract knowledge, which is directed by the principle of the ground of knowing. It is also well known that we seldom find great genius in tandem with pre-eminent reasonableness; on the contrary, persons of genius are often subject to violent emotions and irrational passions. The cause of this is not weakness in the faculty of reasoning, but partly the uncommon energy of that whole phenomenon of will – the man of genius – which expresses itself through vehemence in all his acts of will; and partly the preponderance of perceptive knowledge (gained through the senses and understanding) over abstract knowledge. This produces a decided tendency to the perceptible, which makes an overwhelming impression on these men, an impression so much more vivid than colourless abstraction that it governs their conduct, which consequently becomes irrational. Accordingly the impression of the present moment is very strong with such people, and carries them away into impetuosity, emotion and passion. For that reason, and also because more generally, their intelligence has to some extent freed itself from the service of will, they will in conversation think not so much of the person they are addressing as of the thing they are speaking about, and which is vividly present in their minds; and therefore they are likely to judge or narrate things too objectively for their own interests; they will not pass over in silence what would more prudently be concealed, and so forth. Thus, in the end, they are given to talking to themselves, and in general may exhibit certain weaknesses which are actually akin to madness.

It has often been remarked that genius and madness have an aspect in common, and even converge; and indeed poetical inspiration has been called a kind of madness: *amabilis insania*, Horace calls it (*Odes*. iii. 4). Plato expresses it in the myth of the dark cave (*Rep.* 7), when he says: 'Those who, outside the cave, have seen the true sunlight and the things that have true being (Ideas), cannot afterwards see properly in the cave, because their eyes have grown unaccustomed to the darkness; they can no longer recognise the shadows, and are jeered at for their mistakes by those who have never left the cave and its shadows.' In the *Phaedrus* also, he distinctly says that there can be no true poet without a certain madness; in fact, that everyone appears mad who recognises the eternal Ideas in fleeting things. And, lastly, Pope says –

> Great wits to madness sure are near allied,
> And thin partitions do their bounds divide.[1]

Especially instructive in this respect is Goethe's *Torquato Tasso*, in which he shows us not only the suffering, the martyrdom of genius as such, but also how it constantly passes into madness. Finally, the contiguity of genius and madness is confirmed in fact by the biographies of great men of genius such as Rousseau, Byron, and Alfieri, and by anecdotes from the lives of others.

On the other hand, I must mention that on my frequent visits

---

[1] [In fact, it is Dryden in *Absolem and Architophel* I. 163]

to lunatic asylums I have found individual patients who were unquestionably endowed with great talents and whose genius distinctly appeared through their madness, which, however, had completely gained the upper hand. Now this cannot be ascribed to chance, for on the one hand the number of mad persons is relatively very small, and on the other hand a person of genius is a phenomenon rare beyond all ordinary estimation and appearing in nature only as the greatest exception. We can convince ourselves only by comparing the number of really great men of genius produced by the whole of civilised Europe, both in ancient and modern times, with the two hundred and fifty million who are the constant population of Europe, which renews itself every thirty years. (In estimating the number of men of outstanding genius we must, of course, count only those who have produced works which have retained through all time an enduring value for mankind.) I shall not refrain from mentioning that I have known some persons of decided, though not remarkable, mental superiority, who showed, along with that, a slight trace of insanity. It might seem from this that every advance of intellect beyond the ordinary measure, as an exception to the norm, disposes to madness. In the meantime, however, I will present as briefly as possible my view of the purely intellectual basis of the relation between genius and madness, for this will certainly assist the explanation of the real nature of genius, that is to say, of that mental endowment which alone can produce genuine works of art. But this necessitates a brief discussion of madness itself.

A clear and complete insight into the nature of madness, a correct and distinct conception of what constitutes the difference between the sane person and the insane, has, as far as I know, not as yet been arrived at. Mad people cannot be said to lack either reason or understanding, for they speak and listen, and often draw very accurate conclusions; they also, as a rule, perceive quite correctly what is present, and understand the connection between cause and effect. Visions, like the fantasies of delirium, are no ordinary symptom of madness: delirium falsifies perception, while madness falsifies the thoughts. For the most part, madmen do not err in the knowledge of what is immediately *present*; their confused talk always relates to what is *absent* and *past*, and only through these to their connection with what is present. Therefore it seems to me that their malady specially affects the memory; not indeed that memory fails them entirely, for many of them know a great deal by heart, and sometimes recognise persons whom they have not seen for a long time; but rather that the thread of memory is broken, its continuity disrupted, and no evenly connected recollection of the past is possible. Particular scenes from the past stand out correctly, just like the particular present; but there are gaps in their recollection which they fill up with fictions, and these are either always the same, in which case they become fixed ideas, and the madness that results is called fixed mania or melancholy; or they are always different, momentary fancies, and then it is called folly, *fatuitas*. This is why it is so difficult to question a mad person about his former life when he enters an asylum. The true and the false are increasingly mixed up in his memory. Although the immediate present is correctly known, it becomes falsified through its fictitious connection with an imaginary past; they therefore regard themselves and others as identical with persons who exist only in their imaginary past; they do not recognise some of their acquaintances at all, and thus while they perceive correctly the individual who is actually present, they associate him incorrectly with another one who is absent. If the madness reaches a high degree, there is complete absence of memory, so that the madman is quite incapable of any reference to what is absent or past, and is determined only by the whim of the moment in combination with the fictions which in his mind fill the past. In such a case we are never for a moment safe from personal assault or murder, unless we constantly make the madman aware that he can be overpowered.

The knowledge of the madman has in common with that of the animal that both are confined to the present. What distinguishes them is that the animal has really no idea of the past as such, though the past acts upon it through the medium of habit, so that, for example, the dog recognises its former master even after years, that is to say, seeing his master makes on the dog the same impression as before; but of the time that has passed since it saw him, it has no recollection. The madman, on the other hand, always carries with him in his reasoning an abstract past, but it is a false past that exists only for him, either constantly or only for the moment. The influence of this false past prevents him from using his accurate perception of the present as the animal can. That violent mental suffering, or

unexpected and terrible calamities, should often produce madness, I explain as follows. All such suffering is, as an actual
event, confined to the present. It is thus merely transitory, and
so for the moment is not excessive; it becomes unendurable
only when it is lasting pain; but as such it exists only in thought,
and therefore lies in the *memory*. If now such anguish, such
painful knowledge or reflection, is so tormenting that it is simply
unbearable, and the individual might succumb, then Nature in
alarm seizes upon *madness* as the last hope of saving his life; the
mind so fearfully tortured at once breaks the thread of memory,
fills up the gaps with fictions, and thus seeks refuge in madness
from the mental suffering that exceeds its strength, just as we
cut off a gangrenous limb and replace it with a wooden one. We
may consider as examples the raving Ajax, King Lear, and
Ophelia; for the creations of true genius (the only ones to which
we can refer here as being universally known) are in their
truthfulness to be considered on a par with real people; besides,
in this case, frequent actual experience shows the same thing. A
faint analogy of this kind of transition from pain to madness is
our often trying, as it were mechanically, by some loud exclamation or by bodily movement, to dismiss a painful thought
that suddenly occurs to us, to divert our attention from it, and
forcibly to distract ourselves.

We have supposed that the madman accurately recognises
discreet elements in the present, and also in the past, but that
he mistakes the connection, the relationship of one thing to
another, and therefore falls into error and talks nonsense. Now
this is exactly his point of contact with the man of genius; for he
also fails to recognise the connection of things, since he aban-
dons that knowledge of relations which conforms to the principle of sufficient reason, in order to see in things only their
Ideas, and to seek to comprehend their true nature which
manifests itself to perception, and in regard to which *one* thing
represents its whole species, for which reason, as Goethe says,
one instance is valid for a thousand. The particular object of his
contemplation, or the present which he perceives with extraordinary vividness, appear in so bright a light that the other
links of the chain to which they belong at once recede into the
shade, and this gives rise to phenomena which have long been
recognised as resembling those of madness. A quality that exists
only incomplete and attenuated in the object to hand, the man

of genius will enhance and raise to the Idea of the thing, to perfection: so everywhere he sees extremes, and his own activity tends to extremes; he cannot strike the mean, he lacks sobriety, and the result is as we have said. He knows the Ideas perfectly, but not the individual instances. Thus it has been said that a poet may know mankind profoundly, and may yet have a very imperfect knowledge of men. He is easily deceived, and is a plaything in the hands of the crafty.

§ 37. Genius, then, consists, according to our explanation, in the capacity for knowing independently of the principle of sufficient reason, and hence for knowing not individual things (which have their existence only in their relations) but the Ideas of such things, and of being in relation to these things oneself the correlative of the Idea, and thus no longer an individual, but the pure subject of knowing. Yet this faculty must exist in all human beings in a smaller and different degree; for if not, they would be just as incapable of enjoying works of art as of producing them; they would have no susceptibility for the beautiful or the sublime; indeed, these terms could have no meaning for them. We must therefore assume that there exists in all men this power of knowing the Ideas in things, and consequently of setting aside their personality for the moment, unless indeed there are some men who are capable of no aesthetic pleasure at all. The man of genius excels ordinary men only by possessing this kind of knowledge in a far higher degree, and more continuously. Thus, while under its influence he retains the presence of mind which is necessary to enable him to repeat in a voluntary and intentional work what he has learned in this manner; and this repetition is the work of art.

Through this work he communicates to others the Idea he has grasped. This Idea remains unchanged and the same, so that aesthetic pleasure is one and the same whether it is elicited by a work of art or directly, by the contemplation of nature and life. The work of art is only a means of facilitating the knowledge in which this pleasure consists. That the Idea comes to us more easily from the work of art than directly from nature and the real world, arises solely from the fact that the artist, who knew only the Idea and no longer the actual, has reproduced in his work the pure Idea, has abstracted it from the actual, omitting all chance features which might distract from it. The artist lets us see into the world through his eyes. That he has these eyes, that he knows the inner nature of things apart from all their relations, is the gift of genius, is inborn; but that he is able to lend us this gift, to let us see with his eyes, is acquired, and is the technical side of art.

For this reason, after the account which I have given in the preceding pages of the inner nature of aesthetic knowledge in its most general outline, the following more exact philosophical treatment of the beautiful and the sublime will explain them both, in nature and in art, without separating them further. First of all we shall consider what takes place in a man when he is affected by the beautiful and the sublime; whether he derives this emotion directly from nature, from life, or partakes of it only through the medium of art, makes a difference outwardly but not essentially.

§ 38. In the aesthetic mode of contemplation we have found *two inseparable constituent parts* – the knowledge of the object, not as individual thing but as Platonic *Idea*, that is, as the enduring form of this whole species of things; and the self-consciousness of the knowing subject, not as individual, but as *pure will-less subject of knowledge*. The condition under which both these constituent parts appear always united was found to be the abandonment of the method of knowing which is bound to the principle of sufficient reason, and which, on the other hand, is the only kind of knowledge that is of value for the service of the will and also for science. We shall see, too, that the pleasure which is produced by the contemplation of the beautiful arises from these two constituent parts, sometimes more from the one, sometimes more from the other, according to what the object of the aesthetic contemplation may be.

All *willing* arises from need, therefore from deficiency, and therefore from suffering. The fulfilment of a wish ends it; yet for one wish that is fulfilled there remain at least ten which are denied. Further, the desire lasts long, the demands are infinite; the satisfaction is short and scantily measured out. But even the final satisfaction is itself only apparent; every satisfied wish at once makes room for a new one; both are delusions; the one is known to be so, the other not yet. No attained object of desire can give lasting satisfaction, but merely a fleeting gratification; it is like alms thrown to the beggar, keeping him alive today so that his misery may be prolonged till the morrow. Therefore, as long as our consciousness is filled by our will, as long as we are given up to the urgent prompting of desires with their constant hopes and fears, as long as we are the subject of willing, we can never have lasting happiness nor peace. It is essentially all the same whether we pursue or flee, fear harm or seek enjoyment; the care for the constant demands of the will, in whatever form it may be, continually occupies and sways the consciousness; but without peace no true well-being is possible. The subject of willing is thus constantly stretched on the revolving wheel of Ixion, draws water in the sieve of the Danaids, and is the ever-thirsting Tantalus.

But when some external cause or inward disposition lifts us suddenly out of the endless stream of willing, and snatches knowledge from the slavery of the will, the attention is no longer directed to the motives of willing, but comprehends things free from their relation to the will. Thus, it observes them without personal interest, without subjectivity, purely objectively, and it surrenders to them in so far as they are merely ideas, but not in so far as they are motives. Then all at once the peace which we were always seeking, but which on the former path of the desires, always eluded us comes to us of its own accord, and we experience a sense of well-being. It is the painless state which Epicurus prized as the highest good and as the state of the gods; for we are for the moment set free from the will's base urge; amid the penal servitude of willing we keep the Sabbath; the wheel of Ixion stands still.

But this is just the state which I described above as necessary for the knowledge of the Idea, as pure contemplation, as being absorbed in perception, losing oneself in the object, forgetting all individuality, the suspending of that kind of knowledge which follows the principle of sufficient reason, and comprehends only relations; the state by means of which, at once and inseparably, the perceived particular thing is raised to the Idea of its whole species, and the knowing individual to the pure subject of will-less knowledge, and as such they are both taken out of the stream of time and of all other relations. It is then all one whether we see the sun set from the prison or from the palace.

Inward disposition, the predominance of knowing over willing, can produce this state under any circumstances. This is shown by those admirable Dutch artists who directed this purely objective perception to the most insignificant objects, and established a lasting monument to their objectivity and spiritual peace in their pictures of *still life*, which the aesthetic beholder looks on not without emotion; for they present to him the peaceful, still frame of mind of the artist, free from will, which was needed to contemplate such insignificant things so objectively, to observe them so attentively, and to repeat this perception deliberately; and as the picture challenges the onlooker to participate in this state, his emotion is often increased by the contrast between it and the unquiet frame of mind, disturbed by vehement willing, in which he finds himself. In the same spirit landscape-painters, and particularly Ruisdael, have often painted very insignificant country scenes which produce the same effect even more pleasingly.

The inner power of an artistic disposition can do this on its own; but that purely objective frame of mind is facilitated and assisted from without by congenial objects, by the abundance of natural beauty which invites contemplation and even solicits our attention. Whenever it discloses itself suddenly to our view, it almost always succeeds in snatching us, even if only for a moment, from subjectivity, from the slavery of the will, and in transporting us to the state of pure knowing. This is why the man who is tormented by passions, or want, or care, is so suddenly revived, cheered, and restored by a single unrestricted glimpse of nature: the storm of passion, the pressure of desire and fear, and all the miseries of willing are then at once, and in a marvellous manner, calmed and appeased. For at the moment at which, freed from the will, we surrender to pure will-less knowing, we pass into a world from which everything that influences our will and agitates us so violently has passed away. This liberation of our knowing lifts us as wholly and entirely away from all that, as do sleep and dreams; happiness and unhappiness have disappeared; we are no longer individual; the individual is forgotten; we are only pure subject of knowledge; we are only that *one* eye of the world which looks out from all knowing creatures, but which in man alone can become perfectly free from the service of will. Thus all difference of individuality so entirely disappears that it is all the same whether the perceiving eye belongs to a mighty king or to a wretched beggar; for neither joy nor grieving is carried with us beyond that boundary.

So close to us always lies a tract of ground on which we have eluded all our suffering; but who has the strength to persevere in it? As soon as any single relation to our will, to our person, even of these objects of our pure contemplation, enters consciousness, the magic is at an end; we relapse into the knowledge which is governed by the principle of sufficient reason; we no longer know the Idea, but the particular thing, the link in the chain to which we also belong, and we are again abandoned to all our woe. Most people remain almost always at this standpoint because they entirely lack objectivity, *i.e.*, genius. Therefore they have no pleasure in being alone with nature; they need company, or at least a book. For their knowledge remains subject to the will; they seek, therefore, in objects, only some relation to their will, and whenever they see anything that has no such relation, there sounds within them, like a ground-bass in music, the constant inconsolable cry, 'It is of no use to me'; thus in solitude the most beautiful surroundings have for them a desolate, dark, strange, and hostile appearance.

Lastly, it is this serenity of will-less perception which casts an enchanting glamour over the past and the far-off, and by means of self-deception presents them to us in a light so flattering. For as we think of days long past, days spent in a distant place, it is only the objects of will which our imagination recalls, not the subject of will, which carried with it then its incurable sorrows just as it bears them now; but they are forgotten, because since then they have often given place to others. Now, objective perception acts with regard to what is remembered just as it would in what is present, if we could bring ourselves to surrender to it, renouncing our will. Hence, especially when we are more than ordinarily disturbed by some want, the remembrance of past and distant scenes suddenly flits across our minds like a lost paradise. The imagination recalls only what was objective, not what was individually subjective, and we imagine that that objective stood before us then just as pure and undisturbed by any relation to the will as its image stands in our imagination now; while in reality the relation of the objects to our will gave us pain then just as it does now. We can deliver ourselves from all suffering just as well through present objects as through distant ones as soon as we raise ourselves to a purely objective contemplation of them, and so are able to bring about the illusion that only the objects are present, and not we ourselves. Then, as the pure subject of knowledge, freed from the miserable self, we become entirely one with these objects, and, for the moment, our distress is as foreign to us as it is to them. The world as idea alone remains, and the world as will has disappeared.

In all these reflections I wish to make clear the nature and the scope of the subjective element in aesthetic pleasure – that is the deliverance of knowledge from the service of the will, the forgetting of oneself as individual, and the raising of consciousness to the pure will-less, timeless, subject of knowledge, independent of all relations. With this subjective side of aesthetic contemplation must always appear as its necessary correlative the objective side, the intuitive comprehension of the Platonic Idea. But before we turn to the closer consideration of this, and to the achievements of art in relation to it, it is better that we should pause for a little at the subjective side of aesthetic pleasure, in order to complete our treatment of this by discussing the impression of the *sublime*; this depends entirely upon it, and arises from a modification of it. After that we shall complete our investigation of aesthetic pleasure by considering its objective side.

But first, the following remarks are relevant to what has been said. Light is the most joyous of things; it has become the symbol of all that is good and salutary. In all religions it symbolises salvation, while darkness symbolises damnation. Ormuzd dwells in the purest light, Ahriman in eternal night. Dante's Paradise looks very much like Vauxhall in London, for all the blessed spirits appear as points of light which together form regular figures. The absence of light immediately makes us sad; its return cheers us. Colours immediately excite a keen delight which reaches its highest degree when they are transparent. All this depends entirely upon the fact that light is the correlative and condition of the most perfect mode of knowledge through perception, the only knowledge which does not directly affect the will. For sight, unlike the affections of the other senses, cannot in itself, directly and through its sensuous effect, make the *sensation* of the special organ agreeable or disagreeable; that is, it has no immediate connection with the will. Such a connection can belong only to the perception which arises in the understanding, and then it lies in the relation of the object to the will. In the case of hearing, this is different; sounds can be immediately painful, and they may also be sensuously pleasant, directly and without regard to harmony or melody. Touch, as being one with the feeling of the whole body, is subject even more to this direct influence on the will; and yet there is such a thing as touch which is painless and pleasureless. But smells are always either agreeable or disagreeable, and tastes still more so. Thus the last two senses are most closely related to the will, and therefore they are always the least pure, and have been called by Kant the subjective senses.

Our pleasure in light is, indeed, only pleasure in the objective possibility of the purest and fullest perceptive knowledge, and as such it is derived from the fact that pure knowing, freed and released from all will, is extremely pleasant, and of itself constitutes a large part of aesthetic enjoyment. From our attitude to light we derive, in turn, the incredible beauty which we acknowledge in the reflection of objects in water. That slightest, swiftest, finest interaction between bodies to which we owe by far the most complete and pure of our perceptions, the play of reflected rays of light, is here brought clearly before our eyes, distinct and perfect, in cause and in effect, and on a grand scale; hence the aesthetic delight it gives us, which is entirely based on the subjective ground of aesthetic pleasure, and is delight in pure knowing and its ways.

§ 39. All these reflections are intended to emphasise the subjective part of aesthetic pleasure; that is to say, that pleasure in so far as it is delight in perceptive knowledge as such, as distinct from will. Directly connected with this, there now follows an explanation of that frame of mind which has been called the sense of the *sublime*.

We have already remarked above that one can be most readily transported into the state of pure perception when the objects lend themselves to it, that is, when by their manifold and yet definite and distinct form they easily become representatives of their Ideas; and in this beauty, in the objective sense, consists. This quality belongs preeminently to natural beauty, which thus affords, even to the most insensitive, at least a fleeting aesthetic satisfaction. [. . .] As long as what transports us away from the knowledge of mere relations subject to the will, and towards aesthetic contemplation, and thereby exalts us to the position of the subject of knowledge free from will, is nature's congeniality, this meaningfulness and distinctness of its forms, out of which the Ideas individualised in them appeal to us – while that is so, it is merely *beauty* that affects us and the sense of the *beautiful* that is excited. But the very objects whose meaningful forms invite us to pure contemplation may be generally hostile towards the human will as it exhibits itself in its objectivity – in the human body. If they are opposed to it, if, in their overwhelming power, they threaten it, or, if in the face of their immeasurable greatness they reduce it to nothingness; if, in spite of this, the beholder does not direct his attention to this imminently hostile attitude to his will, but, although aware of it and recognising it, turns consciously away from it, forcibly detaches himself from his will and its relations, and, surrendering to perception, calmly, as pure will-less subject of knowledge contemplates those very objects that are so terrifying to the will, comprehends only their Idea which is alien to all relation, so that he lingers pleasurably over it, and is thereby raised above himself, his person, his willing, and all willing – then he is filled with the sense of the *sublime*, he is in the state of spiritual exaltation; and so the object occasioning such a state is also called *sublime*.

What distinguishes the sense of the sublime from that of the beautiful is that with the beautiful, pure knowledge has gained the upper hand without a struggle, for the beauty of the object (*i.e.*, that property which facilitates the knowledge of its Idea) has banished from consciousness without resistance, and thus imperceptibly, the will and the knowledge of relations which is subject to it, so that what is left is the pure subject of knowledge without even a memory of will. With the sublime, on the other hand, that state of pure knowledge is attained by the same subject's conscious and forcible break with acknowledgedly disadvantageous relations to the will, by his freely and consciously transcending the will and the knowledge relating to it.

This exaltation must not only be consciously won, but also consciously retained, and hence it is accompanied by a constant memory of the will – not of a single particular volition, such as fear or desire, but of human volition in general, in so far as it is universally expressed in its objectivity, the human body. If a single real act of will were to enter consciousness, through actual personal jeopardy and danger from the object, then the individual will, once it had been moved by this actual circumstance, would at once gain the upper hand, and serene contemplation would become impossible. The impression of the sublime would be dissipated because it would yield to anxiety in which the individual's efforts to save himself would displace every other thought.

A few examples will help to clarify this theory of the aesthetic sublime, and remove all doubt about it; and our examples will at the same time show how various are the degrees of this sense of the sublime. It is broadly identical with the sense of the beautiful, with pure will-less knowing, and the knowledge (that necessarily accompanies it) of Ideas which stand outside all relation determined by the principle of sufficient reason; and it differs from the sense of the beautiful only by this additional quality: when the object contemplated is in principle hostile to the will, the sense of the sublime, recognising this hostility, can rise above it. The various degrees of the sublime, and its shading into the beautiful correspond to whether this additional quality is strong, bold, urgent, near, or weak, distant, and faint. I consider it more appropriate to my presentation here that I should first offer examples of these transitional states (between the sublime and the beautiful), and of the weaker degrees of the impression of the sublime, although people whose aesthetic susceptibility overall is not very great, and whose imagination is not lively, will understand only the later examples of the higher and more distinct grades of that impression; hence they should confine themselves to these alone, and disregard my earlier examples of the very weak degrees of the sublime.

Just as man is both impetuous, dark impulse of will (epitomised by the genital organs), and at the same time, eternal, free, serene subject of pure knowing (epitomised by the brain); so, by analogy with this antithesis, the sun is both the source of *light*, the condition of the most perfect kind of knowledge, and thereby of the most delightful of things – and the source of *warmth*, the first condition of all life, *i.e.*, of all phenomenon of will in its higher grades. Hence, what warmth is for the will, light is for knowledge. Light is the biggest jewel in beauty's crown, and has the most decisive influence on the knowledge of every beautiful object. Its mere presence is an indispensable condition of beauty; when it is favourably positioned, it increases the beauty of the most beautiful. Architectural beauty more than any other object is enhanced by favourable lighting; though in these conditions even the most insignificant thing becomes a beautiful object. If, in a harsh winter, when all nature is stiff with cold, we see the rays of the sun when it is low in the sky, reflected by masses of stone, illuminating them without warming, and amenable only to the purest mode of knowledge, not to the will, our contemplating the beautiful effect of the light upon these masses lifts us, as does all beauty, into a state of pure knowing. But in this case, we are gently reminded of the lack of warmth from these rays, and therewith of their deficit in the vitalising principle. This requires us to rise above the will's interest, gently challenges us to persevere in pure knowing, and to turn aside from all willing. Thus our sense of the beautiful passes over into a sense of the sublime. It is the faintest trace of the sublime in the beautiful; and beauty itself emerges here only in a slight degree. The following is an example of the sublime manifest in a degree almost equally slight.

Let us imagine ourselves transported to a very lonely place, with unrestricted horizon, under a cloudless sky, trees and plants in the perfectly motionless air, no animals, no people, no turbulent waterways; the deepest silence. Such surroundings are like a call to seriousness and contemplation, detaching us from all willing and its craving; and just this imparts to such a scene of solitude and stillness a touch of the sublime. For, because it affords no objects, either favourable or unfavourable, for the will which is constant endeavour and acquisition, there remains only the state of pure contemplation, and anyone incapable of this is ignominiously abandoned to the vacancy of unoccupied will, and to the misery of ennui. To a certain extent this is a measure of our intellectual worth, of which, generally speaking, the degree of our ability to endure solitude, or our love of it, is a good criterion. The scene we have sketched affords us, then, an example of the sublime in a low degree, for with the state of pure knowing in its peace and all-sufficiency is mingled here, by way of contrast, a recollection of the dependence and poverty of a will that needs constant activity. This is the species of the sublime for which the boundless prairies in the interior of North America are celebrated.

But let us imagine a plain like this, stripped bare of plants, and showing only naked rocks; then by the total absence of that organic life necessary for our survival, the will is immediately made anxious, the desert assumes a frightening character, our mood becomes more tragic; the elevation to the sphere of pure knowing takes place only after we have more resolutely detached ourselves from the will's interests; and because we persevere in the state of pure knowing, the sense of the sublime appears distinctly.

Surroundings like these may occasion this feeling in a still higher degree: nature shaken by a storm; half-light through threatening black thunder-clouds; huge, bare, overhanging crags which, jutting out this way and that, hem us in; rushing, foaming torrents; absolute barrenness; the wail of the wind sweeping through the gullies. Our dependence, our strife with hostile nature, our will broken in the conflict, is now plain for us to see. Yet, as long as our personal plight does not predominate, but we continue in aesthetic contemplation, the pure subject of knowing, unshaken and unconcerned, looks beyond that strife in nature, beyond that image of the broken will, and quietly comprehends the Ideas even in those very objects which are threatening and terrible to the will. It is in this contrast that the sense of the sublime lies.

But the impression becomes even more powerful, if, when we have before our eyes the struggle of the raging elements on a large scale: when in these surroundings the roar of a waterfall makes it impossible for us to hear the sound of our own voice; or, when we are standing beside the sea when it is lashed by storm, where the waves, high as houses, rise and fall, are driven violently against steep cliffs, toss their foam high into the air; the storm howls, the sea roars, the lightning flashes from black clouds, and the thunder-claps are louder than the storm and sea. Then, in the person who can watch this without being shaken by it, the ambivalence of his consciousness becomes very clear. At one and the same time he feels that he is an individual, the will's frail phenomenon, which the slightest impact of these energies can demolish, that he is helpless against powerful nature, dependent, vulnerable to chance, an infinitesimal dot in relation to stupendous powers; and he feels also that he is the eternal, tranquil, knowing subject which as the condition of the object is therefore the supporter of this same world, and that nature's terrifying struggle is only his idea; the subject itself free and untouched by all desires and necessities, in the tranquil comprehension of the Ideas. This is the complete impression of the sublime, here induced by a glimpse of a power incomparably superior to the individual, a power which threatens him with annihilation.

The impression of the sublime may be induced in quite

another way, by our imagining sheer vastness in space and time – immeasurable vastness which reduces the individual to a nonentity. Retaining Kant's terminology and the distinction he quite properly drew, we can call the first kind the dynamically sublime, and the second the mathematically sublime, although our explanation of the inner nature of the impression is quite different from his, and we can allow neither moral reflections nor hypostases from scholastic philosophy to play a part in it.

If we lose ourselves in contemplation of the infinite greatness of the universe in space and time, meditate on the millennia of years that have passed and are yet to come, or if the night-sky actually brings before our eyes countless worlds, and so forces upon our consciousness the immensity of the universe, we feel ourselves reduced to nothing; as individuals, as bodies vitalised, as transient phenomena of will, we feel ourselves like drops in the ocean, dwindle and disperse into the void. But against this spectre of our own futility, against such mendacious impossibility, there rises up at once the immediate consciousness that all these worlds exist only in our ideation, only as modifications of the eternal subject of pure knowing, which we find ourselves to be as soon as we forget our individuality, and which is the necessary support of all worlds and all eras, and the condition of their existence. The vastness of the world which previously troubled us, now rests in us; our dependence on it is cancelled by its dependence on us. All this, however, does not come at once into reflection, but shows itself merely as the palpable consciousness that in some sense or other (which only philosophy can explain) we are one with the world, and therefore not oppressed, but exalted by its immensity. It is the consciousness of this that the Upanishads of the Vedas express again and again, formulating it in different ways, but most admirably in the saying already quoted above 'I am all these creatures, and besides me there is no other being' [see above]. It is the transcending of our own individual self, the sense of the sublime. [. . .]

§ 40. Since antitheses are mutually illuminating, this may be the right time for me to say that the proper opposite of the sublime is something which would not at first glance be recognised as such: the *charming* or *attractive*. But by this, I understand something that stimulates the will by holding out to it directly its indulgence, its gratification. We saw that the feeling of the sublime arises from the fact that something that brings to the will no advantage may become the object of pure contemplation, so that such contemplation can be maintained only by our persistently turning away from the will, and transcending its interests; this constitutes sublimity of mood. Thus the charming or attractive, on the contrary, draws the beholder away from the pure contemplation required to apprehend the beautiful, because it necessarily excites this will, through objects which directly appeal to it, and thus he no longer remains pure subject of knowing, but becomes the craving and dependent subject of will.

That every beautiful thing which is serene or cheerful should be called charming, results from taking the term too loosely, for lack of proper discrimination: and this I must entirely disregard, and indeed disapprove. But in the sense of the word already established and explained, I find in the province of art only two species of the charming or attractive, and both of them are unworthy of it. The one species, a very lowly one, is found in Dutch paintings of still life, when they are so mistaken as to depict foodstuffs, which, so deceptively rendered, inevitably tempt the appetite. This constitutes stimulation of the will, which puts a stop to all aesthetic contemplation of the subject. Painted fruit we can allow because it presents itself as the further development of the flower, and by way of its form and colour, as a beautiful product of nature, without our being forced to think of it as eatable; but unfortunately we often find, represented with deceptive naturalness, food that has been prepared and set out on the table – oysters, herrings, crabs, bread and butter, beer, wine, and so forth – and that is objectionable.

In historical painting and in sculpture the charming consists in naked figures, of which the pose, the semi-nakedness, and the whole treatment are calculated to excite the passions of the beholder, and thus purely aesthetic contemplation is at once suspended, and the purpose of art is undermined. This mistake corresponds exactly to what we have just deplored in the Dutch paintings. With all the beauty and utter nakedness of their human figures, the ancients are almost always free of this fault, because the artist himself created them in a spirit that was purely objective, and filled with ideal beauty, not in the spirit of subjective, base desire. So in art the charming is to be avoided.

There is also a negative species of the charming or exciting which is even more reprehensible than the positive form which we have just discussed; this is the disgusting or nauseating. It arouses the will of the beholder, as does what is, properly speaking, charming, and thereby destroys pure aesthetic contemplation. But it is a violent aversion and revulsion which it excites; it arouses the will by presenting to it things it abhors. For that reason it has long been recognised as altogether inadmissible in art, where even what is ugly, provided that it is not disgusting, can be tolerated in its proper place, as we shall see later.

§ 41. The course of our study has made it necessary to insert at this point our discussion of the sublime, where we have only half-completed our discussion of the beautiful, having considered only its subjective aspect. For it was merely a special modification of this subjective aspect that distinguished the beautiful from the sublime. This difference between the beautiful and the sublime depends on whether the state of pure will-less knowing, which all aesthetic contemplation presupposes and demands, comes about of itself, without resistance, as a result of the will's merely vanishing from consciousness, because the object invited and drew us towards it; or whether it was attained only through the free, conscious transcending of the will, to which the object contemplated had an unfavourable and even hostile relation, which would put an end to contemplation altogether, if we were to give ourselves up to it. In the object, the beautiful and the sublime are not essentially different, for in every instance the object of aesthetic contemplation is not the individual thing, but the Idea in it which is striving to reveal itself – the idea being the adequate objectivity of will at a particular grade. Its necessary correlative – and independent, like itself, of the principle of sufficient reason – is the pure subject of knowing; just as the correlative of the particular thing is the knowing individual, both of which lie within the province of the principle of sufficient reason.

In calling a thing *beautiful*, we thereby assert that it is an object of our aesthetic contemplation, and this implies two things. On the one hand, it means that the sight of the thing makes us *objective*, that is to say, that in contemplating it we are no longer conscious of ourselves as individuals, but as pure will-less subjects of knowledge; and, on the other hand, it means that we recognise in the object, not the particular thing, but an Idea; and this can happen only in so far as our contemplation of it is not subordinated to the principle of sufficient reason, does not trace the relation of the object to anything outside it (which is always ultimately connected with relations to our own will), but rests in the object itself. For the Idea and the pure subject of knowledge always enter consciousness at once as necessary correlatives, and on their appearance all distinction of time vanishes, for they are both utterly foreign to the principle of sufficient reason in all its forms, and lie outside the relations which are imposed by it; they may be compared to the rainbow and the sun, which have no part in the constant movement and succession of the falling drops. Hence, if, for example, I contemplate a tree aesthetically, *i.e.* with artistic eyes, and so recognise, not it, but its Idea, it becomes at once of no consequence whether it is this tree or its ancestor which flourished a thousand years ago, and likewise whether the observer is this individual or any other that lived anywhere and at any time; the particular thing and the knowing individual are suspended with the principle of sufficient reason, and nothing remains but the Idea and the pure subject of knowing, which together constitute the adequate objectivity of will at this grade. And the Idea dispenses not only with time, but also with space, for the Idea proper is not this spatial form which hovers before me, but its expression, its pure significance, its inner being, which discloses itself to me and appeals to me, and which may be quite the same though the spatial relations of its form be very different.

Since, on the one hand, every given thing may be observed in a purely objective manner and apart from all relations; and since, on the other hand, the will manifests itself in everything at some grade of its objectivity, so that everything is the expression of an Idea; it follows that everything is also *beautiful*. That even the most insignificant things admit of pure objective and will-less contemplation, and thus prove that they are beautiful, is shown by the Dutch pictures of still-life already mentioned above in this context (§ 38). But one thing is more beautiful than another in that it facilitates this pure objective contemplation and meets it half-way; if it even (so to speak) compels it, then we call it *very* beautiful! This is the case sometimes because, as an individual thing, it expresses in its purity the Idea of its species by the very distinct, clearly defined, and significant relation of its parts. It also fully reveals that Idea of the species through the complete range of all the possible manifestations of its species united here in this one thing, so that for the beholder it facilitates the transition from the individual thing to the Idea, and thus, too, the condition of pure contemplation. Sometimes an object is outstandingly beautiful because the Idea itself which speaks to us in it, is a high grade of the will's objectivity, and accordingly it is significant and expressive. So man is more beautiful than anything else, and the loftiest purpose of art is to reveal his nature. Human form and expression are the most important subjects of painting and sculpture, and human conduct the most important subject of literature.

Yet each thing has its own characteristic beauty, not only everything organic which expresses itself in the unity of an individual being, but also everything inorganic and formless, and even every manufactured article. For all these reveal the Ideas through which the will objectifies itself at its lowest grades; they sound, as it were, nature's deepest resounding bass-notes. Gravity, rigidity, fluidity, light, and so forth, are the Ideas which express themselves in rocks, in buildings, in rivers and lakes. Landscape-gardening and architecture can do no more than help them to unfold their qualities distinctly, variously and comprehensively; they can only give them the opportunity of expressing themselves without falsification, and in this way these arts will challenge us to aesthetic contemplation, and facilitate it. On the other hand, this is accomplished only slightly, or not at all, by buildings which art has spoiled, or places which nature has neglected; yet even from them these, nature's universal, fundamental Ideas cannot altogether disappear. Even here they will speak to the thoughtful observer who seeks them out, and even bad buildings and the like are capable of being viewed aesthetically: the Ideas of the most universal properties of their materials are still recognisable in them, only the artificial form which has been given them impedes aesthetic contemplation, rather than facilitates it. Manufactured articles also serve to express Ideas, only it is not the Idea of the manufactured article which speaks in them, but the Idea of the material to which this artificial form has been given. In the language of the scholastics this can be very conveniently expressed in two words: that the manufactured article expresses the Idea of its *forma substantialis*, but not that of its *forma accidentalis*; the latter leads not to Idea, but only to a human concept which was its point of departure. Of course, by 'manufactured article' no work of painting or sculpture is meant. The schoolmen understood, in fact, by *forma substantialis* what I call the grade of the will's objectification in a thing. We shall return shortly, when we consider architecture, to the manifestation of the Idea of the material.

Our view, then, cannot be reconciled with Plato's when he maintains that a table or chair expresses the Idea of a table or chair (*Rep.* x and *Parmen.*); *we* say that they express the Ideas which are already expressed in their mere material as such. According to Aristotle (*Metaph.* xi., Chap. 3), however, Plato himself maintained only Ideas of natural objects: 'Plato taught that there were as many Ideas as natural things'; and in chap. 5 he says that, according to the Platonists, there are no Ideas of house and ring. In any case, Plato's earliest disciples, as Alcinous informs us (*Introductio in Platonicam Philosophiam*, Chap. 9), denied that there were any ideas of manufactured articles. He says: 'However, they define the idea as a timeless prototype of things which exist in nature. For most of Plato's followers do not admit that there are Ideas of man-made objects, like a shield or lyre, or of things which run counter to nature, like fever and cholera, or of individuals, like Socrates and Plato, or even of the meanest things, like dirt and debris, or of relations, such as being bigger and being taller; for the Ideas are the eternal thoughts of God and are in themselves complete.' We may take this opportunity of mentioning another point in which our doctrine of Ideas is very different from Plato's. He teaches (*Rep.* x.) that the object which art intends to present, the model or ideal of painting and poetry, is not the Idea but the particular thing. Our whole exposition up to this point has maintained precisely the opposite, and Plato's opinion is the less likely to lead us astray for its being the source of one of the chief acknowledged errors of this great man, his deprecation and rejection of art, and especially of poetry; his wrong-headed opinion on this he appends to the passage I have quoted above.

§ 42. The knowledge of the beautiful always supposes, simultaneously and inseparably, the pure knowing subject and the known Idea as object. Yet the source of aesthetic satisfaction will lie sometimes more in the apprehension of the known Idea, sometimes more in the serenity and spiritual peace of pure knowing freed from all willing – and thus from all individuality and the pain that proceeds from it. And, indeed, this predominance of one or the other constituent part of aesthetic feeling will depend upon whether the intuitively grasped Idea is a higher or a lower grade of the will's objectivity. Thus in aesthetic contemplation (in real life, or through the medium of art) of natural beauty in the inorganic and vegetable worlds, and in works of architecture, the pleasure of pure will-less knowing will predominate, because the Ideas which are here apprehended are only low grades of the will's objectivity, and are therefore not phenomena of deep significance and rich content. On the other hand, if animals and people are the object of aesthetic contemplation or representation, the pleasure will consist rather in the objective apprehension of these Ideas, which are the most distinct revelation of will; for they exhibit the greatest multiplicity of forms, the greatest richness and deep significance of phenomena, and reveal to us most completely the nature of will, whether in its vehemence, its terribleness, its satisfaction or its subjugation (the latter would be represented in tragedy), or finally in its transformation and self-surrender. This last is the theme of Christian painting, just as the Idea of the will enlightened by full knowledge is the subject of historical painting in general, and of drama. We shall now go through the fine arts one by one, and this will give completeness and distinctness to the theory of the beautiful which we have advanced.

§ 43. [...] If now we consider *architecture* simply as a fine art (and apart from its application to useful ends in which it serves the will, and not pure knowledge, and therefore ceases to be art in our sense), we can assign to it no other aim than that of making more clearly perceptible some of those Ideas which are the lowest grades of the will's objectivity, such as gravity, cohesion, rigidity, hardness, those universal qualities of stone, those first, simplest, most inarticulate manifestations of will; the bass notes of nature; and after these light, which in many respects is their opposite. Even at this low grade of the will's objectivity we see its nature revealing itself in discord; for, properly speaking, the conflict between gravity and rigidity is the sole aesthetic material of architecture; its task is to make this conflict appear with perfect distinctness in a multitude of different ways. It achieves this by depriving these indestructible forces of the shortest way to their satisfaction, and conducting them to it by a circuitous route, so that the conflict is prolonged and the inexhaustible efforts of the two forces become visible in many different ways.

The whole mass of the building, if left to its original tendency, would exhibit a mere heap or clump, bound as closely as possible to the earth, to which gravity (the form in which the will appears here) continually presses, while rigidity (also the will's objectivity) resists. But this very tendency, this effort, is hindered by architecture from obtaining direct satisfaction, and allowed to reach it only indirectly and by roundabout ways. The roof, for example, can press the earth only through columns, the arch must support itself, and can satisfy its tendency towards the earth only through the medium of the pillars, and so forth. But it is precisely through these diversions imposed upon it, and by these very restrictions, that the forces which reside in the crude mass of stone unfold most distinctly and with rich variety; and the purely aesthetic aim of architecture can go no further than this. Therefore the beauty of a building lies in the obvious aptness of every part, not to the outward deliberate human intention (in that the work belongs to practical architecture), but directly to the stability of the whole, to which the position, dimensions, and form of every part must bear an essential relationship so that if it were possible to take away one part, the whole would collapse. For just because each part bears just as much as it conveniently can, and each is supported just where it requires to be and just to the necessary extent, this antagonism develops, this conflict between rigidity and gravity (which constitutes the life of the stone and the expression of its will) becomes completely visible, and these lowest grades of the will's objectivity reveal themselves distinctly. In the same way, the form of each part must be determined not arbitrarily, but by its purpose and its relation to the whole. The column is the simplest form of support, determined simply by its purpose: the twisted column is tasteless; the four-cornered pillar is in fact not so simple as the round column, though it happens that it is easier to make. The forms also of frieze, rafter, arch, and dome are entirely determined by their immediate purpose, and are self-explanatory. The decoration of capitals, etc., belongs to sculpture, not to architecture, which admits it merely as extraneous ornament, and could dispense with it.

It follows that for our understanding and aesthetic enjoyment of a work of architecture, it is absolutely necessary to have immediate knowledge through perception of its matter as regards its weight, rigidity, and cohesion; and our pleasure in such a work would suddenly be very much diminished by the discovery that the material used was pumice-stone; for then it would strike us as a kind of sham building. We would be affected in almost the same way if we were told that it was made of wood, when we had supposed it to be of stone, just because this alters and shifts the relation between rigidity and gravity, and consequently the significance and necessity of all the parts, for these natural forces reveal themselves in a far weaker degree in a wooden building. For that reason no real work of architecture as a fine art can be made of wood, although it lends itself to every shape; this can be explained only by our theory. If we were distinctly told that a building, the sight of which gave us pleasure, was made of different kinds of material of very unequal weight and consistency, but not distinguishable to the eye, the whole building would become as unpalatable as a poem in an unknown language. All this proves that architecture affects us not merely mathematically, but dynamically, and that what speaks to us through it, is not mere form and symmetry, but rather those fundamental forces of nature, those first Ideas, those lowest grades of the will's objectivity.

The regularity of the building and its components is produced in part by the suitability of each member to the stability of the whole, partly it serves to facilitate our visual comprehension of the whole, and finally, regular figures to some extent enhance the beauty because they reveal the laws of space as such. But all this is of subordinate value and necessity, and by no means the chief concern; indeed, symmetry is not always required, as even ruins are still beautiful.

Works of architecture bear a special relationship to light; they gain a double beauty in full sunshine, with the blue sky as a background, and have a quite different effect by moonlight. Thus when a beautiful work of architecture is to be erected, special attention is always paid to the effects of light and orientation. The reason for this is chiefly that all the parts and their relationship are made clearly visible only by a bright, strong light; and besides this, I hold that it is the function of architecture to reveal the nature of light just as it reveals the nature of gravity and rigidity, which are quite contrary to light.

For the light is intercepted, confined, and reflected by the great opaque, sharply outlined, and variously formed masses of stone; and thus it unfolds its nature and qualities in the purest and clearest way, to the great pleasure of the beholders, for light is the most joyous of things, being both the condition for and the objective correlative of the most perfect kind of knowledge through perception.

Now, because the Ideas which architecture brings to clear perception are the lowest grades of the will's objectivity, and since consequently the objective significance of what architecture reveals to us is comparatively small, the aesthetic pleasure of looking at a beautiful building in a good light will lie not so much in the comprehension of the Idea as in the subjective correlative of it which accompanies this comprehension; it will consist preeminently in the fact that, while looking at this building, the beholder is freed from the kind of knowledge characteristic of the individual and which serves the will and follows the principle of sufficient reason, and is raised to that of the pure subject of knowing, free from will. So the aesthetic pleasure will consist principally in pure contemplation itself, free from all the suffering of willing and of individuality. In this respect the antithesis of architecture, and the opposite extreme in the series of the fine arts, is drama, which brings to knowledge the most significant of Ideas. For that reason in the aesthetic pleasure which drama gives, the objective side is predominant.

Architecture is different from painting, sculpture and literature, in that it gives us not a copy, but the thing itself. Unlike those other arts it does not repeat the known Idea (whereby the artist lends his eyes to the beholder) but in architecture the artist merely presents the object to the beholder and facilitates his comprehension of the Idea by bringing the actual, individual object to a distinct and complete expression of its own essential nature.

Unlike the works of the other fine arts, those of architecture are very seldom executed for purely aesthetic purposes, but are generally subordinated to other uses which are foreign to art itself. Thus the architect's achievement consists in implementing the purely aesthetic aims, even under this alien subordination. This he does by cleverly adapting them in a variety of ways to the purpose imposed on them, and by accurately assessing which form of aesthetically architectonic beauty is compatible with, and may be incorporated in, a temple, which with a palace, which with a prison, and so forth. [...]

If architecture is greatly restricted by the demands of necessity and utility, on the other hand it has in them a very powerful support, for, on account of the size and cost of its works, and the narrow sphere of its aesthetic effect, it could not continue to exist merely as a fine art if it had not also, as a useful and necessary profession, a firm and honourable place in human activity. It is the want of this that prevents another art from taking its place beside architecture as a sister art, although from an aesthetic point of view it is quite properly to be classed along with it as its counterpart: I mean the artistic use of water. For what architecture accomplishes for the Idea of gravity when it appears in connection with that of rigidity, hydraulics accomplishes for the same Idea when it is connected with fluidity, *i.e.*, formlessness, the greatest mobility and transparency. Waterfalls foaming and tumbling over rocks, cataracts dispersed into floating spray, fountains rising into tall columns of water, and mirror-like lakes, reveal the Ideas of fluid and heavy matter in precisely the same way as the works of architecture unfold the Ideas of rigid matter. Artistic hydraulics, however, obtain no support from utilitarian hydraulics, for, as a rule, their aims cannot be reconciled; yet in exceptional cases this happens, as for example, in the Trevi fountain in Rome.

§ 44. What the two arts we have spoken of accomplish for these lowest grades of the will's objectivity is performed for the higher grades of vegetable nature by horticulture. The landscape beauty of a place consists, for the most part, in the variety of natural objects which together are present in it, and then in the fact that they are clearly separated, appear distinctly, and yet exhibit a fitting association and alternation. These two conditions are assisted and promoted by the art of gardening, but it has by no means such a mastery over its material as has architecture, and therefore its effect is limited. The beauty it displays belongs almost exclusively to nature: gardening has added little to it; and, on the other hand, where nature is not amenable, it can do little; and when nature works, not for it, but against it, its achievements are negligible.

All around us the plant world offers itself for aesthetic enjoyment without the mediation of art; but in so far as it is an object of art, it belongs principally to landscape-painting; and to this genre all the rest of unknowing nature also belongs. In paintings of still life and of mere architecture, ruins, interiors of churches, etc., the subjective side of aesthetic pleasure is predominant, *i.e.*, our delight lies not principally in our direct comprehension of the represented Ideas, but rather in the subjective correlative of this comprehension, in pure, will-less knowing. For because the painter lets us see these things through his eyes, we at once receive a sympathetic and reflected sense of the deep spiritual peace and of absolute silence of the will, which were necessary in order to immerse knowledge so unreservedly in these lifeless objects and comprehend them with such love, *i.e.*, with such a degree of objectivity. The effect of landscape-painting proper is as a whole, of this same kind; but because the Ideas expressed are more meaningful and significant, as higher grades of the will's objectivity, the objective side of aesthetic pleasure comes more to the fore, balancing the subjective side. Pure knowing, as such, is no longer the paramount consideration, for we are equally affected by the known Idea, the world as idea at an important grade of the will's objectification.

But a far higher grade is revealed through the painting and sculpture of animal subjects. Of the latter we have some important antique remains; for example, horses at Venice, on Monte Cavallo, and on the Elgin Marbles, and at Florence in bronze and marble; the ancient boar, howling wolves, the lions in the Arsenal at Venice, and in the Vatican a whole room almost filled with animals for the most part ancient, etc. In these representations the objective side of aesthetic pleasure is granted a marked predominance over the subjective. The peace of the subject who knows these Ideas, who has silenced his own will, is indeed present, as it is in all aesthetic contemplation; but its effect is not felt, for we are occupied with the restlessness and impetuosity of the will represented. It is the very will that constitutes our own nature that appears to us here in forms in which its manifestation is not, as in us, controlled and tempered by intellect, but is shown in bolder outline and with a clarity that borders on the grotesque and monstrous, and at the same time without dissembling; it is free, naive, open as the day, and precisely this is the basis of our interest in animals. The characteristics of species have emerged in the representation of plants, but showed itself there only in the forms; here it becomes much more significant, and expresses itself not only in the form, but in the action, position, and stance, yet always merely as the character of the species, not of the individual.

This knowledge of the Ideas of higher grades, which comes to us in painting through the mediation of another person, we can gain directly by our purely contemplative looking at plants, and by our observation of animals, and of the latter especially in their free, natural and unrestrained state. The objective contemplation of their manifold and marvellous forms, and of their activity, is an instructive lesson from the great book of nature, and a deciphering of the true *signatura rerum* [*i.e.* signature of things]. We see in them the manifold grades and modes of the manifestation of will, which is in all beings one and the same and has always the same goal: it objectifies itself as life, as existence, in such endless variety, and such different forms, which are all adaptations to the different external circumstances, and may be compared to many variations on the same theme. But if we had to communicate to the observer, for reflection, and in a word, the explanation of their inner nature, it would be best to make use of that Sanskrit formula which occurs so often in the sacred books of the Hindus, and is called Mahavakya, *i.e.*, the great word: '*Tat tvam asi*', which means, 'this living thing you are.'

§ 45. The task of historical painting and sculpture is to express, directly and for perception, the Idea in which the will reaches the highest grade of its objectification. The objective side of the pleasure which beauty gives is dominant here, and the subjective side has receded into the background. It is further to be observed that at the next grade below this, animal painting, the characteristic is entirely one with the beautiful; the most characteristic lion, wolf, horse, sheep, or ox, was always the most beautiful, also. The reason for this is that animals have only the character of their species, rather than individual character. In the representation of people the character of the species is distinct from that of the individual; the former is now called 'beauty' (entirely in the objective sense), but the latter retains the name 'character' or 'expression', and the new difficulty arises of representing both, at once and completely, in the same individual.

Human beauty is an objective expression meaning the fullest objectification of will at the highest grade at which it is knowable, the Idea of man in general, completely expressed in the perceived form. But however much the objective side of the beautiful predominates here, the subjective side still always accompanies it. And just because no object transports us so quickly into pure aesthetic contemplation as the most beautiful human face and form, at the sight of which we are instantly filled with unspeakable satisfaction, and raised above ourselves and all that troubles us; this is possible only because this most distinct and purest knowledge of will transports us most easily and quickly to the state of pure knowing, in which our personality, our will with its constant pain, disappears for as long as the pure aesthetic pleasure lasts. Thus Goethe says [*The Elective Affinities* I, Chap. 6:] 'No ill can touch him who looks on human beauty; he feels himself at one with himself and with the world.' [...]

One would suppose that art achieved the beautiful by imitating nature. But how is the artist to recognise the perfect work which is to be imitated, and distinguish it from the failures, unless he anticipates the beautiful *prior to experience*? And besides this, has nature ever produced a human being perfectly beautiful in all his parts? So it has been supposed that the artist must seek out the beautiful parts distributed among different human beings, and out of them construct a beautiful whole: a perverse and silly surmise. For again the question arises as to which features tell him that precisely *these* forms are the beautiful ones, and that those are not. We also see what progress the old German painters made in achieving the beautiful by imitating nature. Observe their nudes. No knowledge of the beautiful is possible purely *a posteriori*, and from mere experience; it is always, at least in parts, *a priori*, although quite different in kind from the forms of the principle of sufficient reason, of which we are conscious *a priori*. These concern the universal form of the phenomenon as such, as it constitutes the possibility of any knowledge, the universal *how* of all phenomena, and from this knowledge proceed mathematics and pure natural science. But that other kind of knowledge *a priori* which makes it possible to represent the beautiful, concerns not the form but the content of phenomena, not the *how* but the *what* of the phenomenon. That we all recognise human beauty when we see it, but that in the true artist this takes place with such clearness that he shows it as he has never seen it, and surpasses nature in his representation – this is possible only because *we ourselves are* the will whose adequate objectification at its highest grade is here to be judged and discovered. By this means alone have we in fact an anticipation of what nature (which is the same will as constitutes our own being) strives to present. And in the true genius this anticipation is accompanied by so great a degree of intelligence that in the individual object he recognises its Idea, and thus *understands* nature's mere suggestion and articulates clearly what she says incoherently. He imposes on the hard marble that beauty of form which in a thousand attempts she failed to create and he presents it to nature, claiming, as it were, 'That is what you meant to say!' 'Yes, that is it', echoes the connoisseur. Only in this way was it possible for the Greek genius to find the type of human form and establish it as a canon for the school of sculpture; and only by virtue of such anticipation is it possible for all of us to recognise beauty where nature has succeeded. This anticipation is the *Ideal*. It is the Idea in so far as it is known – at least half-known – *a priori*, and it becomes serviceable to art, for it complements what is given *a posteriori* through nature. The artist can anticipate the beautiful *a priori*, and the connoisseur can recognise it *a posteriori* because artist and connoisseur are themselves the 'in-itself' of nature, the will which objectifies itself. For, as Empedocles said, like can be recognised only by like: only nature can understand herself: only nature can fathom herself: and only spirit is susceptible to spirit. [. . .]

A distinctive feature of mankind is that the character of the species is separate from that of the individual, so that to a certain extent every man expresses an Idea peculiarly his own. Therefore the arts, whose aim is the representation of the Idea of man, should treat not only beauty, the character of the species, but also the character of the individual, which is called *character par excellence*. But this is the case only in so far as this character is to be regarded not as something accidental and quite peculiar to the man as a single individual, but as an aspect of the Idea of man which is conspicuous specially in the individual, and which, when it is depicted, contributes to the revelation of the idea of humanity. Thus the character, although as such it is individual, must be comprehended and expressed ideally, that is to say, with emphasis on its significance in regard to the Idea of man generally (which in its way it helps to objectify). Apart from this, the representation is a portrait, a copy of the individual as such, with all his accidental qualities. And even the portrait ought to be, as Winckelmann says, the ideal of the individual.

That *character* which is to be ideally comprehended, allowing preeminence to a particular aspect of the Idea of man, expresses itself visibly in part through permanent physiognomy and bodily form, and in part through transient emotion and passion, the reciprocal modification of knowing and willing, all of which is exhibited in the face and gesture. Since the individual always belongs to humanity, and, on the other hand, humanity always reveals itself in the individual, and with his peculiar ideal significance, beauty must not be eclipsed by character nor character by beauty. For if the character of the species is outweighed by that of the individual, the result is caricature; and if the character of the individual is outweighed by that of the species, the result is an absence of meaning. Therefore the representation which aims at beauty, as sculpture principally does, will yet in some respect always modify this (the character of the species) by the individual character, and will always express the Idea of man in a definite individual manner, giving prominence to one particular side of it. For the human individual as such has to a certain extent the dignity of an Idea of his own, and it is essential to the Idea of man that it should express itself in individuals of special significance. [. . .]

§ 48. Character is, along with beauty and grace, the chief subject of historical painting. By character we mean in general the representation of will at the highest grade of its objectification, when the individual, in emphasising one particular side of the Idea of man, has special significance, and shows this not merely by his physical form, but makes it visible in his face and gesture, by activity of every kind, and the modifications of knowing and willing that occasion and accompany activity. The Idea of man must be presented in this context, and the development of this many-sided idea must be shown to us through representative individuals, and these individuals can, in turn, be made visible in their significance only through various scenes, events, and incidents. This, the endless task of historical painting, is solved by setting before us scenes from every kind of life of greater or lesser significance.

No individual and no action can be without significance; in everyone and through everything the Idea of man unfolds gradually. Therefore no event in human life should be excluded from the sphere of painting. It is thus a great injustice to the excellent painters of the Dutch school to prize merely their technical skill, and to look down upon them in other respects because, for the most part, they depicted subjects from everyday life, rather than the world-historical events or the Bible stories which might be considered more significant. We ought first of all to reflect that the inward significance of an action is quite different from its outward significance, and that these often proceed separately. The outward significance is the importance of an action in relation to its result for and in the actual world; thus according to the principle of sufficient reason. The inward significance is the depth of the insight into the Idea of man which it opens up, in that it brings to light aspects of that Idea which rarely appear, by making individuals who express themselves distinctly and decidedly, disclose their personal characteristics by means of circumstances contrived for this purpose. Only the inward significance is important in art; in history, the outward. They are completely independent of each other; they may appear together, but each may appear alone. An action which is highly significant for history may be intrinsically very ordinary and common; and conversely, a scene from ordinary daily life may be of great intrinsic significance if individual persons, and the inmost recesses of human action and will, appear in it in a bright, clear light. Further, the extrinsic significance can be very different, although the intrinsic meaning is one and the same. Thus, for example, it is all the same, as far as inward significance is concerned, whether ministers of state discuss the fate of countries and nations over a map, or peasants wrangle in a tavern over cards and dice, just as it is all the same whether we play chess with golden or wooden pieces. But apart from this, the scenes and events that make up the life of so many millions of men, their actions, their sorrows, their joys, are on that account important enough to be the object of art, and by their rich variety they must afford material enough for unfolding the many-sided Idea of man. Indeed the very transitoriness of the moment which art has fixed in such a picture (now called *genre*-painting) excites a slight and quite specific pathos; for to fix the fleeting, ever-changing world in the enduring picture of a single event, which yet represents the whole, is an achievement of the art of painting by which it seems to bring time itself to a standstill, for it raises the individual to the Idea of its species.

Finally, the historical and outwardly significant subjects of painting have often the disadvantage that just what is significant in them cannot be presented to perception, but must be supplied by thought. In this respect the nominal significance of the picture must be distinguished from its real significance. The former is the outward significance, which, however, associates itself with it only as an abstraction; the latter is that aspect of the Idea of man which is made manifest to perception through the picture. For example, Moses found by the Egyptian princess is the nominal significance of a painting: it represents a moment of the greatest importance in history; the real significance, on the other hand, that which is actually given to perception, is a foundling child rescued from its floating cradle by a great lady, an incident which may have happened more than once. The costume alone can here indicate the particular historical case to the educated viewer; but the costume is of importance only to the nominal significance and is a matter of indifference to the real significance; for the latter knows only the human being as such, not the arbitrary forms. Historical subjects have no advantage over those which are mere plausible conjecture, and which are therefore to be called, not individual, but merely general. For what is peculiarly significant in the former is not the individual, not the particular event as such, but the universal in it, the facet of the Idea of humanity which expresses itself through it. On the other hand, definite historical subjects are not on this account to be rejected: it is only that the appraisal of such subjects (which, on the part both of the painter and of the beholder, is, properly speaking, artistic) never concerns itself with the individual instance that constitutes the historical, but with the universal which expresses itself in it, that is, with the Idea. [. . .]

We must carefully distinguish pictures whose subject is the historical or mythological aspect of Judaism and Christianity, from pictures in which the real, *i.e.* the ethical spirit of Christianity, is revealed through the depiction of people who are full of this ethical spirit. To depict these is indeed the highest and most admirable achievement of the art of painting; and only the greatest masters of this art succeeded in this, particularly Raphael and Correggio, the latter especially in his earlier pictures. Paintings of this kind are not properly to be classed as historical, for usually they depict no event, no action, but are merely groups of saints, with the Saviour himself, often still a child, with His mother, angels, etc. In their faces, and especially in the eyes, we see the expression, the reflection, of the most perfect knowledge, that which is directed not to particular things but has fully grasped the Ideas, and thus the whole nature of the world and life. And this knowledge in them, reacting upon the will, does not, like other knowledge, convey *motives* to it, but on the contrary has become a *quieter* of all willing. From this has come the complete resignation which is the innermost spirit of Christianity, as of the Indian philosophy; the surrender of all volition, conversion, the suppression of will, and with it of the whole inner being of this world, that is to say, salvation. Thus these eternally great artists expressed the highest wisdom perceptibly in their works. And this is the zenith of all art. It has followed the will in its adequate objectivity, the Ideas, through all its grades, from the lowest in which it is affected and its nature unfolded in so many ways, first by causes, then by stimuli, and finally by motives. And now art ends by representing the will's voluntary extinction by virtue of the great peace which opens up before it, and which proceeds from the perfect knowledge of its own nature.

§ 49. The truth which lies at the foundation of all that we have hitherto said about art, is that the object of art, the representation of which is the aim of the artist, and the knowledge of which must therefore precede his work as its germ and source, is an Idea in Plato's sense, and nothing else; not the particular thing, the object of common apprehension, and not the concept, the object of rational thought and of scholarship. Although the Idea and the concept have something in common in that both as unities represent a multiplicity of real things, the great difference between them has no doubt been made sufficiently clear and evident by what we have said about concepts in the First Book, and about the Idea in this Book. I by no means wish to assert, however, that Plato grasped this difference clearly; indeed many of his examples of Ideas, and his discussions of them, are applicable only to concepts. For the present we leave this question alone and go on our own way, glad when we come upon traces of any great and noble mind, yet not following in his footsteps, but pursuing our own goal. The *concept* is abstract, discursive, undetermined within its own sphere, determined only by its limits, attainable and comprehensible by him who has the faculty of reason, communicable by words without any other mediation, entirely exhausted by its definition. The *Idea*, on the contrary, although defined as the adequate representative of the concept, is always object of perception, and although representing an infinite number of particular things, is yet thoroughly determined. It is never known by the individual as such, but only by him who has raised himself above all willing and all individuality to the pure subject of knowing. Thus it is attainable only by the man of genius, and by the man who, mostly with the help of the works of genius, has raised this power of pure knowing, and is now in a genial frame of mind. [. . .]

The *Idea* is the unity that disperses into multiplicity by virtue of the temporal and spatial form of our intuitive apprehension; the *concept*, on the other hand, is the unity reconstituted out of multiplicity by the abstraction of our faculty of reason; the latter may be defined as *unitas post rem*, the former as *unitas ante rem*. Finally, the distinction between Idea and concept we can express through a simile, by saying that the concept is like a sterile container: things put into it lie there, but no more can be taken out of it (by analytical judgements) than was put in (by synthetical reflection); the *Idea*, on the other hand, develops, in the person who has grasped it, ideas which, in relation to the concept of the same name, are new; it resembles a living organism, evolving, and with the power to engender and produce what had not simply been put into it.

It follows from all that I have said, that the concept – useful as it is in life, and serviceable, necessary and productive as it is in science – is always barren and unproductive in art. The comprehended Idea, on the contrary, is the true and the only source of every work of art. In its powerful originality it is derived only from life itself, from nature, from the world, and only by the true genius or by the person whose momentary inspiration reaches the point of genius. Only in this way, directly, are genuine works conceived, and within them they bear life immortal. Just because the Idea is and remains object of perception, the artist is not conscious in the abstract of the intention and aim of his work; not a concept, but an Idea floats before his mind; therefore he can give no justification for what he does. He works, as ordinary people say, from pure feeling, and unconsciously, indeed instinctively. On the contrary, imitators, mannerists, *imitatores, servum pecus* ['Imitators, the slavish tribe'; Horace, *Epistles*] in art start from the concept; they observe what pleases and affects us in true works of art; understand it clearly, fix it in a concept, and thus abstractly, and then imitate it, openly or clandestinely, with cunning and intention. They suck their nourishment, like parasite plants, from the works of others, and like polyps they become the colour of their food. We might carry this comparison further and say that they are like machines which mince and mix whatever is put into them, but can never digest it, so that the alien elements may always be found again if they are searched out and separated from the mixture; only the man of genius resembles the organic body which assimilates, transforms and reproduces. For he is indeed reared and educated by his predecessors and their works; but he is brought to fruition only by life and the world directly, through the impression of what he perceives; so education and training to a high standard never impair his originality.

All imitators, all mannerists, apprehend in concept the essence of the exemplary achievement of other people; but concepts can never impart inner life to a work. The age, *i.e.*, the dull multitude of any era, knows only concepts and sticks to them, and therefore receives mannered works of art with swift, loud applause: but after a few years these works become unattractive, because the spirit of the age, *i.e.*, the prevailing concepts, have changed, and they are the only soil in which these works of art could take root. Only true works of art, which are drawn directly from nature and life, have eternal youth and enduring power, like nature and life themselves. For they belong to no age, but to mankind, and as on that account they were coldly received by their own age, to which they disdained to adapt themselves, and because indirectly and negatively they exposed the errors of each age, they are recognised belatedly and reluctantly; by the same token, they cannot grow old, but appear to us ever fresh and new, even in the present day. [. . .]

§ 50. We have said that the aim of all art is the communication of the comprehended Idea which, mediated by the artist's mind so that it appears cleansed and isolated from all that is foreign to it, may now be grasped by the man of weaker receptivity and no productive faculty. We have said, too, that in art it is abominable to take the concept as starting-point. Hence we cannot approve the decision to make a work of art intentionally and avowedly the expression of a concept, as is the case in the *Allegory*. An allegory is a work of art which means something different from what it depicts. But the perceptual element, and consequently also the Idea, expresses itself directly and completely, and does not require to be made plain through the mediation of another party. What is in this way indicated and represented by something outside itself, because it cannot itself be made object of perception, is always a concept. Through the allegory a concept is always to be signified, and consequently the mind of the beholder is to be drawn away from the expressed perceptible idea to one which is entirely different, abstract and not perceptible, and which lies quite outside the work of art. The picture or statue is intended to accomplish here what is accomplished far more completely by a written work. What we hold to be the aim of art – representation of a perceivable, comprehensible Idea – is not the aim here. No great perfection in the work of art is required for what is intended. It is enough that we should see what the thing is meant to be, for, as soon as this has been discovered, the purpose has been attained, and the mind is now led away to quite a different kind of idea, to an abstract concept, the goal which had been set.

Allegories in painting and sculpture are, therefore, nothing but hieroglyphics; the artistic value which they may have as perceptible representations, accrues to them not as allegories, but from another quarter. That Correggio's 'Night', Annibale Carracci's 'Genius of Fame', and Poussin's 'Hours' are very beautiful pictures has nothing to do with their being allegories. As allegories they accomplish no more than does an inscription, indeed rather less. Here again we are reminded of the distinction drawn above between the real and the nominal significance of a picture. The nominal is here the allegorical as such, for example, the 'Genius of Fame'. The real is what is actually depicted, in this case a beautiful winged youth, with beautiful boys flying around him; this expresses an Idea. But this real significance affects us only so long as we forget the nominal, allegorical significance; if we think of the latter, we forsake the perception, and the mind is busied with an abstract concept; but the transition from the Idea to the concept is always a descent.

Indeed, that nominal significance, that allegorical intention, often detracts from the real significance, the perceptible truth: for example, the unnatural light in Correggio's 'Night', which, though beautifully executed, has a merely allegorical motive, and is impossible in reality. If, then, an allegorical picture has artistic value, it is quite separate from, and independent of, what it accomplishes as allegory. Such a work of art serves two ends at once: the expression of a concept, and the expression of an Idea. Only the latter can be the purpose of art; the other is an alien purpose, the trifling amusement of making a picture do service also as an inscription, as a hieroglyphic, invented for the pleasure of those to whom the real nature of art can never appeal. It is the same thing as when a work of art is also a useful implement of some kind, in which case it also serves two ends; for example, a statue which is at the same time a candelabrum or a caryatid, or a bas-relief which is also the shield of Achilles. True lovers of art will approve neither the one nor the other. It is true that an allegorical picture may, because of this quality, produce a vivid impression upon the feelings; but when this is the case, an inscription would under the same circumstances produce the same effect. [...]

If then, in accordance with what we have said, allegory in sculpture and painting is a mistaken endeavour serving a purpose alien to art, it becomes quite unbearable when it leads so far astray that the depiction of forced and far-fetched allusions degenerates into absurdity. Such, for example, is a tortoise, to suggest feminine seclusion; the downward glance of Nemesis into the drapery of her bosom, signifying that she can see even what is concealed; Bellori's explanation that Annibale Carracci clothed voluptuousness in a yellow robe because he wished to indicate that her pleasures soon fade and become yellow like straw. If there is absolutely no connection between what is depicted and the concept signified by it – a connection based on subsumption under the concept, or on association of Ideas – but the signs and the things signified are connected in a purely conventional manner under an ordinance which, although binding now, came about by chance: then I call this degenerate kind of allegory *Symbolism*. Thus the rose is the symbol of secrecy, the laurel is the symbol of fame, the palm is the symbol of victory, the scallop-shell is the symbol of pilgrimage, the cross is the symbol of the Christian religion. To this class also belongs all allusions made by mere colour, such as that yellow is the colour of falseness, and blue is the colour of fidelity. Such symbols may often be of use in life, but their merit is foreign to art. They are simply to be regarded as hieroglyphics, or like Chinese writing, and really belong to the same class as armorial bearings, the bush that indicates a public-house, the key by which we recognise the chamberlain, or the leather by which we know miners. [. . .]

Allegory has an entirely different relation to poetry from that which it has to sculpture and painting, and although it is to be rejected in the latter, it is not only permissible, but very serviceable to the former. For in sculpture and painting it leads away from the given perceptible, the proper object of all art, to abstract thoughts; but in poetry the relation is reversed, for here what is directly given in words is the concept, and the first aim is to lead from this to the perceptible, which the listener's imagination must depict. If in sculpture and painting we are led from what is immediately given to something else, this must always be a concept, because here only the abstract cannot be given directly; but a concept may never be the source, and its communication may never be the purpose of a work of art. In poetry, on the contrary, the concept is the material, the immediately given, and therefore we may very well abandon it to conjure up perceptions which are quite different, and in which the purpose is attained. Within the context of a literary work, many a concept or abstract thought may be quite indispensable, although in itself and directly it is quite incapable of being perceived; and then it is often made perceptible by means of some example which is meant to be subsumed under it. This takes place in every trope, every metaphor, simile, parable, and allegory, all of which differ only in the length and completeness of their expression. Thus in the arts which employ language as their medium, similes and allegories are of striking effect. How beautifully Cervantes says of sleep, in order to express the fact that it frees us from all mental and physical suffering, 'It is a cloak that covers the whole person'. How beautifully [Ewald von] Kleist expresses allegorically the thought that philosophers and men of science enlighten mankind, in the line, 'Those whose lamp by night sheds light on all the world.' How strongly and sensuously Homer describes the pernicious Ate when he says: 'She has tender feet, for she walks not on the hard earth, but treads only on the heads of men' (*Iliad*, xix. 91). [...]

§ 51. If with the foregoing reflections on art in general, we turn from sculpture and painting to literature, we shall have no doubt that its aim also is to reveal the Ideas, the grades of the will's objectification, and to communicate them to the hearer with the distinctness and vividness with which the poetic mind comprehended them. Ideas are essentially perceptible; if, therefore, in poetry what is communicated by means of words is only abstract concepts, it is nonetheless clearly the intention to let the hearer perceive the Ideas of life in the representatives of these concepts, and this can take place only with the help of his own imagination. But in order to set the imagination to work for this purpose, the abstract concepts, which are the immediate material of poetry as of the driest prose, must be so assembled that their spheres intersect in such a way that none of them can remain in its abstract universality; but, instead, a perceptible representative comes to the imagination; and this the words of the poet further modify according to his intention. As the chemist obtains solid precipitates by combining perfectly clear and transparent fluids, the writer knows how to precipitate, as it were, the concrete, the individual, the perceptible idea, out of the abstract and transparent universality of the concepts, by the way in which he combines them. For the Idea can be known only by perception; but knowledge of the Idea is the aim of all art. In poetry as in chemistry, skill enables the practitioner always to obtain the precise result he intends. This purpose is assisted by the numerous epithets in poetry, by means of which the universality of every concept is narrowed more and more till the perceptible is attained. Homer attaches to almost every noun an adjective whose concept intersects and considerably reduces the sphere of the first concept, which is thereby brought so much nearer to perception: for example –

> Into the ocean sank the sun's shining light,
> Drawing dark night over the kindly earth.

And –

> The wind blows softly from the cloudless skies.
> Myrtle and bay-tree, tall and silent, rise.

> – [Goethe, Mignon's song in *Wilhelm Meister*]

which for our imagination precipitates from just a few concepts the whole delight of the southern clime.

Rhythm and rhyme are quite special aids to poetry. I can give no other explanation of their incredibly powerful effect than that our imagination has received from time, to which it is essentially bound, some quality on account of which we inwardly follow, and, as it were, join in with every regularly recurrent sound. In this way rhythm and rhyme are partly a means of holding our attention, in that we more willingly follow the recitation; and partly they produce in us a blind, impartial consent to what is read, by which the poem gains a certain emphatic power of conviction, independent of all reasons and reasoning.

By virtue of the universality of the material which poetry uses to communicate the Ideas, and hence by virtue of its concepts, its sphere is wide. The whole of nature, the Ideas of all grades, can be depicted by means of poetry, for according to the Idea it is to communicate, it sometimes adopts the descriptive mode, sometimes the narrative, and sometimes the directly dramatic. If, in the representation of the lower grades of the will's objectivity, sculpture and painting generally surpass poetry, because lifeless nature, and even brute nature, reveals almost its whole being in a single well-chosen moment; man on the other hand, so far as he expresses himself not merely physically and facially, but through a series of actions and the accompanying thoughts and emotions, is the principal subject of poetry, in which no other art can compete with it, for it has an advantage in the continuity and sequentiality which eludes sculpture and painting.

The revelation of that Idea which is the highest grade of the will's objectivity – the representation of man in the sequence of his endeavours and actions – is thus the great subject of poetry. It is true that both experience and history teach us to know man; yet more often men than man, *i.e.*, they record for us empirical observations on social interaction (from which rules for our own conduct emerge) rather than afford us deep insight into the inner nature of man. [. . .] Our own experience is the indispensable condition of understanding literature as of understanding history; for it is, so to speak, the dictionary of the language spoken by both. But history is related to poetry as portrait-painting is related to historical painting; the former gives us the true in the individual, the latter the true in the universal; the former has the truth of the phenomenon, and can verify it from the phenomenal; the latter has the truth of the Idea, which can be found in no particular phenomenon, yet speaks from them all. The poet from deliberate choice presents significant characters in significant situations; the historian takes both as they come. [. . .]

The poet comprehends the Idea, man's inner nature apart from all relations, outside all time, the adequate objectivity of the thing-in-itself at its highest grade. Although even in the historian's perspective, the inner nature, the significance of the phenomena, the germ within all those husks, can never be utterly lost (and he, at least, who seeks it, may still find it and recognise it), what is significant in itself and not in its relations, the real unfolding of the Idea, will be found far more accurately and distinctly in poetry than in history; and therefore, however paradoxical it may sound, far more actual genuine inner truth is to be imputed to poetry than to history. For the historian is obliged to trace the particular event precisely from life as it develops in time, in the complex entangled chains of causes and effects. But he cannot have all the data for this; he cannot have seen all or researched everything. He is deserted at every moment by the original of his picture, or a counterfeit is substituted for the original, and this so often that I think I may assume that in all history there is more of the false than of the true. The poet, on the other hand, has comprehended the Idea of man from some specific aspect which is to be presented here; thus it is the nature of his own self that objectifies itself in it for him. His knowledge, as we argued above when speaking of sculpture, is half *a priori*; his ideal stands before his mind firm, clear, brightly illuminated, and cannot desert him; thus in the mirror of his mind he shows us the Idea purely and distinctly, and his delineation of it down to the last detail is true as life itself. So in the detail in which fact fails them – for example, in the speeches of their heroes – the great classical historians are poets; indeed, their whole manner of handling their material comes close to the epic genre. But it is just this that lends unity to their description, and enables them to retain inner truth even when outward truth was inaccessible, or was even falsified. And as we compared history to portrait-painting (in contradistinction to poetry, which corresponds to historical painting), we find that

Winckelmann's maxim – that the portrait ought to be the ideal of the individual – was followed by the ancient historians, for they depict detail in such a way that that aspect of the Idea of man emerges which expresses itself in that detail. Modern historians, on the contrary, with few exceptions, give us in general only 'a dust-bin and a lumber-room, and, at the most, a political drama' [Goethe, *Faust*, I]. Anyone who want to know man in his inner nature, identical in all its phenomena and developments, to know him according to the Idea, will find that the works of the great, immortal poets present a far truer, clearer picture than the historians can ever give. [. . .] Just as a circle of one inch in diameter and a circle of forty million miles in diameter have precisely the same geometrical properties, so the events and the history of a village and of a kingdom are essentially the same; and we may study man and become acquainted with him as well in the one as in the other. [. . .]

The presentation of the Idea of man, which is the poet's task, may be achieved so that what is presented is also the presenter. This is so in lyric poetry, in the song proper, in which the poet vividly perceives and describes only his own state, so that by reason of the topic it treats, a certain subjectivity is essential to this genre. Again, what is to be presented may be entirely different from the man who presents it, as it is in all other genres in which the poet more or less conceals himself behind his presentation until he vanishes completely. In the ballad, the poet still expresses to some extent his own state through the tone and attitude; therefore, though much more objective than the lyric, it has yet something subjective. This becomes less in the idyll, still less in the novel, almost entirely disappears in the true epic, and finally, in the drama it vanishes without trace, for drama is the most objective and, in more than one respect, the completest and most difficult literary genre. The lyric genre is consequently the easiest, and although art as a whole belongs only to the rare true genius, even a man who is not outstanding overall may produce a beautiful song if, under external stimulus, some inspiration elevates his mental energies; for all that is needed for this is a lively perception of his own state at a moment of emotional excitement. This is proved by many single songs written by individuals who have otherwise remained unknown, especially by the German folk-songs (of which we have an excellent collection in *Des Knaben Wunderhorn*), and also by innumerable love-songs and other folk-songs in every language; for to catch the mood of a moment and embody it in song is the whole achievement of this type of poetry. Yet in the lyrics of true poets the inner nature of all mankind is reflected, and all that millions of past, present, and future men have felt, or will feel in the same recurrent situations, finds its appropriate expression in them. And because these situations, by their constant recurrence, are as permanent as man himself and always evoke the same sensations, the lyrical productions of genuine poets remain through thousands of years true, powerful, and fresh. The poet is, after all, the universal man; all that has ever moved a human heart, all that human nature in any situation has ever produced of itself, all that dwells and broods in any human breast – is his theme and his material, as is, besides this, all the rest of nature. So the poet may just as well sing of voluptuousness as of mysticism, be Anacreon or Angelus Silesius, write tragedies or comedies, present the sublime or the common mind – according to his humour or his vocation. And no one has the right to prescribe to the poet what he ought to be – noble and sublime, moral, pious, Christian, one thing or another – still less to reproach him because he is one thing and not another. He is the mirror of mankind, and brings to its consciousness what it feels and does.

Now if we consider the nature of the song more closely, taking as our examples specimens of high quality which are, at the same time, unadulterated (not those which have some affinity to another type of poetry, such as the ballad, the elegy, the hymn, the epigram, etc.), we shall discover the precise characteristics of the lyric. It is the subject of the will, *i.e.*, his own willing, which fills the singer's consciousness, often as will liberated and gratified (joy), but still oftener as will frustrated (grief), always as an emotion, a passion, an agitated state of mind. Besides this, however, at the same time, the singer, through the sight of surrounding nature, becomes conscious of himself as the subject of pure, will-less knowing, whose imperturbable serenity now forms a contrast with the pressure of will which is always constrained and always craving. The sense of this contrast, of this alternation, is really what the lyric as a whole expresses, and what principally constitutes the lyrical state of mind. In it pure knowing comes to us, as it were, to deliver us from desire and its strain; we follow, but only for an instant; desire, the remembrance of our own personal aims, tears us anew from peaceful contemplation; yet again and again the next beautiful scene in which pure will-less knowledge offers itself to us, lures us away from willing. So in the lyric and the lyrical mood, willing (the personal interest of our aims), and pure perception of the scene before us, are wonderfully intermingled; connections between them are sought and pictured; the subjective mood, the affection of the will, imparts its own hue to the scene, and reciprocally the scene communicates its colour to the will. The true lyric is the impression of the whole of this mingled and divided state of mind. [. . .]

In the more objective kinds of poetry, especially in the novel, the epic, and the drama, the purpose – the revelation of the Idea of man – is accomplished chiefly by two means: by accurate and profound drawing of significant characters, and by the invention of poignant situations in which they reveal themselves. For as it is the chemist's task not only to present the simple elements, pure and genuine, and their principal compounds, but also to expose them to the influence of reagents in relation to which their properties become strikingly visible, so is it the poet's task not only to present to us significant characters as truly and faithfully as nature itself, but, in order that we may get to know them, he must place them in those situations in which their qualities will fully develop and appear distinctly in sharp outline – situations which are for that reason called meaningful. In real life and in history, situations of this kind are rarely brought about by chance, and they stand alone, lost and obscured by the mass of the insignificant. The total significance of the situations ought to distinguish the novel, the epic, and the drama from real life as completely as does the combination and selection of significant characters. In both, however, the strictest truth is a necessary condition of their effect; and lack of unity in the characters, contradiction either within themselves or with the nature of man in general, as well as impossibility, or implausibility verging on the impossible in the events, even in circumstances of secondary importance, offend just as much in poetry as do badly drawn figures, false perspective, or faulty lighting in painting. For both in poetry and painting we demand the faithful mirror of life, of man, of the world – only made more clear by the presentation and more meaningful by the arrangement.

For there is only one purpose in all the arts, the presentation of the Ideas; and their essential difference lies only in which grade of the will's objectification the Idea that is to be presented belongs; and this in turn determines the material of the presentation. So the most divergent art-forms may, when they are compared, shed light on one another. For example, in order to comprehend fully the Ideas which express themselves in water, it is not enough to see it in a placid pool or in the smoothly flowing river; but these Ideas develop fully only when the water appears in all circumstances and exposed to all sorts of obstacles, which by their effect upon it cause it fully to express all its properties. This is why we find it beautiful when it tumbles, rushes, foams, leaps again into the air, or falls in a cataract of spray; or, finally, when it is artificially forced, it strives upwards as a fountain. While showing itself differently in different circumstances, it always faithfully asserts its character; it is just as natural to it to spray upwards as to lie in glassy stillness; it is as ready for the one as for the other, as soon as the conditions prevail. Now, what the engineer does with the fluid matter of water, the architect does with the rigid matter of stone; and the epic or dramatic poet does the same thing with the Idea of man. The common purpose of all art is to unfold and to make clear the Idea which expresses itself in the object of every art, the Idea of the will which objectifies itself at each grade. Man's life, as it shows itself most often in the real world, resembles water as it most often shows itself in pond and river; but in the epic, the novel, the tragedy, selected characters are placed in circumstances in which all their qualities unfold, the depths of the human heart are revealed and become visible in extraordinary and very significant actions. Thus literature objectifies the Idea of man, an Idea which expresses itself in highly individual characters.

Tragedy is to be seen as the high-point of literature, both in its impact and its accomplishment; and it is acknowledged as such. It is very significant for our whole study, and noteworthy that the purpose of this, the highest poetical achievement, is to present the terrible side of life. Man's unspeakable pain and misery, the triumph of malice, the tyranny of mere chance, and the irretrievable fall of the just and innocent, are here presented to us; and in this lies a significant hint as to the nature of the world and of existence. It is the internal conflict of the will which is most completely unfolded here at the highest grade of its objectivity, and shows itself as something to be dreaded. It becomes visible in the suffering of men, which is caused partly by chance and error; in the drama these are personified as the powers that govern the world, and since their malice seems like intentionality, they are personified, too, as fate; partly it proceeds from man himself, through the conflicting desires of individuals, through the malice and perversity of the majority. It is one and the same will that lives and appears in them all, but whose phenomena fight and maul one another. In one individual it appears powerfully, in another more weakly; in one it is reflected upon, and mitigated by the light of knowledge, in another less so, till at last, in the individual instance, this knowledge, purified and heightened by suffering itself, reaches the point at which the phenomenon, the veil of Mâyâ, no longer deceives it. It sees through the form of the phenomenon, the *principium individuationis*. The egoism based on this perishes with it, so that now *motives* hitherto powerful lose their power, and instead the complete knowledge of the nature of the world, which has a *quietening* effect on the will, induces resignation, the surrender not merely of life but of the very will to live.

So in tragedy we see the noblest men, after long conflict and suffering, renounce at the last, and forever, the aims they have so passionately pursued, and all life's pleasures; or else they freely and joyfully surrender life itself. We see Calderón's steadfast prince do this; and Gretchen in *Faust*; so, too Hamlet, whom his friend Horatio would willingly follow but is bade remain a while, and in this harsh world draw his breath in pain, to shed light on Hamlet's fate and to clear his name; so also [Schiller's] Maid of Orleans and Bride of Messina; they all die purified by suffering, *i.e.*, after the will to life has already died in them. In Voltaire's *Mahomet* this is expressed in the concluding words addressed to Mahomet by Palmire as she dies: 'The world is for tyrants: you must live!' On the other hand, the demand for so-called poetic justice rests on an entire misconception of the nature of tragedy, and, indeed, of the nature of the world. It appears unashamedly in all its dullness, in the criticism which Dr Samuel Johnson passed on some of Shakespeare's plays, for he very naively laments the total disregard of it. And this disregard is demonstrable, indeed, for in what have Ophelia, Desdemona, or Cordelia offended? But only the trite, optimistic, Protestant-rationalist – or properly, Jewish – view of life will demand poetic justice, and find its own satisfaction in the satisfaction of poetic justice. The true sense of tragedy is the deeper insight that it is not his own individual sins that the hero atones for, but original sin, *i.e.*, the guilt of existence itself. As Calderón puts it plainly:

> For the greatest crime of man
> Is that he was born

> [*Life is a Dream*]

I shall allow myself only one remark more closely concerning the treatment of tragedy. The presentation of a great misfortune is essential to tragedy. But the many different ways in which this is introduced by the poet may be brought under three categories. It may happen by means of one character's extraordinary (and well-nigh impossible) wickedness; he becomes the author of the misfortune. Examples of this kind are Richard III, Iago in *Othello*, Shylock in *The Merchant of Venice*, Franz Moor [in Schiller's *Die Räuber*], Euripides' Phaedra, Creon in the *Antigone*, etc.. Or again, it may happen through blind fate, *i.e.*, chance and error; a true model of this kind is Sophocles' *Oedipus Rex* and his *Trachinian Maidens*, and in general, most ancient tragedy belongs to this class. Among modern tragedies, *Romeo and Juliet*, Voltaire's *Tancred* and [Schiller's] *The Bride of Messina*, are examples. Lastly, the misfortune may be brought about by the mere attitude of the *dramatis personae* with regard to one another, through their relationship, so that there is no need either for a tremendous error or an unheard-of chance, nor yet for a character whose wickedness reaches the limits of the humanly possible; but characters of ordinary morality, under circumstances such as often occur, are so placed in relation to one another that their situation compels them, knowingly and with their eyes open, to do each other the greatest injury, without the blame falling on one side only.

This last kind of tragedy seems to me far to surpass the other two, for it shows us the greatest misfortune not as an exception, not as something caused by rare circumstances or monstrous characters, but as arising easily and automatically from human action and character, almost as essential to them, and thus brings it frighteningly close to us. In the other two kinds we may look on the prodigious fate and the horrible wickedness as terrifying powers which certainly threaten us, but only from afar, and which we may well escape without taking refuge in renunciation. But the last kind of tragedy shows us that those powers which destroy happiness and life are such that their path to us, too, is always open; we see the greatest sufferings brought about by entanglements whose essence our fate too, might assume, and through actions of which we may also be capable, and so could not complain of injustice; then, shuddering, we feel ourselves already in the midst of hell. The technical execution of this last type of tragedy is also the most difficult, in that the dramatist must produce the maximum impact by placing and assigning the minimum of dramatic means and devices; therefore, even in many of the best tragedies, this difficulty is evaded. Yet one tragedy may be cited as a perfect model of this kind, a tragedy which in other respects is far surpassed by more than one work by the same great master; that is [Goethe's] *Clavigo*. [Shakespeare's] *Hamlet* belongs to a certain extent to this class, as far as the relationship of Hamlet to Laertes and Ophelia is concerned. [Schiller's] *Wallenstein* has also this excellence. [Goethe's] *Faust* belongs entirely to this class, if we regard the episode concerning Gretchen and her brother as the principal action; also Corneille's *Cid*, only that it lacks the tragic conclusion, while, on the other hand, the analogous relationship between Max and Thekla has it [in Schiller's *Wallenstein*].

§ 52. We have now considered all the fine arts in the general way that is consistent with our point of view. We began with architecture, whose aim is to elucidate the will's objectification at the lowest grade of its visibility, in which it shows itself as the dumb unconscious striving of the mass, in conformity with law; and yet it already reveals internal discord and conflict, namely that between gravity and rigidity. We concluded with tragedy, which presents to us at the highest grade of the will's objectification this very conflict with itself on a fearsome scale, and with clarity. We find that one fine art has been excluded from our consideration, and had to be excluded, for in the systematic context of our exposition there was no place for it: I mean *music*. It stands alone, detached from all the other arts. In it we do not recognise the imitation or reproduction of any Idea of the creatures in the world. Yet it is such a great and glorious art, its effect on man's inmost nature is so powerful, and it is so completely and so deeply understood by him in his inmost consciousness as a perfectly universal language whose clarity surpasses even that of the perceptible world itself, that we certainly have more to look for in it than an 'unconscious exercise in arithmetic whereby the mind does not know it is counting', as Leibnitz [Letters] called it. Yet he was quite right in so far as he considered only its immediate external signifi-cance, its exterior. But if it were nothing more, the satisfaction it gives would be like what we feel when a sum in arithmetic comes out right, and could not be that intense pleasure with which we see the deepest recesses of our nature find a voice.

From our stand-point, therefore, where we have an eye to the aesthetic effect, we must attribute to music a far more serious, deeper significance for the inmost nature of the world and our own self; the arithmetical proportions to which music may be reduced we will then recognise as not the thing signified, but merely as the sign. That in some sense music must relate to the world as does a representation to the thing represented, or as does a copy to the original, we may infer by analogy with the other arts, all of which have this character; and they all affect us, on the whole, in the same way as music does, only that the effect of music is stronger, swifter, more compelling and infalli-ble. Further, its imitative relationship to the world must be very deep, infinitely true, and really striking, for it is instantly understood by everyone, and has the appearance of a certain infallibility in that its form may be seen in relation to quite definite rules which can be expressed numerically, and from which it cannot deviate without entirely ceasing to be music. Yet the point of comparison between music and the world, the respect in which its relationship to the world is that of a copy or reproduction, is very obscure. People have practised music in every age without being able to account for this; content to understand it directly, they give up any abstract comprehension of this direct understanding.

By surrendering my mind entirely to the impression of music in its various forms, and then returning to reflection and to the train of thought set out in the present work, I arrived at an explanation of the inner essence of music, and of the nature of its imitative relation to the world (which had necessarily to be presupposed by analogy). This explanation is quite sufficient for myself, and satisfactory to my investigation, and will probably be just as intelligible to anyone who has followed me up to this point, and has agreed with my view of the world. Yet I recognise that it is essentially impossible to prove this explanation, for it accepts and establishes a relationship between music, as idea, and something which by its nature can never be idea; and music will have to be regarded as the copy of an original which can never itself be directly presented as idea. I can therefore do no more than state here, at the conclusion of this Third Book which has been devoted principally to the consideration of the arts, the explanation of the marvellous art of music which satisfies me, and I must leave the assent to, or dissent from, my view to the effect produced upon each of my readers both by music itself and by the whole system of thought communicated in this work. Moreover, I think it necessary that, to assent wholeheartedly to my exposition of the meaning of music, one should often listen to music while pondering on my views on it, and for this, again, it is necessary to be very familiar with the whole of my system of thought.

The (Platonic) Ideas are the adequate objectification of will. To stimulate the knowledge of these by depicting particular things (for works of art are themselves always representations of particular things) is the aim of all the other arts (and is possible only by a corresponding change in the knowing subject). Thus all these arts objectify the will only indirectly by means of the Ideas; and since our world is nothing but the manifestation of the Ideas in plurality, through their entering into the *principium individuationis* (the form of knowledge possible for the individual as such), music, since it takes no account of the Ideas, is entirely independent also of the phenomenal world, ignores it altogether, could to a certain extent exist if there were no world at all; this cannot be said of the other arts. Music is as *direct* an objectification and copy of the whole *will* as is the world itself, indeed, as are the Ideas whose multiplied manifestation constitutes the world of individual things. So music is by no means (as are the other arts) the copy of the Ideas, but the *copy of the will itself*, whose objectivity the Ideas are. This is why the effect of music is so much more powerful and penetrating than that of the other arts, for they speak only of the shadow while music speaks of the essence. Since, however, it is the same will which objectifies itself both in the Ideas and in music, though in quite a different way in each, there must be, not indeed a direct likeness, but a parallel, an analogy, between music and the Ideas whose manifestation in plurality and incompleteness, is the visible world. The tracing of this analogy will serve as an illustration to make this explanation more readily comprehensible, for the obscurity of the subject has made this difficult to explain.

I recognise in the deepest tones of harmony, in the bass, the lowest grades of the will's objectification, inorganic nature, the planet's mass. It is well known that all the high notes, which readily become tremulous and die away more swiftly, follow from the secondary vibration of the deep bass-note. When the low note sounds, the high notes always sound faintly along with it, and it is a law of harmony that only those high notes may accompany a bass-note which actually already, as its *sons harmoniques*, sound along with it of themselves on account of its secondary vibration. This is analogous to our holding, as we must, that all the bodies and organisms of nature came into existence by gradual development out of the planet's mass; this is their support as much as it is their source: and the higher notes bear the same relationship to the bass.

Below a certain maximum depth no sound is audible. This corresponds to the fact that, without form and quality, no matter can be perceived, *i.e.*, without manifesting a force which cannot be further explained, in which an Idea expresses itself; and, more generally, that no matter can be entirely without will. Thus, just as a certain pitch is inseparable from the note as such, so a certain grade of the will's manifestation is inseparable from matter. So bass is for us in harmony what inorganic nature – the crudest mass on which everything rests, and from which every-thing arises and develops – is in the world. Furthermore, in all the parts which together make up the harmony between the bass and the leading voice singing the melody, I recognise the whole gradation of the Ideas in which the will objectifies itself. Those nearer to the bass are the lower of those grades, bodies which, though still inorganic, are manifesting themselves in many ways; the higher represent to me the world of plants and animals. The definite intervals of a scale are parallel to the definite grades of the will's objectification, the definite species in nature. Deviation from the arithmetical correctness of the intervals, through some temperament, or induced by the key selected, is analogous to the individual's departure from the type of the species; indeed, the impure discords which give no definite interval may be compared to the misbegotten offspring of the union of animals of two different species, or of the union of man with animal.

But all these bass and other parts which make up *harmony* lack that coherence and continuity which belong only to the upper voice singing the *melody*; it alone moves quickly and lightly in modulations and runs, while all these others move more slowly and without independent continuity. The deep bass moves most ponderously of all, as representative of the crudest mass. It rises and falls only in large intervals, in thirds, fourths, fifths, never by *one* tone, unless it is a bass inverted by double counterpoint. To move slowly is also physically essential to it; a quick run or trill in the low notes cannot even be imagined. The higher parts, which run parallel to animal life, move more quickly, but still without melodious sequence and meaningful continuity. The incoherent line sung by each of the parts, and their being bound by the laws of harmony, is analogous to the absence in every creature – from the crystal to the most advanced animal – in the whole irrational world, of a coherent consciousness which would make its life into a meaningful whole; for no creature experiences a succession of mental developments, none perfects itself by culture, but everything exists without alteration, always as its species dictates, as determined by inflexible law.

Lastly, in the *melody*, in the high, singing, principal voice leading the whole and progressing with unrestrained freedom, in the unbroken meaningful coherence of *one* thought from beginning to end, and representing a whole, I recognise the highest grade of the will's objectification, man's conscious life and endeavour. Only he, because he is endowed with reason, constantly looks both ahead and behind him on the path of his reality and of the countless possibilities, and so by completing life's course in consciousness, he makes of it a coherent whole. Similarly, only the *melody* has significant intentional connection from beginning to end. So it tells the story of the will enlightened by self-reflection, the will which imprints itself on reality as sequence of actions. But melody says more: it tells the will's secret story, depicts every impulse, every endeavour, its every stirring, everything that the reason includes in the broad negative concept of feeling, and which cannot be admitted any further into its abstract concepts. Therefore it has always been said that music is the language of feeling and of passion, just as words are the language of reason. Plato explains it as 'The movement of melodies which imitates the stirring of the soul' [*Laws*, vii];

and also Aristotle says 'How does it come about that the rhythms and melodies, although only sounds, resemble states of the soul?' [*Prob.*, c. 19].

Now the nature of man consists in this, that his will strives, is gratified and strives anew, and so on for ever. Indeed, his happiness and well-being consist simply in the quick transition from desire to satisfaction, and from gratification to a new desire. For the absence of gratification is suffering, and the empty longing for a new desire is languor, *ennui*. Similarly the nature of melody is a constant digression and deviation from the key-note in a thousand ways, not only to the harmonious intervals, the third and dominant, but to every tone, to the dissonant seventh and to the very wide intervals; yet there always follows a return at last to the key-note. In all these excursions melody expresses the many different forms of the will's striving, but always its gratification, too, by finally returning to a harmonious interval, and still more, to the key-note. The invention of melody, the disclosure in it of all the deepest secrets of human willing and feeling, is the work of genius, whose activity (which is more apparent here than anywhere else) is far from all reflection and conscious intention, and might be called inspiration. Here, as everywhere in art, abstraction is unproductive. The composer reveals the inner nature of the world, and expresses the most profound wisdom, in a language which his reasoning faculty does not understand, just as a person mesmerised talks about things of which he has no understanding when he awakes. Thus in the composer, more than in any other artist, the person is entirely separated and distinct from the artist. Even in the explanation of this wonderful art [*i.e.*, music] abstraction shows its inadequacy and its limitations. I shall try, however, to complete our analogy.

As quick transition from desire to gratification, and from gratification to new desire, is happiness and well-being, so quick melodies without great variations are cheerful; slow melodies, striking painful discords, and winding back only after many bars to the key-note, are sad, by analogy with gratification which is delayed and hard-won. The delay in the new excitation of will, languor, could have no other expression than the sustained keynote, the effect of which would soon be unbearable; very monotonous and meaningless melodies approach this effect. The short catchy tunes of quick dance-music seem to speak only of ordinary pleasure, which is easily attained. On the other hand, the *Allegro maestoso*, in grand phrases, long passages, and wide-ranging variations, signifies a greater, nobler effort towards a distant end and its final attainment. The *Adagio* speaks of the suffering incurred in a great and noble endeavour which despises all trivial contentment. But how wonderful is the effect of the *minor* and *major*! How astounding that the alteration of a semi-tone, the occurrence of the minor third instead of the major, at once and inevitably forces upon us an anxious, painful feeling from which the major releases us again just as swiftly. The *Adagio* in the minor achieves an expression of the keenest pain, and becomes a disturbing lament. Dance-music in the minor key seems to indicate the non-attainment of that trivial contentment which we ought rather to disdain, and seems to speak of attainment, with toil and trouble, of a purpose that is petty.

The inexhaustible variety of possible melodies corresponds to nature's inexhaustible variety of individuals, physiognomies, and ways of life. The transition from one key to an entirely different one, since it completely breaks the connection with what went before, is like death, in so far as the individual ends there; but the will which appeared in this individual lives on, appearing in other individuals whose consciousness, however, has no connection with his.

In pursuing all these analogies which I cite, it must never be forgotten that music has only an indirect relationship to them, and not a direct relationship, for it never expresses the phenomenon, but only the inner nature, the in-itself of all phenomenon, the will itself. Thus it expresses not this or that particular and definite joy, this or that sorrow, or pain, or horror, or delight, or merriment, or peace of mind; but it expresses joy, sorrow, pain, horror, delight, merriment, peace of mind *themselves*, to a certain extent in the abstract, their essential nature, without incidentals and so also without the motives for these emotions. Yet we understand them perfectly in this extracted quintessence. Hence our imagination is so susceptible to music, and now seeks to give form to that invisible yet lively spirit-world which speaks to us directly, and clothe it with flesh and blood, *i.e.*, to embody it in an analogous model. This is the origin of the song with words, and ultimately of opera, and their texts should for that very reason never forsake this subordinate position in order to make themselves the main subject, and the music a mere means of expressing it. This would be a great misconception and a piece of utter perversity, for music always expresses only the quintessence of life and of life's events, but never these themselves, and therefore their differences do not always affect it. It is just this universality – which is the exclusive property of music, and hers in spite of her precise delineation – that gives music its high value as the panacea for all our woes. Thus if music tries to attach itself too closely to the words, and tries to mould itself to episode and instance, it is striving to speak a language which is not its own. No one has kept himself so untainted by error as Rossini; his music *speaks its own language* so distinctly and purely that it needs no words, and makes its full impact when performed by instruments alone.

It follows from all this that we may regard the phenomenal world, or nature, and music as two different expressions of the same thing which is, therefore, itself the only link forging the analogy of the two; and to understand that analogy we must recognise this thing. Music, therefore, if regarded as an expression of the world, is in the highest degree a universal language which is related to the universality of concepts much as they are related to the particular things. Yet its universality is by no means that empty universality of abstraction, but quite of a different kind, and goes hand in hand with utter precision. In this respect it resembles geometrical figures and numbers, which are the universal forms of all possible objects of experience, and applicable to them all *a priori*, and yet are not abstract, but perceptible and utterly precise. All the will's possible expressions, its endeavours and excitements, all that goes on in the human heart and that reason consigns to the broad, negative concept of feeling, may be expressed by the infinite number of possible melodies; but always in the universality of mere form, without the material, always according to the thing-in-itself, not according to the phenomenon, but as the inmost soul, as it were, of the phenomenon, without the body.

The deep relationship which music has to the true nature of all things also explains the fact that suitable music played to any scene, activity, event or circumstance seems to divulge the most secret meaning of that occasion, and to play the part of its most accurate and clearest commentator. This is so truly the case that anyone who surrenders to the impression of a symphony seems to see all the possible events of life and the world pass in procession before him, yet if he reflects, he can cite no similarity between the music and the things that pass before his mind. For music, as we have said, is distinguished from all the other arts by its not being a copy of the phenomenon, or, more accurately, the will's adequate objectivity, but is the direct copy of the will itself, and therefore it presents the metaphysical, and to all phenomenon it presents the thing-in-itself. So we might just as well call the world 'embodied music' as 'embodied will'; this explains why music makes every picture, and indeed every scene of real life and of the world, at once appear more intensely meaningful, and the closer its melody is to the inner spirit of the given phenomenon, the more this is so. It follows that we are able to set a poem to music as a song, or a visual depiction as a pantomime, or both as an opera. Such pictures of human life, set to the universal language of music, are never bound to it or correspond to it with stringent necessity; but bear to it only the relationship borne by an arbitrary instance to a universal concept. They represent, within the bounds of reality, what music expresses in the universality of pure form. For melodies, like general concepts, are to a certain extent an abstraction from the actual.

This actual world, then, the world of particular things, provides the objects of perception, the special and individual, the specific instance, both to the universality of the concepts and to the universality of the melodies. But these two universalities are in a certain respect opposed to each other; for the concepts contain only the forms abstracted first from perception, like the outer skin peeled from things, and thus they are, literally speaking, *abstracta*; music, on the other hand, gives the inmost kernel which precedes all form, or the heart of things. This relationship might be well expressed in the language of the schoolmen, by saying the concepts are the *universalia post rem* whereas music gives the *universalia ante rem*, and the real world the *universalia in re*. To the universal meaning of a melody to which a poem has been set, other examples, selected just as arbitrarily, of the universal expressed in this poem might correspond in the same degree. So the same musical composition suits many stanzas; and this is also what makes the *vaudeville* possible.

But that any affinity at all is possible between a musical

composition and a visual representation rests, as we have said, upon the fact that both are simply different expressions of the same inner nature of the world. When now, in the particular case, such a relationship is actually present, that is to say, when the composer has been able to express in the universal language of music the stirrings of will which constitute the heart of an event, then the melody of the song, the music of the opera, is expressive. But the analogy discovered by the composer between the two must have proceeded from the direct knowledge of the nature of the world, and be unknown to his reasoning, and must not be an imitation produced with conscious intention by means of concepts, otherwise the music does not express the inner nature, the will itself, but merely imitates its phenomenon inadequately. All really imitative music does this; for example, *The Seasons* by Haydn, and many passages of his *Creation* in which phenomena of the perceptible world are directly imitated; and all military music, too. Such music is entirely to be rejected.

The unutterable depth of all music – by virtue of which it drifts over and beyond us as a paradise familiar yet ever remote, comprehensible and yet so inexplicable – rests on its echoing all the emotions of our inmost nature, but entirely without reality and far removed from its pain. So also its essential seriousness (which excludes the absurd from its immediate sphere) is to be explained by the fact that its object is not the idea (solely in respect of which deception and absurdity are possible), but its object is directly the will, and this is essentially the most serious of all things, as being that on which all depends. How rich in content and meaning the language of music is, we see from the repetition-marks as well as from the *da capo*, the like of which would be unbearable in works composed in a language of words, but in music are very appropriate and beneficial, for, in order to grasp it fully, we must hear it twice.

In the whole of this exposition of music I have been trying to bring out clearly that it expresses in a perfectly universal language, in a homogeneous material, (that is, in mere tones), and with the greatest distinctness and truth, the inner nature, the in-itself of the world, which we think of under the concept of will, because will is its clearest manifestation. Further, according to my view and contention, philosophy is nothing but a complete and accurate reproduction and expression of the nature of the world in very general concepts, for only in such is it possible to gain a perspective on that whole nature which will be adequate and applicable everywhere. Thus anyone who has followed me and entered into my mode of thought will not be surprised if I say that, supposing it were possible to give a perfectly accurate, complete, even detailed, explanation of music – that is to say, to reproduce minutely in concepts what it expresses – this would also be a sufficient reproduction and explanation of the world in concepts, or at least equivalent to such an explanation, and thus it would be the true philosophy. Consequently Leibnitz's words quoted above, which on a modest level are quite correct, may be parodied in the following way to suit our loftier view of music: 'music is the unconscious exercise in metaphysics in which the mind does not know that it is philosophising'. [. . .]

BOOK FOUR

BOOK FOUR

The World as Will

SECOND ASPECT

The affirmation and denial of the will to life, once self-knowledge has been attained

At the same time as knowledge appeared, desire arose.

Oupnek'hat, studio Anquetil Duperron, vol. ii. p. 216

§ 53. The last part of our study claims to be the most serious, for it concerns human actions, a subject which affects everyone directly and can be alien or uninteresting to no-one. It is indeed so characteristic of man's nature to relate everything else to action that in every systematic investigation he will always regard the part that has to do with action as the sum of the whole (in so far, at least, as its content interests him), and so he will give his serious attention to this part, even if to no other.

In this respect this next part of our work would, in ordinary language, be called 'practical philosophy' as distinct from the 'theoretical' which has occupied us hitherto. But, in my opinion, all philosophy is always theoretical, because it is essential to it – whatever the immediate subject of its enquiry – to retain a purely contemplative attitude, and to investigate, not to prescribe. On the other hand, to become practical, to direct conduct, to transform character, are old ambitions which, with mature insight, philosophy ought finally to relinquish. For where it is a matter of the worth or worthlessness of a life, where salvation or damnation are in question, it is not the dead concepts of philosophy that are decisive, but the inmost nature of man himself, the Daemon who guides him and who has not chosen him, but been chosen by him, as Plato would say; 'his intelligible character', as Kant expresses himself. Virtue cannot be taught any more than can genius; indeed, for virtue the abstract concept is just as barren as it is in art, and in either case it can be used only as a tool. Hence we would be just as foolish to expect that our moral systems and ethics might inspire virtuous, noble, and holy men, as that our aesthetics might inspire poets, painters, and musicians.

Philosophy can never do more than interpret and explain what is given. It can only bring to the distinct, abstract knowledge of the faculty of reason the nature of the world which expresses itself comprehensibly to everyone in the concrete, that is, as feeling. This, however, it does in every possible respect and from every point of view. Now, as this attempt has been made from other points of view in the three preceding Books, through the general treatment that is proper to philosophy, in this Book human actions will be considered in the same way; and this aspect of the world might, indeed, be found to be the most important of all, not only subjectively, as I remarked above, but also objectively. In considering it I shall faithfully adhere to the method I have hitherto followed, and shall rest my argument on premises already advanced. There is, indeed, just one thought which forms the content of this whole work. I have endeavoured to develop it in relation to all other topics and I shall now do so with regard to human action. I shall then have done all I can to communicate my thought as fully as possible. [. . .]

§ 54. The first three Books will, it is hoped, have conveyed the distinct and certain insight that the world as idea is a mirror which reflects the will. In this mirror the will recognises itself in ascending grades of distinctness and completeness, the highest of which is man, whose nature, however, receives its complete expression only through the integrated series of his actions. The self-conscious integration of these actions is made possible by the faculty of reason, which enables a man constantly to survey the whole in the abstract.

The will, considered purely in itself, is without knowledge and is merely a blind, irresistible impulse, as we see it appear in inorganic and vegetable nature and their laws, and also in the vegetative part of our own life. This will receives, by the accession of the world as idea, which is developed for it, the knowledge of its own willing and of what it is that it wills. And this is nothing but this world, life, precisely as it exists. For that reason we called the phenomenal world the will's mirror, its objectivity. And since what the will wills is always life, just because life is nothing but the representation of that willing for the idea, it is all one and a mere pleonasm if, instead of simply saying 'the will', we say 'the will to life.'

Will is the thing-in-itself, the inner content, the essence of the world. Life, the visible world, the phenomenon, is only the mirror of the will. Therefore life accompanies the will as inseparably as its shadow accompanies the body; and if will exists, so will life, the world, exist. Life is, therefore, assured to the will to life; and as long as we are filled with the will to life, we need have no fear for our existence, even in the presence of death. It is true we see the individual come into being and pass away; but the individual is only phenomenal, exists only for the knowledge which is biased by the principle of sufficient reason, by the *principium individuationis*. Certainly, for this kind of knowledge, the individual receives his life as a gift, rises out of nothing, then suffers the loss of the gift through death, and returns again to nothing. But we desire to consider life philosophically, *i.e.*, according to its Ideas, and in this sphere we shall find that neither the will, the thing-in-itself in all phenomena, nor the subject of knowing, he who perceives all phenomena, is affected at all by birth or by death. Birth and death belong merely to the phenomenon of will, thus to life; and it is essential to this to show itself in individuals which come into being and pass away, as fleeting phenomena appearing in the form of time – phenomena of that which in itself knows no time, but must exhibit itself precisely in the way we have said, in order to objectify its own nature.

Birth and death belong in like manner to life, and hold the balance as reciprocal conditions of each other, or, if one likes the expression, as poles of the whole phenomenon of life. The wisest of all mythologies, the Indian, expresses this by giving to Siva, the very god who symbolises destruction and death (just as Brahma, the most sinful and the lowest god of the Trimurti, symbolises procreation and birth, and Vishnu symbolises preservation) – by giving to Siva as an emblem not only the necklace of skulls, but also the lingam, the symbol of procreation, which appears here as the counterpart of death, thus signifying that procreation and death are essentially correlatives which reciprocally neutralise and cancel each other. It was precisely the same sentiment that led the Greeks and Romans to adorn their costly sarcophagi, just as we still see them, with feasts, dances, marriages, hunting-scenes, fights between wild beasts, bacchanalia with depictions of the most urgent vitality which they present not only in such pleasurable entertainment, but also in lascivious interaction, even going so far as to represent sexual intercourse between satyrs and goats. Clearly the aim was to point with strongest emphasis away from the death of the individual late lamented to the immortal life of nature, and thus to indicate, though without abstract knowledge, that the whole of nature presents both the phenomenon and also the fulfilment of the will to life.

The form of this phenomenon is time, space, and causality, and by means of these, individuation, which implies that the individual must come into being and pass away. But this no more troubles the will to life, of whose manifestation the individual is, as it were, only one particular example or specimen, than the death of an individual grieves the whole of nature. For it is not the individual, but only the species that nature cares about, and for the preservation of which she so earnestly strives, providing for it so extravagantly through the vast surplus of the seed and the great strength of the breeding impulse. The individual, on the contrary, neither has, nor can have, any value for Nature, for her kingdom is infinite time and infinite space, and in these an infinite number of possible individuals. So she is always ready to let the individual fall, and hence it is not only exposed to destruction in a thousand ways by the most trivial chance, but destined for it from the start, and led towards it by Nature herself from the moment it has served its end of maintaining the species. Thus without dissembling Nature declares the great truth that only the Ideas, not the individuals, have, properly speaking, reality, *i.e.*, are complete objectivity of the will. Now, since man is nature itself, and indeed nature at the highest grade of its self-consciousness, but nature is only the objectified will to life, a person who has grasped this point of view and persists in it may well console himself, when contemplating his own death and that of his friends, by turning his eyes to the immortal life of nature, which he himself is. This is the significance of Siva with the lingam, and of those ancient sarcophagi which, through their pictures of the most radiant life, proclaim to the grieving onlooker *natura non contristatur* [nature is not made sorrowful].

That procreation and death are to be regarded as something belonging to life, and essential to this phenomenon of the will, arises also from their both presenting themselves to us merely as more intense expressions of the substance of which all the rest of life consists. For this is nothing but the constant fluctuation of matter even while the form remains fixed; and this is what constitutes the transitoriness of individuals even while the species remains permanent. Constant nourishment and renewal differ from procreation only in degree, and constant excretion differs from death only in degree. The first shows itself most simply and distinctly in the plant. The plant is a constant repetition of the same impulse: the repetition whereby its simplest fibre forms of itself leaf and twig. It is a systematic aggregate of homogeneous interdependent plants, whose constant reproduction is their sole impulse. It ascends to the fuller gratification of this impulse through the grades of its metamorphosis, ultimately attaining to the blossom and fruit, that compendium of its existence and endeavour in which it now by a shorter route reaches its sole aim, and at a stroke accomplishes thousand-fold what hitherto it effected only singly – the repetition of itself. Its development up to the point of fruiting bears the same relationship to that fruit as does writing to printing. With the animal it is clearly the same. The process of nourishing is a constant procreating; the process of procreation is a more intense nourishing. The pleasure which accompanies the act of procreation is, to a more intense degree, pleasure in being alive. On the other hand, excretion, the constant exhalation and discarding of matter, is the same as that which at a higher power is death, the antithesis of procreation. And if we are always content to retain the form without lamenting the discarded matter, we ought to behave in the same way if in death the same thing happens, more intensely and totally, as takes place daily and hourly, and on a small scale, in excretion: if we are indifferent to the one, we ought not to shrink from the other. So from this point of view it appears just as perverse to desire the continuity of one's individuality which is being replaced by other individuals, as to desire the permanence of the body's substance which is always being replaced by new substance. It appears just as foolish to embalm corpses as it would be carefully to preserve one's excreta. As to the individual consciousness which is bound to the individual body, it is absolutely interrupted every day by sleep. Deep sleep is, while it lasts, in no way different from death, into which, in fact, it often passes without interruption, as in the case of freezing to death; it differs only as to the future, that is, with respect to the awaking. Death is a sleep in which individuality is forgotten; everything else wakes again, or, rather, never slept.[1]

Above all, we must distinctly recognise that the form of the phenomenon of will, that is to say the form of life or of reality, is really only the *present*, not the future nor the past. The latter exist only in the concept, exist only in the context of knowledge in so far as it follows the principle of sufficient reason. No man has ever lived in the past, and none will live in the future; the *present* alone is the form of all life, and is, however, also its sure possession which can never be wrested from it. The present always exists, together with its content. Both remain fixed without wavering, like the rainbow on the waterfall. For life is assured to the will, and the present is assured to life. Certainly if we reflect on the thousands of years that have passed by, on the millions of people who lived in them, we ask, What were they? what has become of them? But, on the other hand, we need only recall our own past life and relive its scenes vividly in our imagination, and then ask again, What was all this? what has become of it? As it is with our own life, so is it with the life of those millions. Or should we suppose that the past could receive a new existence because it has been sealed by death? Our own past, even the most recent part of it, and even the day that was just yesterday, is now no more than imagination's empty dream, and the past of all those millions is the same. What was? What is? It is the will, of which life is a mirror, and will-free knowing which glimpses the will clearly in that mirror.

---

[1] The following thoughts, if they are not too subtle, may help to make clear that the individual is only the phenomenon, not the thing-in-itself. Every individual is, on the one hand, the subject of knowing, *ie.*, the complemental condition of the possibility of the whole objective world, and, on the other hand, a particular phenomenon of will, the same will which objectifies itself in everything. But this ambiguity of our being does not rest upon a self-existing unity, otherwise we could be conscious of ourselves *in ourselves, and independent of the objects of knowledge and will.* Now this is simply impossible, for as soon as we turn into ourselves to make the attempt, and seek for once to know ourselves fully by means of introspective reflection, we are lost in a bottomless void; we find ourselves like the crystal ball out of which a voice speaks whose cause is not to be found in it, and wanting to understand ourselves, we grasp, with a shudder, only an insubstantial spectre.

Anyone who has not yet recognised this, or is unwilling to recognise it, must in addition to the question asked above as to the fate of past generations of men, ask this further question, too: Why is he, the questioner, of all people so fortunate as to be in possession of this precious, fleeting, and only real present, while those hundreds of generations of men, and even the heroes and philosophers of those ages, have sunk into the night of the past, and have thus become nothing; but he, his insignificant ego, actually exists? Or more briefly, if just as bizarrely: Why is this 'now', *his* 'now', occurring *now*, and why has it not also occurred long ago? In asking such strange questions, he sees his existence and his time as independent of each other, and the former as projected into the latter. He assumes two nows – one which belongs to the object, the other which belongs to the subject – and marvels at the happy accident of their coincidence. But in truth, only the point of contact of the object (the form of which is time) with the subject (which has no mode of the principle of sufficient reason as its form) constitutes the present, as is shown in the essay on the principle of sufficient reason. Yet all object is the will in so far as it has become idea, and the subject is the necessary correlative of all object. But real objects are only in the present; the past and the future contain only concepts and fancies, therefore the present is the essential form of the phenomenon of the will, and inseparable from it. The present alone is that which always exists and stands fixed and firm. That which, empirically apprehended, is the most transitory of all, presents itself to the metaphysical eye, which looks beyond the forms of empirical perception, as the only thing that endures, the *nunc stans* of the schoolmen. The source and the sustainer of its content is the will to life or the thing-in-itself – which we are. That which constantly becomes and passes away, in that it has either already been or is still to be, belongs to the phenomenon as such by virtue of its forms which make possible this coming into being and passing away. Accordingly we must think *Quid fuit? – Quod est. Quid erit? – Quod fuit* [What was? – that which is. What will be? – that which was], and taking it in the strict meaning of the words, we should understand not *simile* but *idem*. For life is certain to the will, and the present is certain to life. Thus it is that everyone can say, 'I am, once and for all, lord of the present, and through all eternity it will accompany me as my shadow: accordingly I do not wonder where the present has come from, and how it happens to be taking place precisely at this time'.

We can compare time to a constantly revolving sphere; the half that is always sinking would be the past, that which is always rising would be the future; but the indivisible point at the top, which touches the tangent, would be the extensionless present. As the tangent does not revolve with the sphere, neither does the present – the point of contact of the object whose form is time – revolves with the subject – which has no form because it does not belong to the knowable, but is the condition of all that is knowable. Alternatively we can say that time is like a relentless river, and the present like a crag against which the flowing water breaks without sweeping it away. The will, as thing-in-itself, is no more subordinate to the principle of sufficient reason than is the subject of knowledge, which is ultimately, in a certain regard, the will itself or its expression. And just as life, the will's own phenomenon, is assured to the will, so is the present, the sole form of real life. Therefore we have not to search for the past before life, nor the future after death: we have, rather, to know the *present*, the only form in which the will manifests itself. It won't elude the will, nor the will elude it. So the person who is content with life as it is, the person who in every way affirms life, may confidently see it as endless, and banish the fear of death as an illusion that suggests to him the foolish fear that he can ever lose the present, and foreshadows a time in which there is no present; an illusion with regard to time analogous to the illusion with regard to space through which everyone imagines the position on the globe he happens to occupy as on top, and all other places as lower down.

In the same way everyone links the present to his own individuality, and imagines that with that individuality all present will be extinguished; that past and future might then be without a present. But just as on the surface of the globe every place is on top, so, too, the form of all life is the *present,* and to fear death because it snatches the present from us, is no wiser than to fear that we may slide down from the globe precisely when by good fortune we happen to be standing on the top. The form of the present is essential to the objectification of the will. Itself a point without extension, it cuts time, which extends infinitely in both directions, and stands immovably fixed, like an everlasting mid-day without any cool evening, just as the actual sun burns unceasingly, only seeming to sink into the bosom of night. So if a man fears death as his annihilation, it is just as if he were to think that the sun could at evening lament 'Woe is me! for I go down into eternal night.' And conversely, anyone who is oppressed by the burden of life, who desires life and affirms it but abhors its torments, and in particular can no longer endure the hard lot that has fallen to him personally – such a man has no deliverance to hope for from death, and cannot save himself by means of suicide. Only deceptively do the cool shades of Orcus entice him as to a haven of rest. The earth rolls from day into night, the individual dies, but the sun itself shines without intermission, an eternal noon. Life is assured to the will to life; the form of life is the present without end, no matter how the individuals, as phenomena of the Idea, arise and pass away within time, like fleeting dreams. So suicide, even at this early stage, appears to us as a vain, and therefore a foolish, action; when we have advanced further in this study, it will show itself in a light even less favourable.

Dogmas change and our knowledge is deceptive; but nature never errs; she moves confidently, and she never conceals what she is doing. Everything is complete and fulfilled in nature, and nature is complete and fulfilled in everything. She has her centre in every animal. With confidence the animal has found its path into life, just as with confidence it will find its way out; in the meantime it lives without fear of annihilation, and without cares, supported by the consciousness that it is nature herself, and is imperishable as she is. Man alone carries about with him, in abstract concepts, the certainty of his death; yet this, very strangely, can trouble him only at odd moments when some occasion suggests it to his imagination. Against the mighty voice of nature, reflection can do little. In man, as in the animal which does not think, there prevails as his constant condition that confidence that springs from his inmost consciousness that he himself is nature, is the world; and on account of this nobody is noticeably disturbed by the thought of certain and never-distant death, but everyone lives from day to day as though he were destined to live for ever. Indeed, this is carried so far that we may say that no one has a really vivid conviction of the certainty of his death, otherwise there would be no great difference between his frame of mind and that of a condemned criminal. We may say that everyone recognises that certainty in the abstract and theoretically, but lays it aside like other theoretical truths which are not applicable to practice, without really absorbing it into his living consciousness. Anyone who carefully considers this peculiarity of human character will see that the psychological explanations which cite habit and acquiescence in the inevitable, are inadequate, and that its true explanation lies deeper, as we have indicated. The same thing also explains why at all times and among all peoples there arise dogmas of one kind and another relating to the continued existence of the individual after death, and these are respected, although the evidence in support of them must always be very insufficient, and the evidence against them strong and plentiful. But, in truth, this really requires no proof, but is recognised by the healthy understanding as a fact, and confirmed by the confidence that nature lies as seldom as she errs, but frankly displays and naively declares what she does and is, while it is only we ourselves who obscure it by our deludedness, in order to read in it what suits our limited view-point.

But we have now brought to clear consciousness that, although the particular phenomenon of the will has a temporal beginning and end, the will itself as thing-in-itself is not affected by this, nor is the correlative of all object, the knowing but never known subject; and that life is always assured to the will to life: this is not to be numbered with these doctrines of immortality. For permanence has no more to do with the will regarded as the thing-in-itself or with the pure subject of knowing, the eternal eye of the world, than has transitoriness, for permanence and transience are predicates valid only in time, whereas the will and the pure subject of knowing lie outside time. Therefore the egoism of the individual (this particular phenomenon of will enlightened by the subject of knowing) can extract as little nourishment and consolation for his wish to assert himself through endless time from the view we have expressed, as he could extract from the knowledge that after his death the rest of the external world will continue to exist in time – which is just the expression of the same view considered objectively, and therefore temporally. For every individual is transitory only as phenomenon, while as thing-in-itself everyone is timeless, and therefore endless. But it is also only as phenomenon that an individual is distinguished from the other things of the world; as thing-in-itself he is the will which appears in everything, and death removes the illusion which separates his consciousness from that of the others: this is immortality. His exemption from death, which is his due only in so far as he is thing-in-itself, is for the phenomenon one and the same as the continuing life of the rest of the external world.

The inward and merely felt consciousness of what we have just raised to distinct knowledge, prevents, as we have said, the thought of death from poisoning the life of the rational being, in that this consciousness is the basis of that courage which sustains every living thing and enables it to continue to live as if there were no such thing as death, as long as it is focused on life. Yet this consciousness will not prevent the individual from being seized with the fear of death, and trying in every way to escape from it, when it presents itself to him in reality, and specifically to him, even if only in his imagination, and he is compelled to look it straight in the eye. For as long as his perceptive faculty was directed to life as such, he was bound to perceive the intransience in it, too; likewise when death presents itself to him, he is bound to see it for what it is: the temporal end of the individual temporal phenomenon. What we fear in death is by no means the pain, for that lies clearly on this side of death, and, moreover, we often take refuge in death from pain, just as, vice versa, we sometimes endure the most terrible pain merely to escape death for another short while, although dying would be quick and easy. Thus we distinguish between pain and death as between two entirely different evils. What we fear in death is the eclipse of the individual, which it frankly claims to be; and since the individual is a specific objectification of the will to life itself, its whole nature struggles against death.

Now when feeling leaves us so helpless, reason can intervene and for the most part overcome the negative impression made by emotion, for it places us upon a higher vantage-point from which we see the whole rather than the part. Therefore a philosophical knowledge of the nature of the world which had progressed as far as the point we have now reached in this work, but went no farther, could even from this vantage-point overcome the terror of death in so far as, in the given individual, reflection had power over direct feeling. A person who had internalised the truths we have advanced, but had not come to know, either from his own experience or from a deeper insight, that constant suffering is essential to life, who found life gratifying and thoroughly congenial, and could calmly and deliberately desire that his life, as he had hitherto known it, should endure for ever or repeat itself ever anew, and whose commitment to life was so great that, in return for its pleasures, he willingly and gladly accepted all the hardships and miseries to which it is subject – such a man would stand 'with firm, strong bones on the well-grounded, enduring earth', and would have nothing to fear. Armed with the knowledge with which we equip him, he would look death in the face with calm indifference as it hurries towards him on the wings of time. He would regard it as a false illusion, an impotent spectre which frightens the weak but has no power over him who knows that he is himself the will of which the whole world is the objectification or copy, and that therefore he is always certain of life, and also of the present, the actual and only form of the phenomenon of the will. He cannot be terrified by an endless past or future in which he would not be, for this he regards as the empty delusion of the veil of Mâyâ. Thus he would no more fear death than the sun fears the night. [. . .] Finally, there are many men who would adopt this point of view if their insight kept pace with their will, *i.e.*, if, free from all illusion, they were able to understand themselves clearly. For this is, for knowledge, the point of view of *total affirmation of the will to life.*

That the will affirms itself means that, while in its objectivity (*i.e.*, in the world and in life) its own nature is completely and distinctly given it as idea, this knowledge does not by any means inhibit its willing; but this very life, known as it is, is willed as such by the will with knowledge, consciously and deliberately, just as till now the will without knowledge willed it as blind impulse. The opposite of this, the *denial of the will to life*, manifests itself when, once that knowledge is attained, volition ends in that the particular known phenomena no longer act as *motives* for willing, but the whole knowledge of the nature of the world, the mirror of the will, which has evolved through our grasping the *Ideas*, becomes a *quieter* of the will; and so the will passes voluntarily into abeyance. These quite unfamiliar concepts are difficult to understand when expressed in this general way, but it is hoped they will shortly become clear through our discussion of the phenomena – here, modes of conduct – in which, on the one hand, affirmation in its different grades, and on the other hand, denial, expresses itself. For both proceed from knowledge, yet not from abstract knowledge which is expressed in words, but from living knowledge which is expressed in action and behaviour alone, and is independent of the dogmas which as abstract knowledge involve the faculty of reason. To give an account of both of these, and to bring them to the clear knowledge of the faculty of reason, can be my sole aim, and not to prescribe or recommend one or the other, which would be as foolish as it would be useless; for the will in itself is absolutely free and entirely self-determining, and for it there is no law.

But before we proceed to our exposition, we must first explain and more accurately define this *freedom* and its relation to necessity. And also, with regard to life, the assertion and denial of which is our theme, we must insert a few general remarks connected with the will and its objects. By all of this we shall make it easier for ourselves to gain the understanding we want of the ethical significance of modes of conduct, at deeper level. [. . .]

§ 55. That the will as such is *free*, follows from its being, in our view, the thing-in-itself, the content of all phenomena. The phenomena, on the other hand, we recognise as absolutely subordinate to the principle of sufficient reason in its four forms. And since we know that necessity is absolutely identical with consequent from a given ground, and that these are convertible concepts, then all that belongs to the phenomenon, *i.e.*, all that is object for the knowing subject as individual, is in one aspect reason, and in another aspect consequent; and in this last capacity is determined with absolute necessity, and so can in no respect be other than it is. The whole content of Nature, the sum of her phenomena, is thus absolutely necessary, and the necessity of every part, of every phenomenon, of every event, can always be proved, in that it must be possible to find the reason or ground from which this necessity follows as a consequent. This admits of no exception: it follows from the unrestricted validity of the principle of sufficient reason. In another respect, however, the same world is for us, in all its phenomena, objectivity of will. Since the will is not phenomenon, is not idea or object, but thing-in-itself, and is not subordinate to the principle of sufficient reason, the form of all object, it is not determined as a consequent through any reason, knows no necessity, *i.e.*, is *free*. The concept of freedom is thus properly a negative concept, for its content is merely the denial of necessity, *i.e.*, the relation of consequent to its reason, according to the principle of sufficient reason.

Now here lies before us in its most distinct form the reconciliation of that great contradiction, the union of freedom with necessity, which recently has so often been discussed, yet, as far as I know, never clearly and competently. Everything is as phenomenon, as object, absolutely necessary: *in itself* it is will, which is perfectly free for ever. The phenomenon, the object, is necessarily and unalterably determined in that chain of causes and effects which admits of no interruption. That this object exists at all, and the mode in which it exists – that is to say, the Idea which reveals itself in it, or, in other words, its character – is a direct manifestation of will. Thus, in conformity with the freedom of this will, the object might not exist at all, or it might be in its origin and essence something quite different from what it is; then, however, the whole chain of which it is a link, and which is itself a manifestation of the same will, would also be quite different. But once there and existing, it has entered the chain of causes and effects, is always necessarily determined in it, and can, therefore, neither become something else, *i.e.*, change itself, nor yet separate itself from the chain, *i.e.*, vanish.

Man, like every other part of nature, is objectivity of the will; hence all that has been said applies to him too. As everything in nature has its energies and qualities which react in a definite way to definite stimulus, and constitute its character, man also has his *character*, from which the motives necessarily call forth his actions. In this mode of acting his empirical character reveals itself, and in this, in turn, his intelligible character, the will in itself, of which he is the determined phenomenon. But man is the will's most complete phenomenon, and, as we showed in the Second Book, he had to be enlightened with so high a degree of knowledge in order to maintain himself in existence, that in it a perfectly adequate copy or repetition of the nature of the world under the form of the idea became possible: this is the comprehension of the Ideas, the pure mirror of the world, as we learnt in the Third Book. Thus in man the will can attain the full self-consciousness, to distinct and exhaustive knowledge of its own nature as it mirrors itself in the whole world. We saw in the preceding book that art springs from the actual presence of this degree of knowledge; and at the very end of our work it will further appear that when the will applies this same knowledge to itself, a cessation and abnegation of the will in its most perfect manifestation is possible. So the freedom which otherwise, as belonging only to the thing-in-itself, can never show itself in the phenomenon, in such a case does appear also in the phenomenon, and by cancelling the essential nature in which the phenomenon is grounded (while the phenomenon itself continues to exist in time) brings about a conflict of the phenomenon with itself, and by this very means exhibits the phenomena of holiness and self-renunciation. But all this can be fully understood only at the end of this Book.

This gives only a preliminary and general indication of how man is distinguished from all the other phenomena of will by the fact that freedom (*i.e.*, independence of the principle of sufficient reason, which belongs only to the will as thing-in-itself, and contradicts the phenomenon) can nonetheless in the case of man appear also in the phenomenon, where, however, it necessarily shows itself as self-contradiction in the phenomenon. In this sense, not only the will in itself, but man, too, can certainly be called free, and can thus be distinguished from all other beings. But how this is to be understood can become clear only through all that is to follow, and for the present we must disregard it. For, in the first place, we must beware of mistakenly thinking that the action of the individual, determined person is subject to no necessity, *i.e.*, that the compulsion of the motive is less certain than the compulsion of the cause, or than the following of the conclusion from the premises. If we discount the case cited above, which relates only to an exception, the freedom of the will as thing-in-itself by no means extends directly to its phenomenon, not even where this reaches the highest grade of its visibility, and thus it does not extend to the rational animal endowed with individual character, *i.e.*, the person. The person is never free although he is the phenomenon of a free will; for he is the already determined phenomenon of this will's free volition, and, because he enters into the form of every object, the principle of sufficient reason, he develops the unity of that will into a plurality of actions, but on account of the timeless unity of that volition in itself, this plurality exhibits itself with the regularity of a force of Nature. Since, however, it is that free volition that becomes visible in the person and the whole of his conduct, related to him as the concept to the definition, every individual action of the person is to be ascribed to the free will, and directly proclaims itself as such to consciousness. Therefore, as was said in the Second Book, everyone regards himself *a priori* (*i.e.*, here according to his original feeling) as free even in his individual actions, in the sense that, in every given case, every course of action would be possible for him and he recognises only *a posteriori* from experience and from reflection upon experience that his actions follow with absolute necessity from the coincidence of character with motives. Hence the crudest of people, following his feeling, ardently defend complete freedom in individual actions, while the great thinkers of all ages, and indeed the more profound systems of religion, have denied it. But anyone who has come to see clearly that man's whole nature is will, and that man himself is only a phenomenon of this will, and that such a phenomenon has the principle of sufficient reason as its necessary form, knowable even by the subject and appearing here as the law of motivation — such a person will regard it as just as absurd to doubt the inevitability of an action when the motive is presented to a given character, as to doubt that the three angles of any triangle are together equal to two right angles.

[Joseph] Priestley has satisfactorily demonstrated the necessity of individual action in his *Doctrine of Philosophical Necessity*; but Kant, whose achievement in this respect is notable, first proved the coexistence of this necessity with the freedom of the will in itself, *i.e.*, apart from the phenomenon, by establishing the distinction between the intelligible and the empirical characters. I entirely adhere to this distinction, for the former is the will as thing-in-itself in so far as it appears in a definite individual in a definite grade, and the latter is this phenomenon itself as it exhibits itself according to time in the mode of action, and according to space in the physical structure. To make comprehensible the relationship between the two, the best formulation is that which I have already used in the introductory essay: that the intelligible character of every person is to be regarded as an act of will outside time, and therefore as indivisible and unchangeable; and the manifestation of this act of will, developed and protracted in time, space, and all the forms of the principle of sufficient reason, is the empirical character as it shows itself in experience in this man's whole conduct and life. Just as the whole tree is only the constantly repeated manifestation of one and the same tendency which shows itself in its simplest form in the fibre, and recurs and is easily recognised in the composition of the leaf, stem, branch, and trunk, so all a man's deeds are merely the constantly repeated expression, somewhat fluctuating in form, of his intelligible character, and the induction based on the sum of all these expressions gives us his empirical character. [...]

Apart from the fact that, because the will as the true thing-in-itself is actually original and independent, and even in self-consciousness the feeling of its originality and autonomy must accompany its acts, though here these acts are already determined – apart from this fact, there arises the illusion of an empirical freedom of the will (instead of the transcendental freedom that is the only freedom attributable to it), a freedom of its individual actions, from the position of dissociation and subordination which the intellect occupies vis-à-vis the will. [...] The intellect learns the decisions of the will only *a posteriori* and empirically; therefore when a choice is imminent, it has no information as to how the will may decide. For the intelligible character, by virtue of which, when motives are given, only *one* decision is possible and is accordingly necessary, does not come within the knowledge of the intellect, but only the empirical character is known to it through the succession of its individual acts. Therefore it seems to the knowing consciousness (intellect) that in a given case two opposite decisions are possible for the will. But this is just the same thing as if we were to say of a vertical rod that has lost its balance and is swaying, 'It can topple either to the right or the left.' This *can* has merely a subjective significance, and really means 'as far as we can tell from the facts available to us.' Objectively, the direction of the fall is necessarily determined as soon as the rod begins to sway. Accordingly, the decision of one's own will is undetermined only in the eye of the beholder, one's own intellect, and thus merely relatively and subjectively for the subject of knowing. In itself and objectively, on the other hand, in every choice presented to it, its decision is at once determined and necessary. But only through the decision that ensues do we become aware that it was ever determined. [...] The intellect can do nothing more than bring out clearly and fully the nature of the motives; it cannot determine the will itself, for the will is quite inaccessible to the intellect, and even inscrutable.[...]

The assertion of an empirical freedom of the will, a *liberum arbitrium indifferentiae* [free and uncoerced decision of the will] is very closely connected with the doctrine that locates man's nature in a *soul*, which is originally a *knowing*, and really an abstract *thinking* nature, and only in consequence of this a *willing* nature – a doctrine which regarded the will as of a secondary or derivative nature, in place of knowledge, which is really secondary. The will, indeed, came to be regarded as an act of thought, and to be identified, especially by Descartes and Spinoza, with the judgement. According to this doctrine everyone would be what he is only through his knowledge; he would be born as a moral cipher, would come to know the things in this world, and thereupon determine to be this or that person, to act in this way or that way, and could also through new knowledge adopt a new course of action, and so become another person. Further, he would first know a thing to be *good*, and in consequence of this, will it, instead of first *willing* it, and in consequence calling it *good*. It follows from my premises that all this is a reversal of the true relationship. Will is first and original; knowledge follows in second place as a tool belonging to the phenomenon of will. Therefore every person is what he is through his will, and his character is original, for willing is the basis of his nature. Through the knowledge which comes later he learns in the course of experience *what* he is, *i.e.*, he gets to know his character. Thus he *knows* himself in consequence of and in accordance with the nature of his will, instead of (as the old view would have it) *willing* in consequence of, and in accordance with his knowing. According to the latter view he would need only consider how he would like best to be, and so he would be; that is its doctrine of the freedom of the will; for it consists really in this, that a person is his own product produced in the light of knowledge. I, on the contrary, say that he is his own product prior to all knowledge, and knowledge comes later merely to shed light on it. Therefore he cannot resolve to be like this or like that, nor can he become other than he is; but he *is* once for all, and he comes to know in the course of experience *what* he is. According to those other philosophers, he *wills* what he knows; and on my view he *knows* what he wills. [. . .]

The motives which determine the manifestation of the character, or determine the conduct, influence it through the medium of knowledge. But our knowledge is inconstant, and often vacillates between truth and error; yet generally, as life proceeds, the error is progressively corrected, though in very different degrees. Thus a person's behaviour may be visibly changed without entitling us to conclude that his character has been changed. What the person wants, both generally and particularly, the ambition of his inmost nature, and the aim he pursues accordingly, this we can never change by outside influence, by instruction; otherwise we could transform him. Seneca puts it very well: *velle non discitur* ['Willing cannot be learned']; whereby he prefers truth to his Stoic philosophers, who taught διδακτὴν εἶναι τὴν ἀρετήν [Virtue can be taught]. From outside, the will can be affected only by motives. But these can never change the will itself; for they have power over it only on the assumption that it is precisely such as it is. So all the motives can do is to alter the direction of the will's endeavour, *i.e.*, to make it seek by a new route what it constantly, unalterably seeks. Therefore tuition, a perceptive faculty which has been corrected – in other words, influence from without – may indeed teach the will that it erred in the means employed, and accordingly can make the will pursue the goal it aims for (once for all according to its inner nature) on an entirely different path and in an entirely different object from that hitherto pursued. But it can never make the will want something actually different from what it has hitherto wanted; this remains unchangeable, for the will is, after all, only this willing itself, which would otherwise have to be suspended. [. . .]

The influence which knowledge, as the medium of motives, exerts, not indeed upon the will itself, but upon its manifestation in actions, is also the basis of the principal distinction between the action of human beings and that of animals, for the mode of their knowing is different. The animal has knowledge only through perception, whereas man, through the faculty of reason, has also abstract ideas, concepts. Now, although man and animal are with equal necessity determined by their motives, man has, as the animal has not, a complete *choice*, which has often been regarded as a freedom of the will in individual actions, although it is no more than the occasion for a fight to the death between several motives, the strongest of which then, of necessity, determines the will. For this the motives must have assumed the form of abstract thoughts, because it is only by means of these that actual deliberation, *i.e.*, a weighing of conflicting reasons for action, is possible. In animals there can be a choice only between motives presented perceptibly, so that the choice is limited to the narrow sphere of present sensuous perception.

Hence the necessity of the will's determination by the motive, which is like that of the effect by the cause, can be exhibited perceptibly and directly only in animals, because here the spectator, too, has the motives just as directly before his eyes as he has their effect; while in man the motives are almost always abstract ideas to which the spectator is not privy; and, even for the person acting, the necessity of their effect is obscured by their conflict. For only in *abstracto* can several ideas, as judgements and chains of conclusions, co-exist in consciousness, and then, free from all determination of time, work against one another till the stronger overcomes the rest and determines the will. This is the complete *choice* or faculty of deliberation which man has over and above that of animals, and on account of which freedom of the will has been attributed to him, in the belief that his willing is a mere result of the operations of his intellect, without a determined drive which might serve as its basis. In truth, however, the motives work only on the basis and on the assumption of the determined drive, which in his case is individual, *i.e.*, a character. [. . .]

§ 56. This freedom, this omnipotence [of the will] is expressed and reflected in the whole visible world which is its manifestation, and which exists and evolves in accordance with the laws following from the form of knowledge. Now with the dawning of entirely adequate self-knowledge in its most consummate phenomenon [man], this freedom can also express itself anew. Either it wills here, at the summit of reflective awareness and self-consciousness, simply what it used to will when it was blind and did not know itself (whereby knowledge will continue to be its *motive*, both in the particular case and overall); or, conversely, this knowledge becomes for it a *quieter* which appeases and suspends all willing. This is that affirmation and denial of the will to life which was stated above in general terms. As a general, not a particular manifestation of will, in respect of individual conduct, it does not disrupt the development of the character, nor does it find its expression in particular actions; but, either by an ever more marked appearance of the whole mode of conduct it has followed hitherto, or, conversely, by its entire suspension, it expresses in living form the maxims which the will has freely adopted in accordance with the knowledge now attained. [. . .]

First of all, I wish the reader to recall the passage with which we closed the Second Book – a passage occasioned by the question which had arisen there as to the will's aim and object. Instead of the answer to this question, it appeared clearly before us how in all the grades of its manifestation, from the lowest to the highest, the will dispenses altogether with a final aim and object. It always strives, for striving is its sole nature, and even the attainment of its goal does not stop that striving. Therefore it is incapable of any final satisfaction, but can only be restrained, while of itself it goes on for ever. [. . .] It will also be remembered from the Second Book that everywhere the various natural forces and organic forms contest with one another for the matter in which they want to appear, for each of them possesses only what it has wrested from the others. So they carry on a constant struggle for life and death of which the outcome is, chiefly, the resistance by which that striving which constitutes the inner nature of everything, is impeded on every side; it struggles in vain, yet, by its very nature, cannot leave off; toils on laboriously till this phenomenon succumbs, whereupon others avidly seize its place and its matter.

We have long since recognised the striving which constitutes the kernel and in-itself of everything as identical with that which in us, where it manifests itself most distinctly in the light of the fullest consciousness, is called *will*. Its being impeded by an obstacle which places itself between it and its present goal, we call *suffering*, and, on the other hand, its attainment of the goal we call gratification, wellbeing, happiness. We may also transfer this terminology to the phenomena of the unconscious world, for though weaker in degree, they are identical in nature. Then we see them involved in constant suffering, and without any lasting happiness. For all endeavour springs from deprivation – from discontent with one's condition – and is thus suffering as long as it is not satisfied; but no satisfaction is lasting, rather it is always merely the starting-point of a new striving. The striving we see everywhere frustrated in many ways, everywhere in conflict, and therefore we always see it as suffering. Thus, if there is no final goal or purpose in striving, there is no due portion, no purpose in suffering.

But what in perceptionless nature we discover only by paying acute attention and by making a strenuous effort, in perceiving nature presents itself clearly to us in the life of animals, whose constant suffering is easy to demonstrate. But without lingering over this intermediate grade we shall turn to the life of man, in which all this appears with the greatest distinctness, illuminated by the clearest knowledge; for as the phenomenon of will becomes more complete, the suffering also becomes more and more apparent. In the plant there is as yet no sensibility, and therefore no pain. A certain very small degree of each inheres in the lowest species of animal life – infusoria and radiata; even in insects the capacity to feel and suffer is still limited. It appears only later in a high degree with the complete nervous system of vertebrate animals, and increasingly in a higher degree as the intelligence develops. So, as knowledge attains to distinctness and as consciousness intensifies, there is a proportionate increase in pain, which accordingly reaches its highest degree in man; and there again, the more distinctly a man knows, the more intelligent he is, the more pain he feels; and the man who is gifted with genius suffers most. In this sense – that is, with reference to the degree of knowledge in general, not mere abstract rational knowledge – I understand and use here that saying from *Ecclesiastes* 'He that increases knowledge, increases sorrow'.

That philosophical painter or painting philosopher, Tischbein, has very beautifully expressed the precise relationship between the degree of consciousness and that of suffering by depicting it graphically and strikingly in a drawing. The upper half of his page represents women whose children are being taken away from them, and who, in different groups and positions, express in many ways deep maternal pain, anguish, and despair. The lower half of the page shows sheep whose lambs are being taken away. They are arranged and grouped in precisely the same way, so that every human head, every human attitude in the upper half of the page corresponds to an animal's head and attitude in the lower half of the drawing. Thus we see distinctly how the pain possible in the dull consciousness of the animal is related to the violent grief which became possible only through distinctness of knowledge and clearness of consciousness.

So we propose to consider the will's inner and essential destiny in *human existence*. Everyone will easily recognise that same thing expressed in various degrees (though more weakly) in the animal's life, and can be fully convinced by observing the suffering animal world, how essentially *all life is suffering*.

§ 57. At every grade that knowledge illuminates, the will appears to itself as an individual. The human individual finds himself as finite in infinite space and time, and consequently of infinitesimal size compared with these. He is projected into them, and on account of their boundlessness he has always merely a relative, rather than an absolute, *when* and *where* of his existence; for his place and duration are finite parts of what is infinite and boundless.

His real existence is only in the present, and this present flees without hindrance into the past, constantly passing over into death, constantly dying. For his past life, apart from its possible consequences for the present, and the record of his will that is impressed in it, is now entirely done with, dead, and gone; and therefore it must be, from a rational point of view, unimportant to him whether the content of that past was pain or pleasure. But the present in his hands is always becoming the past; the future is quite uncertain and always brief. Thus his existence, even when we consider only its formal side, is a constant headlong rushing of the present into the dead past, a constant dying. But if we look at it from the physical side, too, it is clear that, just as our walking is acknowledged to be merely a falling that is constantly being checked, so the life of our body is only a dying that is continually being checked, a death always postponed: finally, in the same way, the activity of our mind is a constantly deferred *ennui*. Every breath we draw fends off death, the persistent intruder with whom we struggle in this way at every moment, and then again at longer intervals, through every meal we eat, every sleep we take, every time we warm ourselves, etc. In the end, death must conquer, for we fell into his clutches through birth, and he plays only for a little while with his prey before he devours it. We continue our life, however, with great commitment and much care, for as long as possible, just as we blow into a soap-bubble for as long as we can, making it as big as possible, although we know perfectly well that it will burst.

We saw that the inner being of nature without knowledge is a constant striving, without purpose and without respite. And this becomes even clearer to us when we consider animal and man. Willing and striving is his whole being, which may be closely compared to an unquenchable thirst. But the basis of all willing is need, deficiency – in short, pain. Consequently, the nature of animals and of man is subject to pain from its origin and in its essence. If, on the other hand, it lacks objects of desire, because their gratification is immediate and too easy, a terrible emptiness and ennui come over it, *i.e.*, its nature and existence itself becomes an unbearable burden to it. Thus its life swings like a pendulum backwards and forwards between pain and *ennui*, which are the elements of which it is made. This is piquantly expressed in the observation that after man had consigned all pain and torment to hell, there was nothing left for heaven but ennui.

But the constant striving which constitutes the essence of the will's every manifestation establishes itself at the higher grades of objectification primarily through the will's manifesting itself here as a living body, with the iron command to nourish it; and what gives strength to this command is just that this body is nothing other than the objectified will to life itself. Man, as the most complete objectification of that will, is in like measure also the most necessitous of all beings: he is concrete willing and needing through and through; he is a concretion of a thousand needs. With these he stands upon the earth, left to fend for himself, uncertain about everything but his own need and misery. Consequently, concern for the maintenance of that existence will, as a rule, occupy the whole of a man's life, for the demands on him are heavy, and reiterated anew with every day. Closely connected to this is the second claim upon him, that of the propagation of the species. At the same time he is threatened from all sides by dangers of different kinds, which he can escape only by constant watchfulness. Proceeding cautiously and looking about him timidly, he pursues his path, for a thousand accidents and a thousand enemies lie in wait for him. So he walked in the wild state, and so he walks in civilised life; for him there is no security: 'in what darkness and in what dangers is this life lived, as long as it lasts.' [Lucretius II. 15]. The life of the great majority is only a constant struggle for this very existence, with the certainty of losing it in the end. But what enables them to endure this wearisome battle is not so much the love of life as the fear of death, which stands in the background no less ineluctable, and may approach them at any moment. Life itself is a sea full of rocks and whirlpools which man avoids with the greatest caution and care, although he knows that even if he succeeds in getting through with all his efforts and skill, in doing so he comes nearer at every step to the greatest, the total, the inevitable and irremediable shipwreck, death; indeed, he even steers straight towards it. This is the final destination of the toilsome journey, and worse for him than all the rocks he avoided.

Now it is noteworthy that, on the one hand, the suffering and misery of life may well so increase that death itself, in the flight from which the whole of life consists, becomes desirable, and we hasten towards it voluntarily; and again, on the other hand, that as soon as want and suffering leave a man in peace, he is so close to boredom that he needs pleasurable diversion. The striving after existence is what keeps all living things busy and active. But when existence is assured to them, they do not know what to do with it; thus the second thing that sets them in motion is the effort to be rid of the burden of existence, to make it cease to be felt, 'to kill time', *i.e.*, to escape from tedium. Accordingly we see that almost all those who are secure from want and care, now that at last they have thrown off all other burdens, become a burden to themselves, and regard as a gain every hour they succeed in getting through, and thus every deduction from the very life which, till then, they have exerted all their energies to preserve for as long as possible. But boredom is nothing less than an evil to be disdained; in the end it paints real despair on the face. It makes creatures who love one another as little as people do, nonetheless seek one another eagerly, and thus it becomes the source of sociability. Everywhere, if only for reasons of political prudence, public precautions are taken against it, as against other universal calamities. For this evil may drive people to the greatest licentiousness, just as much as its opposite extreme, famine: the populus needs bread and games, *panem et circenses*. The strict penitentiary system of Philadelphia makes mere boredom a means of punishment, through loneliness and inactivity, and it is so terrible that it has led prisoners to commit suicide. Just as want is the constant scourge of the common people, so boredom is the scourge of the fashionable world. In middle-class life ennui is represented by Sunday, just as is want by the six weekdays.

Each and every human life flows onwards between desire and its attainment. The wish is, of its nature, pain; attainment quickly produces satiety: the object of desire merely *seemed* to be that; possession takes away its fascination; the wish, the need, reintroduces itself in a new form; when it does not, then follow desolation, emptiness, boredom, against which the struggle is just as painful as against want. If the intervals between desire and its gratification are neither too short nor too long, the suffering caused by each is reduced to a minimum, and that makes for the happiest life. What we might otherwise call the most beautiful part of life, its purest joy (if only because it lifts us out of real existence and transforms us into its disinterested spectators), is pure knowledge to which all willing is alien, pleasure in the beautiful, true delight in art – this is granted only to a very few, because it demands rare talents, and even to these few it is granted only as a fleeting dream. And then their higher intellectual power makes even those few susceptible of far greater suffering than duller people can ever feel, and places them, too, in lonely isolation among others who are obviously different from them; in this way one thing compensates for the other.

But to the great majority of mankind, purely intellectual pleasures are not accessible. They are almost wholly incapable of the joys which lie in pure knowing, for they are abandoned to willing. If, therefore, anything is to elicit commitment from them, to be *interesting* to them, it must (as is implied in the meaning of the word) in some way excite their *will*, even if it is only through remote and tentative relationship to it; the will must not be uninvolved, for the existence of such people lies far more in willing than in knowing; action and reaction is their sole element. The naive expressions of this characteristic we can decipher in trifling instances and very ordinary occurrences: for example, at any tourist-resort or beauty-spot they may visit, they write their names in order thus to react to, and make some impact on, the place, since it made no impact on them. Again, they cannot easily just look at an unfamiliar rare animal, but must rouse it, tease it, play with it, merely to experience action and reaction; this need for excitement of the will shows itself especially in the devising and playing of card-games in which, truly, the pitiable aspect of mankind finds expression.

But whatever nature and fortune may have done, whoever a man be and whatever he may possess, the pain which is essential to life cannot be thrown off. [. . .] The ceaseless efforts to banish suffering accomplish no more than to make it change its form. This is essentially need, want, concern for the preservation of life. If we succeed (which is very difficult) in banishing pain in this form, it immediately reappears in a thousand others, varying according to age and circumstances, such as the erotic drive, passionate love, jealousy, envy, hatred, anxiety, ambition, avarice, sickness, and so on. If at last it can find access in no other form, it comes in the sad, grey garment of surfeit and boredom against which we try this remedy and that. If, finally, we succeed in driving this away, we shall hardly do so without letting pain in again in one of its earlier forms, and so we start the dance again from the beginning; for all human life is tossed backwards and forwards between pain and boredom. Depressing as this reflection may be, I will draw attention, in passing, to an aspect of it from which we may draw consolation, and which perhaps, even allows us to attain a stoical indifference to our own present ills. For our impatience at these arises for the most part from our recognising them as brought about by chance, by a chain of causes which might easily be different. We do not generally grieve over ills which are absolutely necessary and quite universal; for example, the inevitability of age and of death, and of many daily discomforts. It is rather our reflecting on the accidental nature of the circumstances that brought some sorrow to us, in particular, that gives it its sting. But if we have recognised that pain, as such, is essential to life, and inescapable, and that nothing depends upon chance beyond the shape and form in which pain presents itself; that our present sorrow thus fills a place which, without it, would at once be occupied by another which is now excluded by the present one, so that, essentially, fate can do little to harm us; if such a reflection were to become a living conviction, it might induce a considerable degree of stoical equanimity, and very much reduce our anxious concern for our own well-being. But such powerful dominance of reason over directly-felt suffering seldom or never occurs in actuality. [. . .]

§ 58. All gratification, or what is commonly called happiness, is always really and essentially only *negative*, and never positive. It is not a favour which comes to us of its own accord, or of itself, but must always be the gratification of a wish. The wish, *i.e.*, some want, is the condition which precedes every pleasure. But with gratification the wish, and therefore the pleasure, ceases. Thus the gratification, or the sense of receiving favour, can never be more than the deliverance from pain, from distress; for such is not only all actual, obvious suffering, but also every desire that importunately disturbs our peace, and, indeed, the deadening boredom, too, that makes life a burden to us. But it is so hard to attain or accomplish anything; endless difficulties and efforts stand in the way of every undertaking, and at every step obstacles accumulate. But when finally everything is overcome and attained, nothing can ever be gained but deliverance from some suffering or some desire, so that we find ourselves just as we were before its onslaught.

Only the yearning – that is, pain – is ever given to us directly. But gratification and pleasure we can know only indirectly, by remembering the suffering and deprivation which preceded them, and then gave way to gratification and pleasure. Hence it comes about that we are not fully conscious of the assets and advantages we actually have, nor do we prize them, but take them for granted, for they gratify us only negatively by keeping suffering at bay. Only after we have lost them do we know their value; for yearning, privation, suffering, is the positive, communicating itself directly to us. Thus also we are pleased by the memory of past misery, sickness, shortage, and such like which we have overcome, because this is the only means of enjoying the present assets. And it cannot be denied that in this respect, and from the standpoint of this egoism which is the form of the will to life, the sight or the description of someone else's sufferings affords us satisfaction and pleasure in precisely the way Lucretius beautifully and frankly expresses it at the beginning of the Second Book [of *De Rerum Natura*] – 'When the sea runs high and the water is whipped up by the wind, it is a pleasure to watch from the shore the anxious toil of another person: not because it is pleasant to see someone else harassed, but because it is sweet to see misfortunes from which we ourselves are free.' Yet it will be shown that this kind of enjoyment, derived from an awareness of one's own well-being communicated in this way, lies very close to the source of actual positive malice.

That all happiness is only of a negative, not a positive nature, that for this very reason happiness cannot be lasting satisfaction and gratification, but always merely releases us from some pain or want which must be followed either by a new pain, or by languor, empty longing, and boredom: this is borne out by art, that true mirror of the essence of the world and of life; and it is borne out especially in literature. Every epic or dramatic poem can represent only a struggle, a striving and fight for happiness, but can never present lasting and consummate happiness itself. It conducts its hero through a thousand difficulties and dangers to his destination; as soon as this is reached, poetry swiftly lets the curtain fall; for now there would be nothing left for it to do but to show that the glittering goal in which the hero imagined he would find happiness had only teased him, too, and that after attaining it, he was no better off than before. Because true, lasting happiness is not possible, it cannot be the subject of art. Certainly the purpose of the idyll is the description of such happiness, but one sees, too, that the idyll as such cannot last. In the poet's hands it either becomes epic (and in this case it is a very insignificant epic, made up, most commonly, of petty sorrows, petty delights, and petty endeavours) or else it becomes merely descriptive writing that depicts the beauty of nature, *i.e.*, pure knowing free from will, which is, indeed, of course, the only pure happiness, preceded neither by suffering nor by want, nor inevitably followed by remorse, sorrow, emptiness, or satiety; yet this happiness cannot fill the whole of life, but only moments of it.

What we see in literature we find again in music; in melody we have recognised the universal expression of the innermost story of the self-conscious will, the most secret life, longing, suffering and delight, the ebb and flow of the human heart. Melody is always a deviation from the keynote by a thousand labyrinthine ways, perhaps even striking the most painful discord, and then a final return to the keynote. This return expresses the satisfaction and appeasing of the will, but nothing more can be done with the keynote after that, and if it were to be held longer, it would only become a wearisome and meaningless monotony similar to boredom.

These reflections are meant to make clear the unattainability of lasting satisfaction and the negative nature of all happiness; this is explained at the end of the Second Book where it is shown that the will (of which human life, like every phenomenon, is the objectification) is a striving without aim or end. [. . .] It is really incredible how for most people life passes in a way which, seen from the outside, is meaningless and vacuous, and, felt from the inside, is dull and mindless. It is a weary longing and tormenting, a dreamlike stumbling towards death by way of life's four phases and in the company of a sequence of trivial thoughts. Such people are like clockwork, wound up and going without knowing why; and every time a person is begotten and born, the clock of human life is wound up anew, to repeat the same old tune that it has already played innumerable times, passage after passage, measure after measure, with insignificant variations. Every individual, every human being and his life-span is only one more short dream in the mind of the endless spirit of nature, of the persistent will to life; is only another fleeting form which it playfully sketches on its infinite page – space and time – allows to remain for a moment so brief that it is infinitesimal by comparison, and then rubs out to make room again. And yet – and this is the aspect of life that gives us pause – every one of these fleeting forms, these shallow notions, must be paid for by the whole will to life, in all its passion, with much profound pain, and finally with a bitter death, long feared and making its appearance at the end. This is why the sight of a corpse makes us suddenly so serious. [. . .]

§ 59. [. . .] But perhaps no-one at the end of his life, if he gives the matter sober consideration and is, at the same time, frank, ever wishes to live it over again; he more readily chooses non-existence. The essential content of the famous soliloquy in *Hamlet* amounts to this: that our condition is so wretched that total non-existence would be decidedly preferable. If suicide really offered us this, so that the alternative 'to be or not to be', in the full sense of the word, was offered to us, then it would be without reservation preferable as 'a consummation devoutly to be wished.' But something in us tells us that this is not so: suicide is not the end; death is not absolute annihilation. Similarly what was cited by [Herodotus] the father of history has not yet been refuted, that no-one has ever lived who has not more than once wished that he did not have to live through the following day. Accordingly, the brevity of life, which is so often lamented, may be the best thing about it.

If, finally, we were to show everyone the terrible sufferings and miseries to which his life is constantly exposed, he would be seized with horror; and if we were to conduct the most confirmed optimist through the hospitals, infirmaries, and surgical operating-theatres, through the prisons, torture-chambers, and slave-barracks, over battlefields and places of execution; if we were to open to him all the dark dwellings in which misery cringes from the glance of cold curiosity, and, finally, allow him to look into Ugolino's tower where prisoners starved, then he, too, would finally see just what this 'best of all possible worlds' is like. For where else did Dante get the material for his hell, if not from our real world? And a very proper hell he made of it, too. When, on the other hand, he came to describe heaven and its delights, he was faced with an insuperable difficulty, in that our world offers no material at all for such a thing. So, instead of describing the joys of paradise he could do nothing but repeat to us the instruction given him there by his predecessor, by his Beatrice, and by various saints. From this it is sufficiently clear what kind of a world this is.

Certainly human life, like all inferior merchandise, is embellished on the outside with a false lustre: suffering always hides itself away; on the other hand, everyone displays whatever pomp or splendour he can afford, and the less content he is in himself, the more he desires to appear fortunate in the opinion of others: to such lengths does folly go, and to gain the good opinion of others is a priority in everyone's endeavour, although the utter futility of this is expressed in the fact that in almost all languages vanity, *vanitas*, originally means 'emptiness' and 'nothingness.' But under all this false glamour the miseries of life can so increase – and this happens every day – that death, which had hitherto been feared more than anything else, is eagerly grasped. Indeed, if fate wants to show its full treachery, even this refuge can be denied to the sufferer, and in the hands of furious enemies he may be abandoned to cruel, slow tortures, without relief. In vain the sufferer then calls on his gods for help; without mercy he is left to his fate. But his so being without hope, without relief or release, is only the mirror of the indomitable strength of his will, of which his person is the objectivity.

An external power can no more change or inactivate this will than can a foreign power deliver it from the miseries resulting from the life which is the phenomenal appearance of that will. In this crucial matter, as in everything else, a man must always draw upon his own resources. In vain does he make gods for himself in order to gain from them by prayers and flattery what can be accomplished only by his own will-power. The Old Testament made the world and man the work of a god, but the

New Testament, in order to teach that salvation and redemption from the sorrows of this world can come only from the world itself, saw that it was necessary that this god should become man. It is upon man's own will that everything for him depends, and so it will remain. Sanyassis, martyrs, saints of every faith and name, have voluntarily and gladly endured every torture because in these men the will to live had been suspended; and then even the slow destruction of its phenomenon was welcome to them. But I do not wish to anticipate the development of this exposition.

For the rest, I cannot refrain from stating here that to me *optimism* – when it is not merely the thoughtless talk of those who give room only to words under their low brows – appears not merely as an absurd, but also as a really *wicked* way of thinking, and as a bitter mockery of the unspeakable suffering of humanity. Let no one think that Christianity is conducive to optimism; on the contrary, in the Gospels 'world' and 'evil' are used almost synonymously.

§ 60. [. . .] The *affirmation of the will* is the continuous willing itself, undisturbed by any knowledge; such willing does, in general, occupy human life. For the human body is the objectivity of the will as it appears at this grade and in this individual. And thus his willing, which develops in time is, as it were, a paraphrase of the body, an elucidation of the meaning of the whole and its parts; it is another way of exhibiting the same thing-in-itself as is already manifest in the body. So instead of saying 'affirmation of the will', we may say 'affirmation of the body'. The theme underlying all the many different acts of the will is the satisfaction of the needs which are inseparable from the life of the body in health, are already expressed in it, and derive from the preservation of the individual and the propagation of the species. But indirectly a wide variety of motives in this way are granted power over the will, and bring about many different acts of will. Each of these is only a sample, an instance, of the will which is manifest generally. What kind of a sample this may be, what form the motive may have and impart to the sample, is not essential; the important point here is that something is being willed at all, and with what degree of intensity it is willed. The will can become visible only in the motives, just as the eye manifests its ability to see only in the light. The motive, its form as yet unspecified, stands ready to do the will's bidding like a Proteus who can assume many forms. It constantly promises complete satisfaction, the quenching of the will's thirst. But whenever this is attained, the motive at once appears in another form, and in this it influences the will anew, always according to the degree of the will's intensity and to its relationship to knowledge, which through these very samples and instances are revealed as empirical character.

From the first accession of consciousness a person finds that he wills, and the connection between his knowledge and his will remains, as a rule, constant. He seeks first to become thoroughly acquainted with the objects of his willing, and then with the means of attaining them. Now he knows what he has to do, and, as a rule, he does not strive to acquire other factual information. He moves and acts; the consciousness that he is to work towards the goal of his willing keeps him alert and active; his thought is concerned with the choice of means. Such is life for almost everyone; they desire, they know what they desire, and they strive after it with sufficient success to keep them from despair, and sufficient failure to save them from boredom and its consequences. From this comes a certain serenity, or at least unconcern, which wealth or poverty really does not alter; for the rich and the poor do not enjoy what they *have* (for this, as we have shown, has only a negative effect) but what they hope to *attain* by their efforts. They press forward with much earnestness, and indeed with an air of importance, just as children also pursue their play.

It is always an exception when this way of life suffers disruption, as may happen when – following from perception independent of the service of the will, and directed to the inner nature of the world more generally – there results either the aesthetic challenge to contemplate or the ethical challenge to renounce. Most people are pursued by want all through life, without ever being allowed to reflect. On the other hand, the will is often inflamed to a degree that is superfluous to the affirmation of the body. This excessive degree is demonstrated by the violent emotions and powerful passions in which the individual not only asserts his own existence, but denies and tries to cancel out that of others when it stands in his way.

The maintenance of the body by its own energies is so slight a degree of the affirmation of will, that if it voluntarily remained at this degree, we might assume that with the death of this body, the will which appeared in it would also be extinguished. But even the gratification of the sexual impulse goes beyond the affirmation of one's own brief existence, and affirms life for an indefinite time beyond the death of the individual. Nature, always true and consistent, and here even naïve, sets out very frankly for us the inner significance of the sexual act. Our own consciousness, the intensity of the impulse, teaches us that in this act the most decided *assertion of the will to life* expresses itself, pure and without further addition (such as, for example, the denial of other individuals); and now, as the consequence of this act, a new life appears in time and the causal series, *i.e.*, in nature; the begotten presents himself to the begetter, different from him in the phenomenon, but in himself, or according to the Idea, identical to him. So it is through this act that every species of living creature bonds to form a whole, and is perpetuated as such. Procreation is, as far as the begetter is concerned, only the expression, the symptom, of his decided affirmation of the will to live: for the begotten, it is not the cause of the will which appears in him (for the will in itself knows neither cause nor effect) but, like every first cause, procreation is merely the occasional cause of the phenomenal appearance of this will at this time, in this place. As thing-in-itself, the will of the begetter and that of the begotten are not different one from the other, for only the phenomenon, not the thing-in-itself, is subordinate to the *principium individuationis*.

Along with that affirmation which extends beyond our own body to the delineation of a new body, suffering and death, since they belong to the phenomenon of life, have also been asserted anew; and the opportunity for redemption – an opportunity made possible by a faculty of knowledge brought to its most consummate perfection – is for this time declared abortive. Here lies the profound reason for the shame associated with the business of procreation. This view is mythically expressed in the Christian dogma that we are all partakers in Adam's first transgression (which, clearly, is only the gratification of sexual passion), and through it are guilty of suffering and death. Here doctrine goes beyond the viewpoint consistent with the principle of sufficient reason, and recognises the Idea of man of which the unity, lost in its dispersal into innumerable individuals, is re-established through the all-embracing bond of procreation. Accordingly it regards every individual as, on one hand, identical with Adam, the representative of the affirmation of life, and to that extent subject to sin (original sin), suffering, and death; on the other hand, knowledge of the Idea [of man] enables doctrine to regard every individual as identical with the Saviour, the representative of the denial of the will to life, and, to that extent, as partaking in His self-sacrifice, saved through His merits, and delivered from the bonds of sin and death, *i.e.*, of the world (Rom. v. 12–21). [. . .]

The sexual impulse proves itself the decided and strongest affirmation of life also by the fact that to man in a state of nature, as to the animals, it is the ultimate purpose, the highest goal of life. Self-preservation is his first ambition and as soon as he has made provision for that, he strives only after the propagation of the species: as a merely natural being he can attempt no more. Nature, too, whose essence is the will to life itself, with all her strength impels both man and animal to propagate. After that it has achieved its purpose with the individual, and is quite indifferent to its death, for as the will to life it cares only for the preservation of the species, and the individual is nothing to it. [. . .]

The genitals are, far more than any other external part of the body, subject merely to the will and not at all to knowledge. Indeed, the will shows itself here almost as independent of knowledge as in those parts of the body which, responding merely to stimuli, serve vegetative life, reproduction, in which the will works blindly as in Nature devoid of understanding. For generation is only reproduction passing over to a new individual – reproduction at the second power, as it were – just as death is only excretion at the second power. Consequently the genitals are properly the *focus* of will, and consequently the opposite pole of the brain, the representative of knowledge, *i.e.*, the other aspect of the world, the world as idea. The genitals are the life-sustaining principle; to time they guarantee life without end. As such they were revered among the Greeks in the *phallus*, and among the Hindus in the *lingam*, which are thus the symbol of the affirmation of the will. Knowledge, on the other hand, affords the possibility of the suspension of willing, of redemption through freedom, of overcoming and annihilating the world. [. . .]

§ 61. We recall from the Second Book that in the whole of nature, at all the grades of the will's objectification, there was inevitably a constant conflict between the individuals of all species; and in this the inner self-contradiction of the will to life expressed itself. At the highest grade of the objectification, this phenomenon, like everything else, will show itself with enhanced clarity, and so it can be more fully deciphered. For this purpose we shall next trace the source of *egoism*, the starting-point of all conflict.

Time and space we have called the *principium individuationis*, because only through them and in them is plurality of the homogeneous possible. They are the essential forms of natural knowledge, *i.e.*, knowledge springing from the will. Therefore the will manifests itself everywhere in the plurality of individuals. But this plurality applies not to the will as thing-in-itself, but only to its phenomena. The will itself is present, whole and undivided, in every one of these, and sees around it the innumerably repeated image of its own nature; but this nature itself, the actually real, it finds directly only in its inner self. Therefore everyone wants everything for himself, wants to possess, or at least to control, everything; and anything that opposes him, he would like to destroy. To this is added, in the case of such beings as have knowledge, that the individual is the support of the knowing subject, and the knowing subject is the support of the world, *i.e.*, that the whole of nature outside the knowing subject, and all other individuals, too, exist only in his idea; therefore he is conscious of them only as his idea, thus merely indirectly, as of something which is dependent on his own nature and existence; for with his consciousness the world necessarily disappears for him, *i.e.*, its being and non-being become synonymous and indistinguishable. Thus every knowing individual truly is, and finds himself as, the whole will to live, or the inner being of the world itself, and also as the integral condition of the world as idea, consequently as a microcosm to be valued on a par with the macrocosm. Nature itself, which is truthful at all times and in all places, gives him this knowledge straight from the source and independently of all reflection, with simple and direct certainty.

Now, from these two essential conditions just cited may be explained how every individual, though infinitesimally small and reduced to insignificance in the boundless world, nonetheless makes itself the centre of the world, considers his own existence and well-being before everything else; indeed, from the natural standpoint, is ready to sacrifice everything else for this – is ready to annihilate the world in order to safeguard his own self, this drop in the ocean, a little longer. This disposition is *egoism,* which is essential to everything in nature. Yet it is through just this same egoism that the inner self-contradiction of the will reveals itself so terrifyingly; for this egoism exists in and feeds from that opposition of the microcosm and macrocosm, or from the fact that the will's objectification has for its form the *principium individuationis* through which the will manifests itself in the same way in innumerable individuals, and indeed, in each of these individuals it manifests itself in both aspects (Will and Idea) entirely and completely. Thus, while each individual is given to itself directly as the whole will and the whole subject of ideas, all the other individuals are given to him initially only as his ideas; for that reason his own being and its preservation is of more importance to him than that of all the others together. Everyone looks upon his own death as upon the end of the world, while he accepts the death of his acquaintances as a matter of comparative indifference, if he is not in some way personally concerned in it. In consciousness, intensified to the highest grade, human consciousness, egoism, too, must like knowledge, pain and pleasure, have reached its highest grade, and the conflict of individuals, to which it predisposes, must appear in its most terrible form.

And indeed we see this everywhere before our eyes, in small things as in great. Now we see it in its terrible aspect in the lives of great tyrants and villains, and in wars that have devastated the world; and again we see its absurd side, in which it is the theme of comedy, and appears specially as haughtiness and vanity. La Rochefoucauld understood this better than anyone else, and presented it in the abstract. We see it both in the history of the world and in our own experience. But it appears most distinctly of all when any crowd of people is released from all law and order; then we are shown at once in the distinctest form the *bellum omnium contra omnes* [war of everyone against everyone] which Hobbes has so well described in the first chapter of *De Cive*. We see not only how everyone tries to seize from someone else what he wants himself, but how often one will destroy the whole happiness or life of another in pursuit of an insignificant increase in his own well-being. This is the highest expression of egoism; its manifestations in this regard are surpassed only by those of actual wickedness, which seeks, quite disinterestedly, the injury and suffering of others, without any advantage to itself. Of this we shall speak soon. [. . .]

§ 62. It has already been argued that the first and simplest affirmation of the will to life is only the affirmation of one's own body, *i.e.*, the expression of the will through acts in time, in so far as the body, in its form and design, exhibits the same will in space, and no further. This affirmation shows itself as preservation of the body by the use of its own energies. Directly related to this is the gratification of the sexual impulse; indeed this belongs to it, in so far as the genitals belong to the body. Hence *voluntarily* to renounce the gratification of that impulse without a motive as basis for this renunciation, is, at a low grade, a denial of the will to life, is a voluntary renunciation of it, consequent on the advent of knowledge which acts as *quieter*. Accordingly such denial of one's own body shows itself as a contradiction by the will of its own phenomenon. For although here also the body objectifies in the genitals the will to perpetuate the species, this propagation is not willed. For this very reason, because it is a denial or abnegation of the will to life, such renunciation is a hard and painful self-conquest; we will return to this later.

But since the will exhibits that *self-affirmation* of one's own body in innumerable neighbouring individuals, it very easily extends in one individual, by virtue of the egoism characteristic of them all, beyond this affirmation to the *denial* of the same will manifest in another individual. The will of the first breaks into the territory of the will's affirmation in someone else, by the individual's either destroying or injuring this other body itself, or else by its compelling the energies of the other individual's body to serve his will, instead of the will manifest in that other body. Thus if from the will manifesting itself as another body, he takes away the energies of this body, and so increases the energy serving his own will beyond the quota of his own body, he consequently affirms his own will beyond its own body by means of the negation of the will appearing in another body.

This trespassing on the sphere of affirmation has always been clearly recognised, and the concept denoted by the word *wrong*. For both parties recognise the fact instantly, not, indeed, as we do here in clear abstraction, but as feeling. He who suffers wrong feels the trespass into his own body's sphere of affirmation, through another individual's denying it, as a direct and mental pain which is entirely separate and different from the accompanying physical suffering experienced as a result of the act, or from vexation at the loss. On the other hand, the insight forces itself on the perpetrator of this wrong that he is in himself the same will as appears in that body also, and which affirms itself with such vehemence in the one phenomenon that, transgressing the limits of its own body and its powers, it becomes the denial of this very will in the other phenomenon, and so, regarded as will in itself, it fights against itself by this very vehemence, and excoriates itself. To the perpetrator of the wrong, too, this insight presents itself in the flash of a moment, not *in abstracto*, but as an obscure feeling; and this is called qualms of conscience, or, in this case, more accurately, the feeling of having done wrong.

Wrong, the notion of which we have analysed in its most general and abstract form, expresses itself in the concrete more completely, characteristically, and palpably in cannibalism. This is its most distinct and conspicuous type, the horrifying picture of the greatest conflict of the will with itself at the highest grade of its objectification, which is man. Murder is, after cannibalism, the most distinct expression of wrong; hence the committing of murder is followed instantly, and with fearful distinctness, by qualms of conscience (the significance of which we have just given abstractly and drily) which inflicts a wound on our peace of mind that a lifetime cannot heal. For our horror at the murder committed, like our shrinking beforehand from the committing of it, corresponds to that infinite clinging to life with which everything living, as phenomenon of the will to life, is suffused.[...] Intentional mutilation, or mere injury of another body, indeed, every blow, is to be regarded as in its nature the same as murder, and differing from it only in degree. Further, wrong is shown in the subjugation of another individual, in forcing him into slavery, and, finally, in the seizure of another's goods, which, in so far as these goods are regarded as the fruit of his labour, is just the same thing as making him a slave, and stands in the same relationship to it as bodily harm does to murder.

For *property*, which is not taken from a man without *wrong*, can, according to our explanation of wrong, be only that which has been wrought by a man's own energies. Therefore by taking this from him, we really take the powers of his body from the will objectified in it, to make them the will objectified in another body. For only in this way does the wrong-doer, by seizing, not the body of another, but a lifeless thing quite different from it, break into another person's sphere of will-affirmation, in that the energy, the work of this other body, are, as it were, intimately associated and identified with this thing. [. . .]

Other cases of wrong are invariably attributable to my compelling another individual to serve my will instead of his own, to act according to my will instead of according to his own. On the path of violence I attain this end through physical causality, but on the path of cunning I achieve it by means of motivation, *i.e.*, by means of causality that has passed through knowledge. For I present to the other man's will *fictitious motives*, on account of which he follows *my* will, while believing that he is following *his own*. Since knowledge is the medium in which the motives lie, I can accomplish this only by falsifying his knowledge, and this is the *lie*. The lie always aims at influencing another's will, not merely his knowledge, for itself and as such, but only as a means, so far as it determines his will. For my lying, in so far as it proceeds from my will, requires a motive; and only someone else's will can be such a motive, not his knowledge in and for itself; for as such it can never have an influence upon *my* will, therefore it can never move it, can never be a motive of its aims. But only the willing and doing of another can be this, and his knowledge indirectly through it. This holds true not only for all lies that have sprung from obvious self-interest, but also for those which stem from pure malice which wants to exult in the painful consequences of the error into which it has led someone else. Indeed, mere empty boasting aims at influencing the will and action of others more or less, by increasing their respect or improving their opinion of the boaster. The mere refusal of a truth, *i.e.*, of a statement generally, is in itself no wrong, but telling a lie, an untruth, is certainly always an injustice. The person who refuses to show the right path to the traveller who has lost his way does him no wrong, but the person who directs him to the wrong path certainly does. It follows from what has been said that every *lie*, like every act of violence, is as such wrong because as such it aims, as violence does, to extend the authority of my will to other individuals, and so to affirm my will by denying theirs.

But the most complete lie is the *broken contract*, because here all the conditions mentioned are completely and distinctly present together. For when I enter into a contract, the action promised by the other party is directly and explicitly the motive for my reciprocal action. The promises were deliberately and formally exchanged. The truth of the declarations made is, it is assumed, within the power of each party to make. If the other breaks the contract, he has deceived me, and by introducing merely fictitious motives into my knowledge, he has bent my will according to his intention; he has extended the control of his will to another individual, and thus has committed a complete wrong. On this is founded the moral lawfulness and validity of *contracts*. [. . .]

The concept of wrong is the original and positive, and the concept of right, which is opposed to it, is the derivative and negative; for we must keep to the concepts, and not to the words. As a matter of fact, there would be no talk of right if there were no such thing as wrong. The concept *right* comprises merely the negation of wrong, and every action is subsumed under it which does not trespass upon the boundary set above, *i.e.*, is not a denial of someone else's will in the interest of affirming our own more vigorously. Hence that boundary-line divides, as regards a purely *moral* definition, the whole field of possible actions into such as are wrong or right. Whenever an action does not encroach, in the way argued above, on the sphere of someone else's affirmation of his will, thereby denying it, it is not wrong. So, for example, the refusal to help another in urgent need, the serene contemplation of another's death from starvation while we ourselves have more than enough, is certainly cruel and diabolical, but it is not wrong. Yet it can be said with confidence that anyone capable of carrying unkindness and callousness so far will certainly also commit every wrong as soon as his desires demand it and no compulsion prevents it.

But the concept of *right* as the negation of wrong is applied chiefly (and doubtless it also originated) in cases in which an attempted injustice is fended off by force. This self-defensive action cannot itself be wrong, and consequently is right, although the force used, if considered independently and in isolation, would be wrong. Here it is justified only by the motive; that is, it becomes right. If an individual goes so far in affirming his own will that he encroaches upon the sphere of the will's affirmation essential to my person as such, and in so doing denies mine, then my fending off of his encroachment is only the denial of that denial, and thus on my side is nothing more than the affirmation of the will which in its essence and origin is manifest in my body, and is already implicitly expressed by the mere phenomenon of this body; consequently is not wrong, and is therefore right. That is to say: I have then a *right* to deny another's denial with the force necessary to inactivate it, and it is easy to see that this may extend to the killing of the other individual, whose encroachment, his violent intrusion upon me, I may ward off by counteraction slightly more forceful than this action, without my doing any wrong, and consequently, by right. [. . .]

§ 63. [. . .] The world in all the plurality of its parts and forms is the phenomenon, the objectivity, of the one will to life. Existence itself, and the kind of existence, both in its totality and in every part, comes from the will alone. The will is free; it is almighty. In everything the will appears just as it determines itself, in itself, and outside time. The world is only the mirror of this willing; and all the finitude, all the suffering, all the misery it contains, belong to the expression of what the will wills, are as they are because the will so wills. Thus every creature is perfectly justified in existing: first of all in his existing at all, and then more specifically in existing as a species and as a particular individuality, just as it is and in an environment such as it is, in a world such as it is, ruled by chance and error, in a world that is temporal, transient, and always suffering; and in all that happens to every creature, or indeed can happen to it, justice is always done. For the will belongs to it; and as the will is, so is the world. Only this world itself can bear the responsibility for its own existence and nature – no-one else bears that responsibility; for how could anyone else have assumed it? If we want to know what people are worth morally, both as a whole and in general, we have only to consider their fate as a whole and in general. This is want, wretchedness, affliction, misery, and death. Eternal justice reigns; if they were not, as a whole, worthless, their fate, as a whole, would not be so sad. In this sense we may say that the world itself passes judgement on the world. If we could lay all the world's misery in one pan of the weighing-scales, and all the world's guilt in the other, the pointer would certainly indicate that they are equally heavy.

It is true, however, that the world does not present itself to knowledge (which has sprung from the will with the purpose of serving that same will, and is given to the individual as such), in the same way as it finally reveals itself to the inquirer as the objectivity of the one-and-only will to life, which he himself is. But the eye of the uncultured individual is clouded, as the Hindus say, by the veil of Mâyâ. To him is shown, instead of the thing-in-itself, only the phenomenon in time and space, in the *principium individuationis*, and in the other forms of the principle of sufficient reason. And in this form of his limited knowledge he sees not the inner nature of things, which is one, but its phenomena, as separated, disunited, innumerable, very different, and indeed opposed. To him pleasure appears as one thing, and pain as quite another thing: this man as a tormentor and a murderer, that man as a martyr and a victim; wickedness as one thing and evil as something else. He sees one man live a life of joy, abundance, and pleasure, while at his door another man dies miserably of want and cold. Then he asks, 'Is there no justice? Is there no punishment, no reward?' And he himself, under that compulsion of the will which is his origin and his nature, seizes upon the pleasures and enjoyments of life, firmly embraces them, not knowing that by this very act of his will he is grasping and holding close to him all those pains and sorrows which he shudders to see. He sees the ills and he sees the wickedness in the world, but far from recognising that both of these are only different aspects of the manifestation of the one will to life, he regards them as very different, and even as quite opposed, and often seeks to escape by wickedness, *i.e.*, by causing suffering to someone else, from ills, from the suffering of his own individuality, for he is entangled in the *principium individuationis*, deluded by the veil of Mâyâ.

Just as on a raging sea which stretches boundlessly in every direction and, howling, causes a mountainous swell to rise and fall, there sits a boatman in his small boat, trusting the frail vessel, so sits the human individual, serene amid a world of torment, propped up by and relying on the *principium individuationis*, or the way in which the individual knows things as phenomenon. The boundless world full of suffering, both in the infinite past and in the infinite future, is alien to him, indeed for him it is a fantastic tale; only his infinitesimal person, his extensionless present, his momentary comfort, has reality for him; and he does everything to maintain this, as long as truer insight does not open his eyes. Till then will stir only in the inmost depths of his consciousness a very obscure presentiment that all of this is, after all, not really so alien to him, but has a connection with him from which the *principium individuationis* cannot protect him. This presentiment is the source of that ineradicable terror common to all human beings (and indeed, perhaps even to the more intelligent animals) which suddenly seizes them if by any chance they become perplexed by the *principium individuationis* in that the principle of sufficient reason, in some one of its forms, seems to be admitting of an exception: for example, if it seems as if some change were taking place without a cause, or that some deceased person were alive again, or if in any other way the past or the future were to become present, or the distant to become near. The immense horror at anything of the kind is founded on the fact that they suddenly become perplexed by the forms of knowledge of the phenomenon, the only means by which their own individuality is kept separate from the rest of the world. But this separation lies only in the phenomenon, and not in the thing-in-itself; and it is on this latter that eternal justice rests.

In fact, all temporal happiness stands, and all prudence moves, on ground that is not at all solid. They defend the person from accidents and supply its pleasures; but the person is merely phenomenon, and its difference from other individuals, and exemption from the sufferings which they endure, are due merely to the form of the phenomenon, the *principium individuationis*. According to the true nature of things, everyone has to regard all the suffering of the world as his own, and indeed regard all merely potential suffering as actually his, as long as he is the steadfast will-to-life, that is, as long as he asserts life with all his energy. A happy temporal life (whether freely given by chance or cunningly wrested from it) amid the sufferings of countless other people – this, as seen with the insight that penetrates the *principium individuationis*, is only the beggar's dream that he is a king, but it is a dream from which he must awake in order to find out that only a fleeting illusion had separated him from the suffering of his life.

Eternal justice eludes the eye that is taken up with the knowledge which follows the principle of sufficient reason in the *principium individuationis*; such an eye fails to see it altogether, unless it salvages it in some way by fictions. It sees the wicked man, after misdeeds and cruelties of every kind, live sumptuously and leave the world without impeachment. It sees the oppressed man drag out to its end a life full of suffering, and no-one offers to be his avenger or vindicator. But the only person who will grasp and comprehend eternal justice is the one who lifts himself above the knowledge that proceeds along the lines of the principle of sufficient reason, knowledge which is bound to individual things, and who recognises the Ideas, sees through the *principium individuationis*, and becomes aware that the forms of the phenomenon do not apply to the thing-in-itself. It is also he alone who, by dint of the same insight, can understand the true nature of virtue, as it will soon become apparent to us in connection with the present inquiry; although for the practice of virtue this knowledge in the abstract is by no means necessary.

So it will become clear to anyone who has attained to this knowledge that, because the will is the in-itself of all phenomena, the misery both experienced by oneself and inflicted upon others – on one hand passive misfortune and on the other hand, active wickedness – always affect the one and the same inner being, even if the phenomena in which the one and the other present themselves exist as quite different individuals, and are even separated by wide intervals in time and space. He sees that the difference between the person who inflicts suffering and the one who must bear it is only phenomenon, and has no bearing on the thing-in-itself which is the will living in both. Deceived by the knowledge bound to its service, the will fails to recognise itself here, and in promoting the wellbeing of *one* of its phenomena, produces great suffering in *another*. So in its passion it sinks its teeth into its own flesh, not knowing that it is injuring only itself.

Thus, through the medium of individuation, the will reveals its own inherent self-conflict. The inflicter of suffering and the sufferer are one. The former errs in believing he does not share the suffering; the latter, in believing he does not share the guilt. If the eyes of both were opened, the inflicter of suffering would see that he lives in everything that in this wide world suffers pain, and which, if endowed with reasoning, wonders in vain why it was called into existence for such great suffering, through no fault of its own that it can discern. And the sufferer would see that all the wickedness which is, or ever was, committed in the world flows from that will which constitutes *his* own nature also, is manifest also in *him*, and that through this phenomenon and its affirmation he has taken upon himself all the sufferings arising from such a will, and justly endures them as long as he is this will. With this insight the poet Calderón says, reprovingly:

> Man's greatest offence
> Is that he ever was born. [*Life a Dream*]

How should it not be an offence, since, in accordance with an eternal law, it is punishable by death? In these lines Calderón has done no more than to express the Christian dogma of original sin.

The living knowledge of eternal justice, of the balance that inseparably connects the *malum culpae* with the *malum poenae*, requires the complete transcending of individuality and presupposes the principle of this possibility. It will always remain inaccessible to the majority of men, as will, too, the pure and distinct knowledge of the nature of all virtue, which is akin to it, and which we are about to discuss. Accordingly it is in the Vedas (which are allowed only to the three regenerate castes) or in their esoteric teaching that the wise forefathers of the Hindu people have expressed this as directly as it can be expressed through concept and language, and as their style of exposition, which is still pictorial and even rhapsodic, permits; but in the religion of the people, or exoteric teaching, they communicate it only by means of myths. The direct exposition we find in the Vedas, the fruit of the highest human knowledge and wisdom, the kernel of which has at last become accessible to us in the Upanishads as the greatest gift of this century. It is expressed in various ways, but especially by making the apprentice a spectator of the procession of all the beings in the world, living and lifeless, while over each of them is pronounced that word which has become a formula, and as such has been called the Mahavakya: *Tatoumes*, or more correctly, *Tat twam asi,* which means, 'This thou art' *(Oupnek'hat* I. 60 ff).

But for the people that great truth, in so far as in their limited intelligence they could comprehend it, was translated into the mode of knowledge which follows the principle of sufficient reason. This mode of knowledge is indeed, from its nature, quite incapable of apprehending that truth pure and in itself, and even stands in direct contradiction to it, yet in the form of a myth it received a substitute for it which was sufficient as a guide for conduct. For the myth enables the mode of knowledge in accordance with the principle of sufficient reason, to comprehend through figurative depiction, which itself is always alien to it, the ethical significance of conduct. This is the purpose of all systems of religion, for as a whole they are the mythical clothing of the truth which is inaccessible to the crude human intellect. In this sense that myth might, in Kant's language, be called a postulate of the practical reason; but so considered, it has the great advantage of containing absolutely no elements but such as lie before our eyes in the realm of reality, and therefore of being able to support all its concepts with perceptions. What is here meant is the myth of the transmigration of souls. It teaches that all sufferings which in life one inflicts upon other beings must be expiated in a subsequent life in this world, through precisely the same sufferings; and this even to the extent that someone who does no more than kill an animal must, at some point in endless time, be born as the same kind of animal and suffer the same death. It teaches that the consequence of wicked conduct is a future life, in this world, in creatures which suffer and are scorned, and, accordingly, that one will then be born again in lower castes, or as a woman, or as an animal, as Pariah or Chandala, as a leper, or as a crocodile, and so forth.

All the torment which the myth threatens it supports with concrete cases observed from real life, through suffering creatures which do not even know what they have done to deserve their misery, and it does not need to call in the assistance of any other hell. As a reward, on the other hand, it promises re-birth in better, nobler forms, as Brahmans, wise men, or saints. The highest reward, which awaits the noblest deeds and the completest resignation, which is also given to the woman who in seven successive lives has voluntarily died on the funeral pile of her husband, and no less to the person whose pure mouth has never uttered a single lie – this reward the myth can express only negatively in the language of this world, in the often-repeated promise that they shall never be born again, *Non adsumes iterum existentiam apparentem*; or, as the Buddhists, who recognise neither Vedas nor castes, express it, 'Thou shalt attain to Nirvana', *i.e.*, to a state in which four things no longer exist – birth, age, sickness, and death.

Never has a myth more closely allied itself (and never will one ally itself more closely) to the philosophical truth which is accessible to so few, than this ancient doctrine of the noblest and oldest of peoples. Degenerate as this race may now be in many respects, this doctrine still holds sway as the universal belief of the people, and has a decided influence on life to-day as it had four thousand years ago. Hence, Pythagoras and Plato admiringly took up that *ne plus ultra* of mythical representation, adopted it from India or Egypt, respected it, applied it, and (we know not in how far) even believed it themselves. We, on the contrary, now send to the Brahmans English clergymen and pietistical Moravian linen-weavers in order, out of compassion to set them right, to tell them that they are created out of nothing, and that they ought gratefully to rejoice in that. But what will happen to us is the same as what happens to the man who fires a bullet at a rock-face. In India our religions will *never* take root. The primeval wisdom of the human race will not be displaced by what happened in Galilee. On the contrary, Indian philosophy flows back to Europe, and will produce a fundamental change in our scholarship and in our thinking. [. . .]

§ 65. [. . .] The explanation of the concept *true* has already been given in the essay *On the Principle of Sufficient Reason* chap. v. § 29 *et seq.* By means of our Book Three, in its entirety, the content of the concept *beautiful* was adequately explained for the first time ever. We now wish to trace the meaning of the concept *good*, which can be done with very little trouble. This concept is essentially relative, and signifies *the suitability of an object to some one of the will's endeavours.* Accordingly everything agreeable to the will in any of its manifestations, and fulfilling the will's purposes, is thought of through the concept *good*, however different such things may be in other respects. Thus, we say 'good meal', 'good roads', 'good weather', 'good weapons', 'good omen', and so on; in short, we call everything 'good' that is just as we wish it to be. Hence what may be good in the eyes of one man may be just the reverse in those of another. The conception of the good falls into two sub-categories – that of the directly instantaneous satisfaction of each act of volition, and that of satisfaction which is merely indirect and relates to the future, *i.e.*, the agreeable and the useful.

As long as we are speaking of creatures without understanding, the concept of the opposite of 'good' is expressed by the word *bad*, more rarely and abstractly by the word *evil*, which thus denotes everything that does not correspond to the will's ambition in each instance. Like all other beings that can enter into a relationship with the will, persons who favour the will's currently desired aims, who further and befriend them, are called *good*, in the same sense and always retaining the relative noticeable, for example, in the expression, 'I find this good, but you don't.' Those, however, who are naturally disposed not to obstruct the willing of other people, but rather to facilitate their ambitions, and who are thus consistently helpful, benevolent, friendly, and charitable, are called *good* persons on account of their general attitude to the will of others. In the case of creatures that have understanding (animals and people) the contrary concept is denoted in German and, within the last hundred years or so, in French also, by a different word from that which is used in speaking of creatures without understanding, namely, in German, *böse*; in French, *méchant*; while in almost all other languages this distinction does not exist; and *kakos, malus, cattivo, bad*, are used of people as of inanimate things which are opposed to the aims of a definite individual will.

Thus, having started entirely from the passive element in the good, the inquiry could only proceed later to the active element, and investigate the conduct of the person who is called *good*, not this time in relation to others, but to himself. It could specially set itself the task of explaining both the purely objective esteem which such conduct produces in others, and the peculiar self-contentment which it clearly produces in the 'good' person, for he purchases this even with sacrifices of another kind; and it could also explain, on the other hand, the inner pain which accompanied the evil disposition no matter how many outward advantages it brought to the one who nurtured it. It was from this source that the ethical systems arose, both the philosophical and those supported by religious doctrine. Both sought constantly in some way or other to associate happiness with virtue, the former either by means of the principle of contradiction, or even that of sufficient reason, and thus, always sophistically, to make happiness either identical with, or the consequence of, virtue; but the latter by asserting the existence of worlds other than the one which can possibly be known to experience. But according to our enquiry, the inner nature of virtue will prove to be a striving in the opposite direction to that of happiness, which is that of well-being and of life.

It follows from what has been said above that the *good* is, according to its concept τῶν πρός τί [something belonging to the relative]; thus every good is essentially relative, for it has its essential nature only in its relation to a desiring will. *Absolute good* is, therefore, a contradiction in terms; highest good, *summum bonum*, means the same thing: a final gratification of the will, after which no new desire would arise; a last motive, the attainment of which would bring the will's enduring satisfaction. According to the line of thought we have so far followed in this Fourth Book, such a thing is unthinkable. It is as unlikely that any gratification can make the will stop willing ever anew as it is that time should begin or end; for the will there is no permanent fulfilment which completely and for ever satisfies its craving. It is the vessel of the Danaides; there is for it no highest good, no absolute good, but always a merely temporary good. If, however, we wish to give an honorary position – or as it were, an emeritus position – to an old expression which from custom we would not like to discard altogether, we may, metaphorically and figuratively, call the complete self-suspending and denial of the will, true will-lessness, the only thing that for ever hushes and appeases its impulse, gives that contentment which can never again be disturbed, alone redeems the world, and which we shall now soon consider at the close of our whole study – we may call it the absolute good, the *summum bonum*, and regard it as the only radical cure for the disease for which all other goods – that is, all wishes fulfilled, all happiness attained – are only palliatives or anodynes. In this sense the Greek τέλος, like *finis bonorum*, too, is even more apposite. So much for the words *good* and *bad*; now let us return to our main theme.

If a person is always inclined to do *wrong* as soon as the occasion presents itself, and no external power restrains him, we call him *bad*. According to our explanation of wrong, this means that such a person not only affirms the will to life as it is manifest in his own body, but in this affirmation goes so far that he denies the will manifest in other individuals. This is shown by his craving their powers for the service of his own will, and by his trying to destroy their existence when they oppose his will's ambitions. The ultimate source of this is a high degree of egoism, the nature of which has already been analysed above. Two separate things become clear here at once. In the first place, that in such a person an extremely vehement will to life expresses itself, a willing that goes far beyond the affirmation of his own body; and, in the second place, that his knowledge, entirely given over to the principle of sufficient reason and involved in the *principium individuationis*, cannot get beyond the difference which this latter principle establishes between his own person and everyone else. For that reason he seeks his own well-being alone, completely indifferent to that of everyone else, whose existence is completely alien to him, and separated from his own by a wide gulf; indeed, he regards them as mere masks without reality. And these two qualities are the basic elements of the bad character.

This great vehemence of will is of itself and immediately a constant source of suffering. In the first place, because all volition as such arises from yearning for something one does not possess; that is, from suffering. (Therefore, as will be remembered from the Third Book, the momentary silencing of all volition, which occurs as soon as we give ourselves over to aesthetic contemplation, as pure will-less subject of knowledge, the correlative of the Idea, is one of the principal elements in our pleasure in the beautiful.) Secondly, because, through the causal connection of things, most of our desires must remain unfulfilled, and the will is more often thwarted than satisfied; therefore much intense volition always entails much intense suffering. For all suffering is nothing but unfulfilled and thwarted volition; and even the pain of the body, when it is injured or destroyed, is as such possible only because the body is nothing but the will itself become object.

Now on this account, because much intense suffering is inseparable from much intense volition, the facial expression of very bad people bears the stamp of inward suffering; even when they have attained every external happiness, they always look unhappy as long as they are not transported by some momentary ecstasy, or are not pretending. The end result of this inward torment, which is immediately essential to them, is the delight in the suffering of others which springs not from mere egoism but is disinterested, and which constitutes *wickedness* proper, and can rise to the pitch of *cruelty*. The suffering of others, as cruelty conceives of it, is not just a means of attaining the objectives of its own will, but is in itself an objective.

The fuller explanation of this phenomenon is as follows. Since man is a manifestation of will illuminated by the clearest knowledge, he is always measuring the actual satisfaction of his will as he feels it with the merely possible satisfaction of it which knowledge holds out to him. Hence arises envy: every privation is infinitely intensified by the enjoyment of others, and relieved by knowledge that others also suffer the same privation. Those ills which we suffer as a community, and which are inseparable from human life, trouble us little, just as those which appertain to the climate, to the whole country. Our bringing to mind sufferings greater than our own eases our pain; our seeing the sufferings of others alleviates our own. Now a person filled with an exceptionally intense impulse of will, who with burning eagerness would like to grab everything in order to slake the thirst of his egoism, will learn, as he inevitably must, that all satisfaction is merely apparent. He will learn that his ambition once attained never fulfils the promise held out by the object of his desire, that is to say, the final appeasement of the will's fierce impulse. He will find, on the contrary, that once fulfilled, the wish only changes its form, and now torments him in a new form; and, indeed, that when at last all his wishes are exhausted, the will's passion itself remains, even without any conscious motive, and makes itself known to him with desperate pain as a feeling of terrible *desolation* and *emptiness*. All this in a person manifesting ordinary degrees of volition is felt only in a smaller measure, and produces only the ordinary degree of melancholy, whereas in the person who is a manifestation of will to the point of extraordinary wickedness there must arise an excessive inward misery, an eternal unrest, an incurable pain. He will then seek indirectly the alleviation which he has not been able to find directly. He will seek to mitigate his own suffering by the sight of the suffering of others, which at the same time he recognises as an expression of his power. The suffering of others now becomes for him an end in itself, and is a spectacle in which he delights; and so the phenomenon of actual cruelty and blood-thirstiness comes about, which history so often shows us in its Neros and Domitians, in the African Deys, in Robespierre, and the rest.

The desire for revenge is closely related to wickedness. It

recompenses evil with evil, not in the interests of the future (as is the nature of punishment), but merely on account of what has happened, what is past, as such; and so it is without hope of personal gain; it is not a means, but an end; that end is to revel in the torment which the offender must now himself suffer at the hands of the avenger. What distinguishes revenge from pure wickedness, and to some extent excuses it, is an appearance of justice. For if the same act, which is now revenge, were to be done legally – that is, according to a rule previously determined and known, and in a social group which had sanctioned this rule – it would be punishment, and hence justice.

Besides the suffering which has been described (and which is inseparable from wickedness because it springs from the same root in a very vehement will), there is associated with wickedness another specific pain quite different from this, which is felt in the case of every bad action – whether it be merely injustice stemming from egoism, or pure wickedness – and according to its duration this is called *the pang of conscience*, or *remorse*. Now the reader who clearly recalls the content of this Fourth Book hitherto, and especially the truth argued at the beginning of it – that life itself is always assured, as its mere copy or mirror, to the will to life – and also the exposition of eternal justice, will find that the 'pang of conscience' can mean only the following; in other words its content, abstractly expressed, is as follows, in which two parts are distinguishable, which, however, come together again perfectly, and must be thought of as one.

However closely the veil of Mâyâ may envelop the mind of the bad person, that is to say, however firmly he may be enmeshed in the *principium individuationis*, according to which he regards his person as absolutely different and separated by a wide gulf from all others – an insight to which he clings with all his might, since only that suits and supports his egoism: and in just this way, indeed, knowledge is almost always corrupted by will – there arises, nonetheless, in the inmost depths of his consciousness the secret presentiment that such an order of things is only phenomenal, and that things are in themselves, at deeper level, quite different. He has a dim foreboding that, however much time and space may separate him from other individuals and the innumerable miseries they suffer (and suffer even through him), and however much time and space may represent these misfortunes and misfortunates as quite alien to him, yet in themselves, and apart from the idea and its forms, it is the one will to life that appears in them all, which failing to recognise itself, turns its weapons against itself, and, in seeking to enhance the well-being of one of its phenomena, imposes very great suffering on another. He dimly sees that he, the bad person, is precisely this whole will; that consequently he is not only the tormentor but also the tormented, from whose suffering he is separated and spared only by a deceptive dream, the form of which is space and time. But the dream, he knows, will be dispelled, and in reality he must pay for the pleasure with the pain, and that all suffering which he recognises as only possible affects him really as the will to life, in so far as the possible and actual, the near and the distant in time and space, are different only for the knowledge of the individual, only by means of the *principium individuationis*, not in themselves. This is the truth which mythically, *i.e.*, adapted to the principle of sufficient reason, and by that route translated into the form of the phenomenal, is expressed in the transmigration of souls. Yet it has its purest, unalloyed expression precisely in that obscurely felt yet inconsolable misery called remorse.

But remorse springs also from a second immediate insight, which is closely allied to this first – namely the recognition of the strength with which the will to live asserts itself in the wicked individual, which far exceeds the bounds of his own individual phenomenon, and goes so far as to deny absolutely the same will appearing in other individuals. Consequently the inner horror of the wicked man at his own deed, which he tries to conceal from himself, contains – besides that presentment of the nothingness and mere illusiveness of the *principium individuationis*, and of the distinction established by the principle between him and others – also the knowledge of the vehemence of his own will, the force with which he has seized life and sunk his teeth in it, that very life whose terrible aspect he sees before him in the torment of those he has oppressed, a life to which he is nonetheless so grotesquely attached that by that very intimate self-identification he himself becomes the perpetrator of the most horrible actions as a means of more fully affirming his own will. He recognises himself as the concentrated manifestation of the will to life, feels to what degree he is in life's clutches and a prey, too, to the innumerable sufferings which are essential to it, for life has infinite time and infinite space to erase the distinction between the possible and the actual, and to change all the sufferings of which as yet he merely *knows* into sufferings he has actually *felt*. The millions of years of constant rebirth continue to exist, like the whole past and future, only as an abstraction; yet only occupied time, the form of the phenomenon of the will, is the present, and for the individual, time is always new: he always feels he has newly come into being. For life is inseparable from the will to life, and the only form of life is the present. Death (we beg leave to repeat the simile) is like the setting of the sun which is then only apparently swallowed up by the night, but in reality, being itself the source of all light, burns without intermission, brings new days to new worlds, and is always rising and always setting. Beginning and end effect only the individual, through the medium of time, the form of the phenomenon for the idea. Outside time lies only the will, Kant's thing-in-itself, and the adequate objectification of this, Plato's Idea. For that reason suicide affords no escape; what everyone in his inmost consciousness *wills*, that he must *be*; and what everyone *is*, that he *wills*.

Thus, besides the merely felt knowledge of the illusiveness and nothingness of the forms of the idea that separate individuals, it is the self-knowledge of one's own will and of its degree that gives conscience its sting. A man's career delineates the picture of the empirical character, whose original is the intelligible character, and the wicked man takes fright at this picture. It matters not whether the picture is delineated on a big scale so that the world shares his horror, or on a scale so small that he alone sees it, for it immediately concerns only him. The past would be, as mere appearance, a matter of indifference, and could not trouble the conscience if the character did not feel itself to be, as long as it does not deny itself, free from all time, and unalterable by it. Therefore things which are long past still weigh on the conscience. The prayer, 'Lead me not into temptation', means, 'Let me not see who I am.' In the violence with which the evil person affirms life, and which is made plain to him in the sufferings which he inflicts on others, he measures how far he is from the surrender and denial of that will, which is the only possible deliverance from the world and its miseries. He sees how far he belongs to it, and how firmly he is bound to it; what others suffer he *recognises,* but that has failed to move him; he is in the grip of life and of the suffering he *feels*. Whether this will ever break and overcome the vehemence of his will, remains uncertain.

This exposition of the significance and inner nature of the *bad*, which as mere feeling (*i.e.*, *not* as distinct, abstract knowledge) is the content of *remorse*, will gain in clarity and comprehensiveness as a result of our similarly studying the *good* as a quality of human will, and finally through our turning our attention to absolute resignation and holiness, which proceed from it when it has attained its highest grade. For opposites are always mutually illuminating, and the day at one and the same time reveals both itself and the night, as Spinoza has so well expressed it.

§ 66. A theory of morals which is not properly argued – in other words, mere moralising – can effect nothing, because it does not motivate. A theory of morals which *does* motivate can do so only by working on self-love. But what springs from this latter has no moral worth. It follows that no genuine virtue can be produced through moral theory or abstract knowledge of any kind, but that such virtue must spring from that intuitive knowledge which recognises in the individuality of others the same essence as in our own.

For virtue certainly proceeds from knowledge, but not from the abstract knowledge that can be communicated through words. If it were so, virtue could be taught, and by here expressing in abstract language its nature and the knowledge which lies at its base, we should have effected the ethical improvement of everyone who comprehended this. But it does not happen like this at all. On the contrary, ethical discourses and preaching will no more produce a virtuous man than have all the systems of aesthetics since Aristotle produced a poet. For the real inner nature of virtue, abstraction is unproductive, just as it is in art, and it is only in a completely subordinate position that it can be of use as a tool in the elaboration and preserving of what has been ascertained and inferred by other means. *Velle non discitur* [willing cannot be learned]. Abstract dogmas are, in fact, without influence upon virtue, *i.e.*, upon the goodness of one's disposition. False dogmas do not perturb it; true ones will scarcely assist it. Truly, it would be very bad if the chief business in human life, its ethical value, that value which counts for eternity, were dependent upon anything of which the attainment is so much a matter of chance as is the case with dogmas, religious doctrines, and philosophical theories. Dogmas are of value to morality only in that the person who has become virtuous from insight of another kind (which is shortly to be discussed) finds in dogma a ready formula whereby he can offer, to his own faculty of reason, an explanation (albeit mostly fictitious) for his non-egoistical behaviour. His reason (*i.e.*, the man himself) does not *understand* the nature of this behaviour, but he has accustomed his reason to express itself content with this explanation.

On *conduct*, on outward action, dogmas may certainly exercise a powerful influence, as can custom and example (the latter because the ordinary person does not trust his judgement, being conscious of its weakness, but follows only his own experience, or someone else's experience); but the disposition is not altered thereby. All abstract knowledge gives only motives; but, as was shown above, motives can alter only the direction of the will, not the will itself. All communicable knowledge, however, can affect the will only as a motive. Thus, however dogmas may steer the will's course, what the person wills, actually and overall, still remains the same. Only in respect of the ways in which it is to be attained has he had second thoughts, and imaginary motives direct him just as real ones would. So in respect of ethical merit, it is all the same whether he gives generously to the poor, firmly persuaded that in a future life he will receive everything ten times over in return, or expends the same sum on the improvement of an estate which will yield interest, albeit late, but all the more surely and substantially. And anyone who for the sake of orthodoxy commits the heretic to the flames is as much a murderer as the bandit who does it for gain; and indeed, as regards inward circumstances, so also is anyone who slaughters the Turks in the Holy Land, if, like the burner of heretics, he really does so because he thinks that he will thereby earn a place in heaven. For these people are concerned only for themselves, for their own egoism, just like the bandit, from whom they are distinguished only by the absurdity of their means. From without, as has been said, the will can be approached only through motives, and these merely alter the way in which it expresses itself, without ever altering the will itself. *Velle non discitur* [Willing cannot be learned].

When the doer of good deeds claims to be acting in accordance with dogmas, we must always distinguish whether these dogmas really are the motives for those good deeds, or whether, as I said above, they are merely the ostensible explanation by which he seeks to satisfy his own reason in respect of a good deed which really springs from quite a different source, a deed which he performs because he is *good*, though he does not know how to explain it rightly, since he is no philosopher, and yet wishes to offer *some* motive for his behaviour. But this difference is very hard to discern, because it lies deep within us. Hence we can scarcely ever pass a correct moral judgement on the conduct of others, and very seldom on our own.

The deeds and modes of action of an individual and of a nation may be very much modified through dogmas, example and custom. But in themselves all deeds (*opera operata*) are merely empty figures, and only the disposition which leads to them gives them moral significance. This, however, may be exactly the same while the outward appearance is very different. With an equal degree of wickedness one man may die on the wheel, and another in the bosom of his family. It may be the same degree of wickedness which in one nation is writ large in murder and cannibalism, and in another expressed delicately and subtly in miniature, through court intrigues, oppression, and machinations of every kind; the essence is the same. It is conceivable that a politically perfect state, or perhaps indeed complete faith in a doctrine of rewards and punishments here-after, might prevent every crime; thereby much would be gained politically, but nothing morally; only the mirroring of the will in life would be obstructed.

Thus genuine goodness of disposition, disinterested virtue, and pure nobility of mind do not result from abstract knowl-edge. Yet they do proceed from knowledge; but it is a direct intuitive knowledge, which can neither be reasoned away, nor arrived at by reasoning, a knowledge which, just because it is not abstract, cannot be communicated, but must arise in each for himself, and which thus finds its own appropriate expression not in words, but only in deeds, in action, in the course of a human life. Although here we are seeking the theory of virtue, and have therefore also to express abstractly the nature of the knowledge which is fundamental to it, we will be unable to convey that knowledge itself in this statement. We can only give the concept of this knowledge, and thus always start from action in which alone it becomes visible, and refer to action as its only adequate expression. We can only explain and interpret this expression, *i.e.*, we can articulate in abstract terms what really takes place in it.

Before we speak of actual *goodness* as distinct from wickedness, which we have already presented, we must touch on the mere negation of wickedness as an intermediate stage: this is *justice*. What right and wrong are has been fully argued above; therefore we can briefly say here that a person who voluntarily acknowledges and respects that merely moral limit between wrong and right, even where no state or other authority guarantees – consequently a person who, according to our explanation, never carries the affirmation of his own will so far as to deny the will manifest in another individual – is *just*. Thus, he will not, in order to increase his own well-being, inflict suffering upon others, *i.e.*, he will commit no crime, he will respect the rights and the property of others. We see that for such a just man the *principium individuationis* is no longer, as for a bad man, an absolute wall of partition. We see that he does not, like the bad man, affirm merely his own manifestation of will and deny all others; that other persons are for him not mere masks, and their nature quite different from his own; but he shows by his behaviour that he also *recognises* his own nature – the will to life as a thing-in-itself – even in the alien manifestation which is given to him only as idea; so with that other manifestation he identifies himself, up to a certain point, the point at which he will commit no injustice – that is, do no injury. Now to this same degree he sees through the *principium individuationis*, the veil of Mâyâ, in so far as he places the other being on a par with himself: he does the other no harm.

When we examine the kernel of this justice, we find in it the intention not to go so far in the affirmation of one's own will as to deny the manifestations of will in others by compelling them to serve one's own. One will therefore wish to do as much for the benefit of others as one enjoys at their hands. The highest degree of this disposition to justice (which, however, is always allied with real goodness whose character is now not merely negative) leads a man even to doubt his right to inherited property; to want to maintain his body solely by his own energy, mental and physical; to feel every service rendered by others, every luxury, as a reproach; and ultimately, of his own free will, to embrace poverty.

Voluntary justice springs, as we have found, from our seeing to some degree through the *principium individuationis*, while the unjust person remains entirely caught up in this. We may see through it not only in the degree required for justice, but also in the higher degree which moves us to positive benevolence and beneficence, and to philanthropy. And this may happen irrespective of the strength and energy of the will manifest in such an individual. Knowledge can always counterbalance it in him, teach him to resist the temptation to do wrong, and even produce in him every degree of goodness, and, indeed, of resignation. Thus the good man is by no means to be regarded as having been in the first place a weaker manifestation of will than the bad man: it is knowledge which masters the blind impulse of will within him. There are individuals who, on account of the weakness of the will appearing in them, merely seem to have a good disposition, but what they are will soon show itself in their incapacity for the self-conquest adequate to performing a deed that is just or good.

If, however, as a rare exception, we meet a man who possesses a considerable income, but uses very little of it for himself and gives all the rest to the needy, while he does without many pleasures and comforts himself, and we seek to explain the action of this man, we shall find - apart altogether from the dogmas through which he tries to make his actions intelligible to his reasoning - that the simplest general explanation and the essential character of his conduct is that *he makes less distinction than is usually made between himself and others*. In the eyes of some, this same distinction is so great that to the malicious person the suffering of other people is a direct pleasure, and to the unjust it is a ready means to self-contentment. The merely just person is content not to cause suffering; and, in general, most people know of, and are acquainted with, the countless sufferings of others close to them, but do not make up their minds to alleviate these, because to do so would require some sacrifice. Thus, in every one of these people a compelling distinction seems to hold sway between his own ego and that of others; but on the contrary, to the noble man of our hypothesis, this distinction is not so significant. The *principium individuationis*, the form of the phenomenon, no longer envelops him so closely, but the suffering which he sees in others touches him almost as closely as his own. So he tries to strike a balance between the two, denies himself pleasures, practises renunciation, in order to relieve the sufferings of others. He becomes aware that the distinction between himself and others, which to the wicked person is so great a gulf, belongs only to a fleeting, deceptive phenomenon. He recognises directly and without argument that the in-itself of his own manifestation is also that of others, namely the will to life, which constitutes the inner nature of each and everything, and lives in all; indeed, that this applies also to the animals and the whole of nature, and hence he will not cause suffering even to an animal.[2]

He can now no more let others starve, while he himself has more than enough and to spare, than is any one likely to suffer hunger one day in order the next day to have more than he can eat. For the person who performs works of charity, the veil of Mâyâ has become transparent, and the illusion of the *principium individuationis* has left him. He recognises himself, his will, in every being, and consequently also in the sufferer. He is now free from the perversity with which the will to life, not recognising itself, here in one individual enjoys a fleeting, deceptive pleasure, while in another it suffers and starves, and so both inflicts and endures misery, not knowing that, like Thyestes, it avidly devours its own flesh and blood; and then, on the one hand, laments its undeserved suffering, and on the other hand transgresses without fear of Nemesis, always merely because caught up in the *principium individuationis*, and thereby in the kind of knowledge which is governed by the principle of sufficient reason, it does not recognise itself in the phenomenon

[2] Man's right over the energies and the life of animals is based upon the animal's suffering less pain in dying or in toiling than man would suffer by being deprived of that animal's meat or of his energy in work: and the animal's pain is deemed to be less than man's because susceptibility to suffering increases in proportion to clarity of consciousness. Hence man may carry the assertion of his existence to the extent of denying the existence of animals, and the will to life as a whole endures less suffering in this way than if the situation were reversed. This at once determines the extent of the use man may legitimately make of the animals' energies; a limit, however, which is often transgressed, especially in the case of beasts of burden, and of hounds used in hunting; and to this the activity of societies for the prevention of cruelty to animals is especially opposed. In my opinion, that right does not extend to vivisection, particularly of the higher animals. On the other hand, the insect does not suffer so much through its death as a man suffers from its sting. The Hindus have no perception of this.

outside its own, and therefore does not perceive eternal justice. To be cured of this illusion and deception of Mâyâ, and to perform works of charity, are one and the same. But the latter is the sure sign of that knowledge.

The opposite of the bad conscience, the origin and significance of which is elucidated above, is the *good conscience*, the satisfaction we feel after every disinterested deed. It arises from the way in which such a deed, proceeding as it does from the direct recognition of our own inner being in the phenomenon of another being, in turn also endorses this insight for us: the knowledge that our true self exists not only in our own person, this single specific manifestation, but in everything that lives. By this insight the heart feels that it is expanded, just as by egoism it is contracted. Egoism concentrates our involvement upon the particular manifestation of our own individuality, in the course of which our intelligence always presents to us the countless dangers which constantly threaten this manifestation, and anxiety and care becomes the key-note of our disposition; but the insight that everything living is essentially just as much our own inner nature as is our own person, extends our involvement to everything living; and in this way the heart is expanded. Through this reduction in our self-involvement our anxious self-concern is attacked at its very root, and restricted; hence the calm, confident serenity which a virtuous disposition and a good conscience grant, and the clear development of this with every good deed, in that the deed itself authenticates for us the basis for that disposition. The egoist feels himself to be surrounded by phenomena which are alien and hostile, and all his hope is centred on his own good. The good man lives in a world of friendly phenomena, and the well-being of any one of these is his own. Thus, although the knowledge of man's lot in general does not make his disposition a cheery one, his habitually recognising his own nature in all living beings gives him, on the other hand, a certain equanimity, and even serenity of disposition. For concern extended to countless phenomena cannot cause such anxiety as concern concentrated upon *one*. The accidents which befall individuals collectively balance out overall, while those which happen to the particular individual bring happiness or unhappiness.

Thus, though others have set down moral principles which they offer as prescriptions for virtue, and rules to be followed, I cannot do this, as I have already said, because I have no 'ought' or law to prescribe to the eternally free will. Yet on the other hand, in the context of my inquiry, what to a certain extent corresponds and is analogous to that undertaking is the purely theoretical truth (of which my whole exposition may be seen as merely an elaboration) that the will is the in-itself of every phenomenon, but is itself, as such, free from the forms of the phenomenal, and consequently from plurality. This truth, in so far as it has relevance to conduct, I cannot better express than by the formula already quoted from the Vedas: 'Tat twam asi!' (This thou art!). Anyone who can say this to himself with clear insight and firm inner conviction, about every being with whom he comes in contact, can be confident of all virtue and eternal bliss, and is on the straight path to salvation. [. . .]

§ 68. [. . .] We saw earlier that hatred and malice are conditioned by egoism, and that egoism is based on the entanglement of knowledge in the *principium individuationis*. Conversely we found that the penetration of that *principium individuationis* is the source and the essence of justice, and then, if we take a further step, we find it is the source and essence of love and nobility of character to the highest degree. Only this penetration, by cancelling the distinction between our own individuality and that of others, makes possible and explains perfect goodness of disposition, to the point of unselfish love and the most generous self-sacrifice for the benefit of others.

If, however, this penetration of the *principium individuationis*, this direct recognition of the will's identity in all its manifestations, is present with a high degree of clarity, it will at once show an even more extensive influence on the will. If that veil of Mâyâ, the *principium individuationis*, is lifted from a person's eyes to such an extent that he no longer makes the egotistical distinction between himself and another person but participates in the sufferings of other individuals as in his own, and so is not only benevolent in the highest degree, but even ready to sacrifice his own individuality if others can be saved thereby, then it follows that such a person, who recognises in all beings his own inmost and true self, must also regard the infinite suffering of everything that lives and suffers as his own, and take upon himself the pain of the whole world. No suffering is any longer alien to him. All the miseries of others which he sees and is so seldom able to alleviate, all the miseries of which he knows indirectly, and even those of which he learns as being merely possible, make on his mind the same impact as his own sufferings do. It is no longer the alternating joy and sorrow which befalls him personally that he has in view, as is the case with the person still caught up in egoism; but, since he sees through the *principium individuationis*, everything is equally close to him. He recognises the whole, grasps its nature, and finds that it is caught up in a constant passing away, vain striving, inward conflict, and continual suffering. He sees, wherever he looks, suffering mankind, the suffering animal kingdom and a world that is fading away. But all this is now as close to him as only his own self is to the egoist. Why should he now, with such knowledge of the world, affirm this very life through constant acts of will, and thereby bind himself ever more closely to it, press it ever more firmly to himself? Thus he who is still caught up in the *principium individuationis*, in egoism, knows only specific, individual things and their relevance to himself and these constantly become the renewed *motives* of his volition. But, on the other hand, that knowledge of the whole, of the nature of the thing-in-itself, which has been described, becomes a *quieter* of all and every volition. The will now turns away from life; it now shudders at the pleasures in which it recognises the affirmation of life. The person now attains to the state of voluntary renunciation, resignation, true calm and perfect will-lessness.

At times when our own suffering is a heavy burden, or we keenly feel another's pain, we others, who are still wrapped in the veil of Mâyâ, may at close quarters recognise life's vanity and bitterness. Then we would like by total and permanent renunciation to break the sting from our desires, close the door upon all suffering, and purify and sanctify ourselves; yet the illusion of the phenomenon soon ensnares us again, and its motives activate the will anew; we cannot tear ourselves free. The allurement of hope, the flattery of the present, the sweetness of pleasure, the well-being which falls to our lot, amid the lamentations of a suffering world governed by chance and error, draws us back to it and attaches our bonds anew. For that reason Jesus says: 'It is easier for a camel to go through the eye of a needle, than for a rich man to enter into the kingdom of God.' [Matthew xiv.24]

If we compare life to a circuit around which we must run without stopping – a circuit of red-hot coals, with a few cool places here and there – then the person caught up in delusion finds consolation in the cool spot, on which for the moment he is standing, or which he sees in front of him, and he continues to run round the track. But the person who sees through the *principium individuationis*, and recognises the real nature of the thing-in-itself, and thereby recognises the whole, is no longer open to such consolation; he sees himself in all places at once, and withdraws from the race. His will turns round, no longer asserts its own nature reflected in the phenomenon, but denies it. This change announces itself in the transition from virtue to *asceticism*. For it is no longer enough for such a man to love others as himself, and to do as much for them as for himself: he feels revulsion at the being of which his own phenomenal existence is an expression, at the will to live, the kernel and inner nature of that world which he recognises as full of misery. He therefore disowns this nature which appears in him and is expressed through his body, and his action gives the lie to his phenomenal existence and appears in open contradiction to it. Essentially nothing but a manifestation of will, he ceases to will anything, guards against attaching his will to anything, and seeks to consolidate in himself the greatest indifference to everything. His body, being healthy and strong, expresses the sexual impulse through the genitals; but he denies the will and gives the lie to the body: he desires no sexual gratification under any condition. Voluntary and complete chastity is the first step in asceticism or the denial of the will to life. It thereby denies the assertion of the will which extends beyond the individual life, and gives notice that with the life of this body, the will, whose manifestation it is, will be suspended. Nature, always truthful and undissembling, declares that if this maxim became universal, the human race would die out; and I think I may assume, in accordance with what was said in the Second Book about the connectedness of all the will's manifestations, that with its highest manifestation, the weaker reflection of it (that is, the animal world) would also pass away, just as the twilight vanishes once day has broken. Once knowledge had been entirely suspended, the rest of the world would of itself disappear into nothingness. [. . .]

Asceticism then further shows itself in voluntary and intentional poverty, which comes about not only *per accidens*, through the giving-away of one's possessions to alleviate the sufferings of others, but is here an end in itself, meant to serve as a constant mortification of will, so that the will should not again be stimulated by gratification of desire, the sweetness of life, against which self-knowledge has conceived a revulsion. Anyone who has reached this point still always feels, as a living body, as concrete manifestation of will, the natural disposition towards every kind of volition; but he deliberately suppresses it by forcing himself to refrain from doing all he would like to do, and on the contrary, to do all he would like not to do, even if this has no purpose beyond that of serving to mortify his will. Since he himself denies the will which appears in his own person, he will not object if another does the same, *i.e.*, inflicts wrongs upon him. Hence every suffering coming to him from without, by chance or through the malice of others, is welcome to him. Every injury, ignominy, and insult he receives gladly as the opportunity to ascertain that he no longer affirms the will, but gladly joins forces with every foe against the will's manifestation which is his own person. So he bears such ignominy and suffering with inexhaustible patience and mildness, without ostentation returns good for all the evil, and he no more allows the fire of wrath to reawaken within him ever again than he allows the fire of the desires.

He mortifies not only the will itself, but also its visible form, its objectivity – the body. He nourishes it sparingly, lest its robust good health and its full bloom should reanimate and more vigorously stimulate the will, of which it is merely the expression and the mirror. So he has recourse to fasting, and resorts even to chastisement and self-inflicted torture so that by constant privation and suffering he may gradually break and exterminate the will, which he recognises and abhors as the source of his own suffering existence and the world's. When at last death comes, bringing disintegration to this manifestation of the will (whose essential being here had, through its voluntary self-denial, long since died, except for its frail residue which appeared as the vital element of this body) it is most welcome, and is joyfully received as a deliverance long desired. In this person it is not, as in others, merely the phenomenon which ends with death, but the inner nature itself is suspended, which had existed here still only in the manifestation, and weakly; now this last brittle bond breaks too. For anyone who ends like this, the world has ended at the same time.

And what I have here described with feeble tongue and only in general terms is no philosophical fable that I have improvised myself and only today; no, it was the enviable life of so many saints and great souls among Christians, and still more among Hindus and Buddhists, and also among the faithful of other religions. However different were the dogmas impressed on their faculty of reason, the same inward, direct, intuitive knowledge, which is the only source of all virtue and holiness, expressed itself identically in the way of life. For here, too, the great distinction shows between intuitive and abstract knowledge; and it is a distinction which is important and fundamental to our whole study, although till now neglected. The gulf between intuitive and abstract knowledge is wide, and with regard to insight into the nature of the world, this gulf can be crossed only by philosophy. For intuitively or *in concreto*, every person is conscious of all philosophical truths, but to bring them to his conceptual awareness, to reflection, is the business of the philosopher, who neither ought nor can do more.

Thus it may be that the inner nature of holiness, self-renunciation, mortification of self-will, asceticism, is here for the first time expressed in the abstract and free from all myth, as *denial of the will to life*, emerging after the consummate knowledge of its own nature has become a quieter of all volition. On the other hand, it has been known directly and expressed in practice by all those saints and ascetics who, though with the same insight, used very different language according to the dogmas which their reason had accepted, with the result that an Indian holy man, a Christian saint, or a Lama must each give a very different account of his conduct – which is, however, of no material consequence here. A holy man may be full of the absurdest superstition, or, on the contrary, he may be a philosopher: it is all the same. His conduct alone proves that he is a holy man, for, with respect to its morality, it proceeds from knowledge of the world and its nature which is not abstractly, but intuitively and directly, apprehended, and is, merely for the satisfaction of his reason, interpreted by him through some dogma or other. So it is no more necessary that the saint should be a philosopher than that the philosopher should be a saint;

just as it is not necessary that a supremely handsome person should be a great sculptor, or that a great sculptor should himself also be a handsome person. More generally, it is odd to require of a moralist that he should commend no virtue other than that which he himself possesses. To reproduce the whole nature of the world abstractly, universally, and distinctly in concepts, and to lay it down in storage as a reflected image in concepts of reason which keep well and always lie ready for use; this, and nothing else, is philosophy. [. . .]

A closer and more complete knowledge of what we, within the abstract, general style of our presentation, term 'the denial of the will to life' will be further greatly assisted by our studying the ethical prescripts given with this purport and by people inspired by it; and at the same time, these will show how old our viewpoint is, however new its purely philosophical expression may be. The most obvious example is Christianity, the ethics of which are entirely in the spirit we have indicated, and lead not only to the highest degrees of philanthropy, but also to renunciation. The germ of this latter aspect of it was already very clearly present in the writings of the Apostles, but not until later was it fully developed and expressed. We find the Apostles bidding us to love our neighbour as ourselves, to practise charity, to recompense hatred with love and well-doing, to exercise patience, meekness, to endure all possible insults without resistance, to practise abstemiousness in eating and drinking, to suppress passion, to resist sexual desire (if possible, altogether). We see here the first stages of asceticism, or of actual denial of the will. This last expression denotes what in the Gospels is called 'denying ourselves and taking up the cross' (Matt. xvi. 24, 25; Mark viii, 34, 35; Luke ix. 23, 24, xiv, 26, 27, 33). This tendency soon developed more and more, and was the origin of penitents, anchorites, and monasticism – an origin which in itself was pure and holy, but for that very reason inappropriate to the great majority of people; hence what developed out of it could only be hypocrisy and travesty, for *abusus optimi pessimus* ['the worst is the abuse of the best']. In more developed Christianity we see that seed of asceticism unfold into the full flower in the writings of the Christian saints and mystics. Besides the purest love, these also preach complete resignation, voluntary and absolute poverty, genuine unconcern, total indifference to all worldly things, dying to our own will and being born again in God, utter self-oblivion, and self-immersion in the contemplation of God. [. . .]

But we find what we have called 'the denial of the will to life' still more fully developed, more comprehensively expressed, and more vividly presented in the ancient Sanskrit writings than could be done in the Christian Church and the Western world. That this important ethical view of life could here attain to a fuller development and a more distinct expression is perhaps to be ascribed chiefly to its not being restricted by an element quite alien to it, as is Jewish doctrine within Christianity. The sublime founder of Christianity had necessarily to accommodate and adapt to this Jewish doctrine, partly consciously, partly, it may be, unconsciously. Thus Christianity is made up of two very different elements, of which I should like to call the purely ethical part primarily, and indeed exclusively, the Christian, and distinguish it from the Jewish dogmatism which preceded it. If, as has often been feared, and especially at the present time, that excellent and salutary religion should some day fall into a total decline, I should seek the reason for this solely in its consisting not of one simple element, but of two originally different elements which have been combined only through accident of history. As a result of their unequal relationship and their unequal reaction to the spirit of the new age, the elements of this compound might separate. In such a case, disintegration would have to follow, but even then the purely ethical part would inevitably still remain unimpaired, because it is indestructible.

Our knowledge of Hindu literature is still very imperfect. Yet, as we find their ethical teaching variously and powerfully expressed in the Vedas, Puranas, imaginative literature, myths, legends of their saints, maxims and codes of conduct, we see that it prescribes love of our neighbour, with total renunciation of all self-love; love generally, not confined to mankind, but embracing all living creatures; charity to the point of giving away our hard-won daily earnings; endless patience towards all who offend us; the requital of all wickedness, however base, with goodness and love; voluntary and joyful endurance of all ignominy; abstinence from all meat; absolute chastity and renunciation of all sensual pleasure for him who strives after true holiness; the rejection of all possessions, the forsaking of one's home and family, deep unbroken solitude spent in silent contemplation, with voluntary penance and terrible slow self-torture for the absolute mortification of the will, torture even to the point of voluntary death by starvation, or by exposing oneself to crocodiles, or flinging oneself over the sacred precipice in the Himalayas, or being buried alive, or, finally, by throwing oneself beneath the wheels of the huge wagon [juggernaut] conveying the images of the gods amid the singing, shouting, and dancing of bayadères. And even now these precepts, whose origin goes back more than four thousand years, are followed (and by some individuals, followed even to the last extreme) although the Hindu race is in many respects degenerate.

A religion which demands the greatest sacrifices, and which has yet remained so long in practice in a nation that embraces so many millions of people, cannot be an arbitrarily invented whim, but must have its basis in human nature. But besides this, if we read the life of a Christian penitent or saint and that of a Hindu saint, we cannot cease to wonder at the harmony we find between them. Despite such radically different dogmas, customs, and circumstances, the aspiration and inner life of the two is the same. And the same harmony prevails in the rules prescribed for both of them. For example, Tauler speaks of the absolute poverty which one ought to seek, and which consists in giving away and divesting oneself completely of everything from which one might draw comfort or worldly pleasure – clearly because all this constantly gives new nourishment to the will, which it is our intention to destroy utterly. And as an Indian counterpart of this, we find in the precepts of Fo that the Saniassi, who ought to be without a dwelling and entirely without property, is further finally told not to lay himself down often under the same tree, lest he should conceive a preference or liking for it above other trees. The Christian mystics and the teachers of the Vedânta philosophy agree also in this respect, that they both regard all outward works and religious exercises as superfluous for the person who has achieved perfection. So much agreement in spite of such different times and different peoples is a factual proof that what is expressed here is not, as trite optimism likes to assert, an eccentricity and perversity of the mind, but an essential aspect of human nature, an aspect seldom seen only because of its excellence.

I have now cited the sources from which one may get to know, drawn directly and from life, the phenomena in which the denial of the will to life exhibits itself. In some respects this is the most important point of our whole study; yet I have explained it only quite generally, for it is better to refer to those who speak from direct experience, than to allow the size of this book to expand unduly as a result of my feebler repetition of what they have said.

I wish to add only a little more to the general description of their condition. We saw above that the wicked man, by the vehemence of his volition, suffers constant, consuming, inward pain, and finally, if all objects of volition are exhausted, quenches the fiery thirst of his wilfulness by the sight of another's suffering. On the other hand, the person in whom the denial of the will to life has dawned, however poor, joyless, and full of privation his condition may be to an outside observer, is filled with inward joy and the true peace of heaven. It is not the restless pressure of life, the jubilant delight conditional upon keen suffering either before or after it, such as make up the routine of the person who grasps life cheerfully. It is, instead, an unshakeable peace, a profound tranquillity and inward serenity, a state which we cannot look at without the greatest longing when it is brought before our eyes or our imagination, for we at once recognise it as that which alone is right, infinitely surpassing everything else. And thereupon our better self calls out to us the great *sapere aude* [dare to be wise!]. Then we feel that every fulfilment of our wishes won from the world is, after all, only like the alms which keep the beggar alive today so that he may be hungry again tomorrow. Resignation, on the other hand, is like an inherited estate: it removes its owner for ever from all anxiety.

We remember from the Third Book that the aesthetic pleasure in the beautiful consists largely in our being lifted, for that moment when we enter the state of pure contemplation, above all willing, that is, above all desires and cares. We become, as it were, freed from ourselves. We are no longer the individual whose knowing serves its constant willing, no longer the correlative of the particular thing, for whom objects become motives; but instead we are, purified from will, the eternal subject of knowing, the correlative of the Platonic Idea. And we know that these moments in which, released from the sullen pressure of will, we seem to rise out of the earth's heavy atmosphere, are the most blissful we know. From this we can understand how blessed must be the life of a person whose will is assuaged not merely for moments, as in the enjoyment of the beautiful, but for ever; indeed, it is utterly extinguished but for the last glimmering spark that maintains the body, and will be extinguished with it. Such a person, who, after many bitter struggles with his own nature, has finally conquered outright, remains only as a pure, knowing being, the undimmed mirror of the world. Nothing more can trouble him, nothing can move him, for he has cut all the thousand cords of will which keep us bound to the world, and which, as desire, fear, envy, anger, tear and pull us hither and thither, inflicting constant pain. He now looks back, smiling and at rest, on the delusions of this world, which were once able to move and hurt his spirit also, but which now stand before him as indifferently as the chess-men when the game has ended, or as the masks and fancy costume, discarded now in the morning, which last night at the carnival teased and troubled us. Life and its forms now pass before him as a fleeting illusion, as a light morning dream in the mind of the sleeper already half-awake, a dream through which reality already shimmers, and which can no longer deceive; and like this morning dream, they finally vanish without violent transition. These reflections help us to understand what Madame de Guyon means when, towards the end of her autobiography, she often expresses herself thus: 'Everything is indifferent to me; I *cannot* will anything more: often I know not whether I exist or not' [*Vie de Madame de Guyon*, Cologne 1720, II.13]. [. . .]

But we should not think that once the denial of the will to life has come about (by way of the knowledge which has become a quieter of the will) it will never again falter, and that we can pause to rest on it as on a property that we have acquired. Rather, it must be fought for again and again by constant battle. For since the body is the will itself (only in the form of objectivity, or as manifestation in the world as idea), as long as the body lives, the whole will to live exists potentially, and constantly strives to become actual, and to burn again with all its ardour. Thus that peace and felicity we have described is found in the life of saintly people only as the flower that grows from their constantly overcoming the will, and we see the continual battle with the will to life as the ground from which this flower grows: for on earth no-one can have lasting peace. So we see that the stories of the inner life of saints are full of spiritual conflicts, temptations, and the sense of having been deserted by divine grace, that is to say, full of the kind of knowledge which, making all motives ineffectual, as a universal quieter soothes all volition, gives peace most profound, and opens the gateway to freedom. For that reason also we see those who, having once attained to the denial of the will to life, strive with all their might to keep themselves on this path by self-imposed renunciation of every kind, by a penitential and austere way of life, and by seeking out whatever is disagreeable to them: all in order to suppress the will which is constantly raising its head anew. Finally, it is because they already know the value of redemption, that they feel anxiety to retain the hard-won salvation, and they experience scruples of conscience about every innocent enjoyment, or about every little stirring of their vanity, which even here dies last of all; for it is the most indestructible, the most active, and the most foolish of all human tendencies. By the term *asceticism*, which I have already used fairly often, I mean in its narrower sense this *intentional* breaking of the will by foregoing the agreeable and seeking out the disagreeable, the freely chosen life of penance and self-chastisement for the continual mortification of the will.

We see this practised by someone who has already achieved denial of the will, so that he may persist in it; but any suffering at all, such as inflicted by fate, is a second path ($\delta\varepsilon\acute{\nu}\tau\varepsilon\varrho o\varsigma$ $\pi\lambda o\tilde{\nu}\varsigma$) to that denial. Indeed, we may assume that most people reach it only in this way, and that it is the suffering which is personally experienced, not that which is merely known, which most frequently produces complete resignation, often not until death is near. For only for a few is mere knowledge sufficient to bring about the denial of the will – the knowledge, that is, which, by seeing through the *principium individuationis*, first produces perfect goodness of disposition and universal philanthropy, and then ultimately enables them to recognise all the suffering of the world as their own. Even for someone approaching this point it is almost always so that the tolerable condition of his own body, the flattery of the moment, the enticement of hope and the gratification of the will which presents itself ever anew, that is, the satisfaction of desire, is a constant obstacle to the denial of the will, and a constant temptation to the renewed affirmation of it. For that reason, all these enticements have been in the context personified as the devil. Thus in most cases the will must have been broken by great personal suffering before its self-denial evolves. Then we see the person who has passed through all the stages of increasing distress, while putting up the most vehement resistance, and brought to the verge of despair, suddenly retire into himself, recognise himself and the world, change his whole nature, rise above himself and all suffering, as if purified and sanctified by it, in unassailable peace, felicity, and sublimity, willingly renounce everything he till now most passionately desired, and joyfully embrace death. It is the silver of the denial of the will to life, the gleam of silver which suddenly emerges from the refiner's fire of suffering. It is salvation.

Even those who were very wicked we sometimes see purified to this degree by great grief; they have become different people and are completely transformed. Hence their former misdeeds now no longer trouble their consciences; yet they willingly atone for them by death, and gladly see the end of the manifestation of that will which is now alien and repugnant to them. This denial of the will, induced by great unhappiness and by despair of any relief, Goethe has clearly depicted for us in the tale of Gretchen's sufferings in his immortal masterpiece *Faust*. I know no parallel to this in literature. It is a perfect example of the second path to the denial of the will, leading not, as the first, through the mere recognition of the sufferings of a whole world which one voluntarily makes one's own, but through one's own overwhelming pain, personally felt. Many tragedies end by taking their vehemently willing heroes to the point of total resignation, at which the will to life and its phenomenon usually end together; but no account I know presents us as clearly with the essence of that transformation, free from all that is incidental, as the part of *Faust* I cite.

In real life we see unfortunate people who have to drain the full cup of suffering in going, without hope but with their mental powers intact, to their death on the scaffold – a death that is ignominious, violent, agonising – and they are in this way very often transformed. We should not assume that there is so great a difference between their character and that of most people as their fate suggests, but should attribute this fate for the most part to circumstances; yet they are guilty and, to some degree, bad. We see, however, many of them, after they have entirely lost hope, transformed in the way I have indicated. They now show actual goodness and purity of disposition, true abhorrence of doing anything in the least degree bad or unkind. They forgive their enemies, even if it is through them that they innocently suffered; and not with words merely and out of a sort of hypocritical fear of the judges in the lower regions, but in reality and with heart-felt earnestness, and they want no revenge. Indeed, their sufferings and death in the end become dear to them, for the denial of the will to life has evolved; they often decline deliverance when it is offered, and die gladly, peacefully, and with other-worldly serenity. Life's last secret has revealed itself to these people amid their overwhelming pain: the secret that ills and wickedness, suffering and hate, the tormented and the tormentor, however different they may appear to the knowledge which follows the principle of sufficient reason, are in themselves one, the manifestation of that one will to life which objectifies its self-conflict by means of the *principium individuationis*. They have learned to know both aspects in full measure, the wickedness and the misery it causes; and since in the end they see the identity of the two, they now reject them both at once; they deny the will to life. Through what myths and dogmas they give account to their reasoning faculty for this intuitive and direct knowledge, and for their own transformation is, as I have said, unimportant. [. . .]

The approach of death and the absence of hope are not, however, strictly necessary to such purification through suffering. Even without them we can be brought by force, through great misfortune and pain, to recognise the self-contradiction within the will to life, and we may gain insight into the vanity of all striving. Hence people who have led a very eventful life exposed to the force of the passions – kings, heroes, and adventurers – have been seen suddenly to change, take to resignation and penance, become hermits or monks. To this class belong all tales of genuine conversions. An example is that of Raymon Lully, who had long wooed a fair lady, and was at last bidden to her chamber, anticipating the fulfilment of all his desires. There opening her bodice, she showed him her bosom hideously eaten away by cancer. From that moment, as if he had looked into hell, he was changed; he left the court of the King of Majorca, and went into the desert to do penance. [. . .]

It follows that the denial of the will to life – what is called total resignation, or holiness – always springs from the quieter of the will which consists in recognising its inner conflict and its essential vanity, the same conflict and vanity as express themselves in the suffering of everything that is alive. The difference, which we have represented as two paths, consists in whether that recognition is induced by suffering which is merely and purely *known* (and which we freely make our own by penetrating the *principium individuationis*), or by suffering which is directly *felt* by us personally. True salvation, redemption from life and suffering, cannot even be imagined without total denial of the will. Till then, everyone is nothing but this will itself, whose manifestation is an ephemeral existence, an always vain, constantly frustrated endeavour; and the phenomenal world, to which all irrevocably and in like manner belong, is full of suffering. For we found above that life is always assured to the will to life, and its one real form is the present, from which these surely can never escape — as surely as that birth and death reign in the phenomenal world. Indian myth expresses this by saying 'they are born again.' The great ethical difference in characters means that the bad man is infinitely far from attaining the knowledge from which the denial of the will results, and therefore he is in truth *actually* exposed to all the miseries which appear in life as *possible*; for even his present fortunate physical condition is merely a phenomenon conveyed by the *principium individuationis*, and a delusion of Mâyâ, the beggar's happy dream. The sufferings, which under vehement impulse of his will he inflicts upon others are the measure of the suffering which, in his personal experience, cannot break *his* will and lead it to ultimate denial of itself. All true and pure love, on the other hand, and even all spontaneous justice, results from our seeing through the *principium individuationis*; and our doing so with perfect clarity brings about complete sanctification and redemption. The phenomenon of these is the state of resignation described above, the imperturbable peace which accompanies this resignation, and the most exalted joyfulness in death.

§ 69. *Suicide*, the arbitrary termination of one's individual phenomenon, could not be more different from the denial of the will to life which is the single outstanding act of the will's freedom in the phenomenon, and is thus, as Asmus calls it, the transcendental change. (Within the limits of our study, we have now adequately defined the denial of the will.) Suicide, far from being denial of the will, is a phenomenon of the will's strong affirmation; for the essence of negation lies in shunning not life's sufferings, but its pleasures. The suicide wills life, and is dissatisfied only with the conditions under which it has been given to him. Hence he surrenders not the will to life, but only life, by destroying the individual phenomenon. He wills life, wants the body's unrestricted existence and affirmation; but the complication of circumstances does not permit this, and for him great suffering is the result. The will to life finds itself so much inhibited in this particular manifestation that it cannot let its ambition unfold. It therefore makes a decision in accordance with its own nature, which lies outside the forms of the principle of sufficient reason, and to which every individual phenomenon is therefore indifferent, in that it remains untouched by all coming into being and passing away, and is the inner life of all things. For that same firm inner assurance which allows us all to live free from the constant dread of death (namely, the certainty that the will can never lack a phenomenal existence), supports our action even in suicide. Thus the will to life is manifest just as much in committing suicide (Siva) as in the comfort of self-preservation (Vishnu) and in the sensual pleasure of procreation (Brahma). This is the inner meaning of the *unity of the Trimurti*, which every human being is in his totality, though in time it raises now one, now another, of its three heads.

Suicide stands in the same relation to the denial of the will as the individual thing does to the Idea. The person committing suicide denies only the individual, not the species. We have already found that, as life is always assured to the will to life, and as sorrow is inseparable from life, suicide, the arbitrary destruction of a single phenomenal existence, is a vain and foolish act; for the thing-in-itself remains unperturbed by it, just as the rainbow remains constant, however swiftly the drops which sustain it for the moment may take the place one of another, successively. But, beyond this, it is also the masterpiece of Mâyâ, as the most flagrant example of the self-contradiction of the will to life. As we recognised this contradiction in the will's lowest manifestations, in the constant struggle of all the manifestations of natural forces, and of all organic individuals, for matter, time and space; and as we saw this antagonism become increasingly prominent with terrible clarity in the ascending grades of the will's objectification, so at last in the highest grade, the Idea of man, it reaches the point at which not only the individuals which express the same Idea extirpate one another, but even the same individual declares war against itself. The vehemence with which it wills life, and revolts against what hinders it, namely, suffering, brings it to the point of destroying itself; so that the individual will, by its own act of will, puts an end to that body which is merely its particular visible expression, rather than permit suffering to break the will. Just because the suicide cannot give up willing, he gives up living. The will affirms itself here even in putting an end to its own manifestation, because it can no longer affirm itself otherwise. But because it was the very suffering which he evades that, as mortification of the will, could have lead him to self-denial and hence to redemption, the suicide is in this respect like a sick man who, after the initiation of painful surgery, which could completely cure him, will not allow the operation to be completed, but prefers to retain his sickness. Suffering approaches and, as such, offers the opportunity for the denial of will; but the suicide rejects it, by destroying the will's manifestation, the body, in order that the will may remain unbroken.

This is the reason why almost all ethical teachings both philosophical and religious, condemn suicide, although they themselves can give only curious, sophistical reasons for this condemnation. But if ever a human being restrained himself on grounds of moral impulse from committing suicide, the inmost meaning of this self-conquest (whatever the abstractions in which his reasoning may have clothed it) was this: 'I will not evade suffering, for suffering can help to put an end to the will to life whose manifestation is so full of misery, by so reinforcing my dawning insight into the true nature of the world that this may become the final quieter of my will, and may free me for ever.'

It is well known that from time to time cases occur in which the act of suicide extends to the children: the father first kills the children, whom he dearly loves, and then kills himself. Now, if we consider that conscience, religion, and all received notions teach him to recognise murder as the gravest crime, and that, in spite of this, he commits this crime in the hour of his own death, and without any possible egotistic motive, then the deed can be explained only in the following way. Here the will of the individual recognises itself immediately in the children. However, hampered by the delusion of regarding the phenomenon as being-in-itself, and at the same time profoundly affected by his insight into the misery of all life, he now imagines that along with the phenomenon he is putting an end to the thing-in-itself. Hence he intends to save from life and its misery both himself and the children in whom he directly sees himself live all over again.

It would be an aberration precisely analogous to this to suppose that one might achieve the same as is achieved through voluntary chastity by frustrating nature's purposes in fecundation; or indeed if, taking into consideration life's inevitable suffering, parents were to favour the destruction of their new-born children, instead of doing everything possible to safeguard life for those just struggling into it. For if will to life exists, it cannot – as the only metaphysical reality, or the thing-in-itself – be broken by any physical force; but that force can destroy only its manifestation in this place and at this time. The will to life cannot itself be suspended except through *knowledge*. Thus the only path to salvation is the one by which the will may appear without restriction, so that in this manifestation it may *recognise and know* its own nature. Only as the result of this knowledge can the will suspend and cancel itself, and thereby end the suffering inseparable from its manifestation: but this cannot be done by physical force, like the destruction of the seed, or like the killing of the new-born child, or like suicide. For nature guides the will to the light, because only in the light can it find its salvation. Thus Nature's purposes are to be promoted in every way as soon as the will to life, which is its inner being, has made its decision.

One particular type of suicide seems to be quite different from the usual kind, though it has perhaps not yet been adequately documented. It is voluntary starvation motivated by the highest degree of asceticism. But its occurrence has always been accompanied by much religious fanaticism, and even by superstition, and thereby obscured. Yet it seems that the absolute denial of will may reach the point at which the will is insufficient even to support the body's natural functions by assimilating food. This kind of suicide is far from arising from the will to life; indeed, such a completely resigned ascetic ceases to live only because he has entirely ceased to will. No way of dying other than by starvation is in this case conceivable (except, perhaps, a way resulting from some particular superstition); for the intention to cut short the torment would itself be a stage in the affirmation of will. The dogmas which satisfy the reasoning of such a penitent delude him with the notion that a being of a higher nature has decreed the fasting to which his own inner tendency drives him. [...] Between this voluntary death resulting from extreme asceticism and ordinary suicide resulting from despair, there may be various intermediate stages and combinations, and this admittedly is difficult to explain; but human nature has depths, obscurities, and complications which are extremely hard to illuminate and unravel.

§ 70. One might regard the entire exposition (now concluded) of what I call the denial of the will as irreconcilable with the earlier explanation of necessity, which is relevant just as much to motivation as to every other form of the principle of sufficient reason. In consequence of necessity, motives are, like all causes, only occasional causes as a result of which the character unfolds its inner nature and reveals it with the inexorability of a natural law; it was on this account that earlier we absolutely denied freedom as *liberum arbitrium indifferentiae*. Far from contradicting this here, I would call it to mind. In truth, real freedom, (*i.e.*, independence of the principle of sufficient reason) belongs to the will only as a thing-in-itself and not to its manifestation, whose essential form everywhere is the principle of sufficient reason, the element or sphere of necessity. But the only circumstance in which that freedom can become directly visible in the manifestation, too, is when it makes an end of what is manifest; and because the mere manifestation – in so far as it is a link in the chain of causes, namely the living body – still continues to exist in time which contains only phenomena, the will which manifests itself through this phenomenon then stands in contradiction to it in denying what the phenomenon expresses. In these circumstances the genital organs, for example, as the visible form of the sexual impulse, are alive and well, yet no sexual gratification is desired, not even secretly. Although the whole body is only the visible expression of the will to life, the motives pertaining to this will are no longer active; indeed, the dissolution of the body, the end of the individual and therewith the greatest obstacle to the natural will, is welcome and desired.

Now, the contradiction between our asserting, on one hand, that the will is necessarily determined by motives in accordance with the character, and our asserting, on the other hand, that the will can be utterly suspended, whereby the motives become impotent – this contradiction is only the repetition in the reflection of philosophy of this *real* contradiction which results from the direct encroachment of the freedom of the will-in-itself, which knows no necessity, into the sphere of the necessity of its manifestation. But the key to reconciling these contradictions lies in the fact that the state in which the character is removed from the power of motives proceeds not directly from the will, but from a changed mode of knowledge. So long as the knowledge is merely that which is entrammeled in the *principium individuationis* and simply follows the principle of sufficient reason, the power of the motives is irresistible. But when the *principium individuationis* is seen through, and when the Ideas, and indeed the inner nature of the thing-in-itself, are directly recognised as the same will in everything, and from this recognition ensues a universal quieter of volition, then the individual motives become ineffective because the mode of knowledge pertaining to them is overshadowed and superseded by quite a different mode, and has passed into abeyance. Therefore the character can never change partially, but must, with the consistency of a law of Nature, implement in every detail the will it manifests as a whole. But this totality, the character itself, may be completely suspended or cancelled through the modification of knowledge, as we have outlined it above. It is this suspending or cancelling which Asmus (whom we have quoted above) marvels at, and defines as the 'catholic, transcendental change'; and it is the same thing as that which in the Christian Church was very appropriately called *rebirth*, and the insight from which it follows is what was called *the work of grace*. Just because it is not a question of a change, but of an entire suspending of the character, those characters affected, however different they may have been before it, show after it a great similarity in their conduct, though each of them, according to his notions and dogmas, still *talks* very differently.

In this sense, then, the old philosophical doctrine of the freedom of the will, which has constantly been contested and constantly maintained, is not without ground, and the Church dogma of the work of grace and the rebirth is not without sense and significance. But we now unexpectedly see the two coalesce as one, and we can also now understand in what sense the excellent Malebranche could say, 'La liberté est un mystère' [freedom is a mystery], and he was right. For precisely what the Christian mystics call *the work of grace* and *the rebirth* is for us the single direct expression of *the freedom of the will*. It appears only when the will, having attained to a knowledge of its own true nature, receives from this a *quieter,* and is thereby removed from the influence of the motives which lies in the province of another mode of knowledge, the objects of which are merely phenomena.

The potential for freedom which thus expresses itself is man's greatest prerogative (and it eternally eludes the animal), because its precondition is the reason's self-conscious deliberation, which, independent of the impression made by the present, enables him to survey the whole of life. The animal is entirely without the potential for freedom, as, indeed, it is without the potential for actual and thus deliberate free choice once it has passed beyond the stage at which motives are in complete conflict, since for such free choice the motives would have to be abstract ideas. Hence, with the same necessity with which a stone falls to the earth, the hungry wolf buries its fangs in the flesh of its prey, without being able to recognise that it is itself the mauled as well as mauler. *Necessity* is the *kingdom of nature; freedom* is the *kingdom of grace.*

Now because, as we have seen, that *suspending of the will* by the self comes from knowledge, but all knowledge and insight are as such independent of volition, that denial of will also, that passage to freedom, cannot be won by force of strategy, but comes from the intimate relationship of knowing and volition in man, and so comes suddenly, as if unbidden, from outside him. For this very reason the Church has called it *the work of grace*; and just as the Church makes the effect of grace further depend on the acceptance of grace, so the effect of the quieter, too, is in the last resort a free act of will. And because in consequence of such a work of grace the whole nature of man is changed and turned inside out from its foundation – so that he no longer wills any of what he previously willed so intensely, so that it really is as if a new man were actually taking the place of the old – the Church called this consequence of the work of grace *rebirth*. For what it calls the *natural man*, to which it denies all capacity for goodness, is the very will to life which must be denied if redemption is to be achieved from an existence such as ours. For behind our life something else is hiding, something we can reach only after we have shaken off this world.

Considering the idea of man in its unity (rather than considering individuals according to the principle of sufficient reason), Christian theology symbolises *nature, the affirmation of the will to life, in Adam.* His sin, bequeathed to us (that is, our being one with him in the Idea which in time is represented by the bond of procreation) makes us all partakers of suffering and eternal death. On the other hand, Christian doctrine symbolises *grace, the denial of the will, salvation* in God incarnate. Being free from all sinfulness, that is, from all willing of life, He cannot, like us, have resulted from the most pronounced affirmation of the will, nor can he, like us, have a body which is simply a concretion of will, manifestation of the will; but born of a pure virgin, he has only a phantom body. This last is the teaching of the Docetae, that is, of certain Church Fathers, who in this respect are very consistent. [. . .] Augustine writes that sin is already present in new-born children, but shows itself only after they have grown up. Yet the origin of this sin is to be traced to the will of the sinner. This sinner was Adam, but we all existed in him; Adam became wretched and in him we are all held to become wretched. Certainly, the doctrine of original sin (affirmation of the will) and of salvation (denial of the will) is the great truth which constitutes the essence of Christianity, while most of what remains is only the clothing of it, the drapery or accessories. Accordingly, Jesus Christ ought always to be conceived in the universal, as the symbol or personification of the denial of the will to life, but never individually, whether according to his mythical story in the Gospels, or according to the presumably true story which lies at its foundation. For neither the one nor the other will easily satisfy us entirely. It is merely the vehicle of that former version for the people, who always demand something factual. That in recent times Christianity has forgotten its true significance, and degenerated into banal optimism, does not concern us here.

It is, moreover, an original and Biblical doctrine of Christianity – which Augustine, with the approval of the heads of the Church, defended against the platitudes of the Pelagians, and which Luther aimed to purify from error and to emphasise, this being the chief ambition he explicitly claims in his book, *De Servo Arbitrio* – the doctrine that *the will is not free,* but from the start is subject to the inclination to evil. Thus the deeds of the will are always sinful and imperfect, and can never fully satisfy justice; and, finally, these works can never save us, but faith alone, a faith which itself springs not from deliberate intention and free choice, but comes to us as from outside ourselves, without our co-operation, through the *work of grace*. [. . .]

In the doctrine mentioned above we recognise the truth that is in complete agreement with the outcome of our own investigations. For we see that true virtue and holiness of disposition have their origin not in deliberate exercise of willing (works), but in knowledge, insight (faith), just as we, too, developed it from our key thought. If it were works, born of motives and deliberate intention, that led to salvation, then, however one might turn it, virtue would always be only a shrewd, methodical, far-seeing egoism. But the faith to which the Christian Church promises salvation is this: that, as through the Fall of the first man we are all partakers of sin and subject to death and perdition, so, too, through the divine mediator, through grace and His taking upon Himself our terrible guilt, are we all redeemed, without having done anything to deserve this ourselves, personally. For works, which may proceed from a person's intentional (*ie.* motive-determined) action, can never justify us, from the very nature of that action, just because it is *intentional*, and produced by motives, *opus operatum*. Thus in this faith there is implied, first of all, that our condition is in its origin and in its essence an incurable one, from which we need *redemption*; then, that we ourselves essentially belong to evil, and are so firmly mortgaged to it that the works we perform according to law and precept, *i.e.*, according to motives, can never satisfy justice nor redeem us; but that redemption is won only through faith, *i.e.* through an altered mode of knowing, and this faith can come only through grace, thus as though from outside ourselves. This means that the salvation is one quite alien to our person, and indicates that a denial and surrender of this person is necessary to salvation. Works, the observance of the law as such, can never justify, because they are always action from motives. [. . .]

Here I have introduced these tenets of Christian theology which are in themselves alien to philosophy, merely to show that the ethics emerging from our whole study (and which precisely agrees with, and is integrated with, all its parts), although in its expression perhaps new and startling, is in its real nature by no means so, but fully agrees with authentic Christian doctrine, and was, indeed, in essence implied in it. It also agrees just as precisely with the doctrines and ethical teachings of the sacred books of India, teachings which are presented in forms that are quite different again. At the same time, the calling to mind of the dogmas of the Christian Church served to explain and illustrate the apparent contradiction between the inevitability with which character expressed itself under the stimulus of certain motives (the kingdom of Nature) on the one hand, and the freedom of the will in itself, to deny itself, and to suspend the character with all the inevitability of the motives based on this character (the kingdom of grace), on the other hand.

§ 71. In concluding this general account of ethics, and with it the whole development of that one thought which it has been my purpose to impart, I by no means wish to conceal a criticism that relates to this last part of my exposition, but rather to point out that it inheres in the nature of the material, and that it cannot be helped. It is this, that after our study has finally reached the point at which in perfect holiness we see the denial and surrender of all volition – and thereby the redemption from a world whose whole existence presented itself to us as suffering – this appears to us as a transition into *empty nothingness*.

On this I must first remark that the concept of *nothing* is essentially relative, and always refers to a definite 'something' which it negates. This quality has been attributed (by Kant) merely to the *nihil privativum*, which is indicated by − as opposed to +. This −, from an opposite point of view, might become +, and in opposition to this *nihil privativum* has set up *nihil negativum* which would in every respect be nothing; and as an example of this we have used the logical contradiction which cancels itself out. But more closely considered, no absolute nothing, no actual *nihil negativum* is even thinkable; but everything of this kind, when considered from a higher standpoint or subsumed under a wider concept, is always merely a *nihil privativum*. Every nothing is such only when thought of in relation to something else, and presupposes this relation, and thus also this something else. Even a logical contradiction is only a relative nothing. It is not a thought of reason, but it is not on that account an absolute nothing; for it is a combination of words; it is an example of the unthinkable, which is necessary in logic in order to prove the laws of thought. So, if for this purpose we seek such an example, we will hold fast to the nonsense as being the positive which we are in search of, and pass over the sense as the negative. Thus every *nihil negativum* or absolute nothingness, if subordinated to a higher concept, will appear as a mere *nihil privativum* or relative nothing, which can, moreover, always exchange signs with what it negates, so that the former would then be thought of as negation, and it would itself be thought of as assertion. [. . .]

What is generally accepted as positive, which we call *being*, and the negation of which is expressed by the concept *nothing* in its most general sense, is precisely the world as idea, which I have shown to be the objectivity and mirror of the will. We ourselves are this will and this world, and to it belongs all ideation, as one aspect of them. The form of the Idea is space and time, hence everything which for this point of view is being, must *be* in some place and at some time. Then the concept – the material of philosophy – and finally the word – the sign of the concept – also belong to the idea. Denial, suspension, conversion of the will are also the suspension and the disappearance of the world, its mirror. If we no longer glimpse the will in this mirror, we ask in vain where it has gone, and then, because it has no longer any *where* and *when*, we lament that it has strayed into nothingness, and is lost.

An opposite viewpoint, if it were possible for us, would exchange the signs, to designate as 'nothing' what for us is being, and to designate as 'being' what for us is nothing. But as long as we ourselves are the will to life, this latter – 'nothing' as the 'being' – we can know and define only negatively, because Empedocles' old motto that 'like can be known only by like' deprives us at this very point of all knowledge, just as, conversely, on just this ultimately depends the possibility of all our actual knowledge, *i.e.*, the world as idea, or the will's objectivity. For the world is the will's self-knowledge.

If, however, it should be absolutely insisted upon that in some way or other a positive knowledge should be gained of what philosophy can express only negatively as the denial of the will, we could only refer to that state experienced by all those who have attained to complete denial of the will, and which has been variously denoted by the names 'ecstasy', 'rapture', 'illumination', 'union with God', and so forth. But this state cannot properly be called knowledge, because it has no longer the form of subject and object, and is, moreover, accessible only to one's own experience and cannot be communicated at second hand.

We, however, who are committed to the standpoint of philosophy, must be satisfied here with negative knowledge, content to have reached the outer limits of the positive. If we have recognised the inner nature of the world as will, and in all its phenomena we have recognised only the objectivity of will; and if we have followed this objectivity from the mindless impulse of obscure natural energies till it ensues in the completely conscious action of man, then we will not evade the consequence that with the free denial, the surrender of the will, all those phenomena are also suspended. That constant strain and stress without purpose and without rest, at all the grades of objectivity, that strain and stress in which and through which the world consists; the variety of forms succeeding one another in gradation; the whole manifestation of the will; and, finally, also the universal forms of this manifestation, time and space, and also its ultimate fundamental form, subject and object – all are suspended. No will: no idea, no world.

Before us, certainly, remains only nothingness. But what resists this disintegration into nothing, our nature, is simply only the will to life, and we ourselves are that will, just as the will is our world. That we so abhor annihilation is simply another way of saying that we so want life, and that we are nothing but this will, and know nothing besides it. But we turn our eyes away from our own pitiable and preoccupied condition to those who have overcome the world, in whom the will, having attained to perfect self-knowledge, found itself again in everything, and then freely denied itself, and who then merely wait to see the last trace of it vanish with the body which it animates. Then, instead of the restless strain and stress, instead of our passing continually from wish to fear, and from joy to sorrow, instead of the never-satisfied yet never-dying hope which, for the person who wills, constitutes life's dream, we shall see that peace which 'passeth all understanding', that total tranquillity of mind, that profound calm, that unshakeable confidence and serenity. Merely reflected in the face, as Raphael and Correggio have depicted it, this is a divine message, complete and trustworthy. Only knowledge remains, the will has vanished.

But we look with profound and painful longing on this condition, in contrast with which our own hopeless plight stands fully illuminated. Yet this is the only thought which can give us lasting consolation, when, on the one hand, we have recognised incurable suffering and endless misery as essential to the will's manifestation, the world; and, on the other hand, we see the world disintegrate once the will has been suspended, leaving us only empty nothingness. So, in this way, by contemplating the lives of holy men – whom we are rarely privileged to meet in person but whom we encounter through written records and (where its authenticity is hall-marked) through art – we must dispel the gloomy impression of that nothingness which looms behind all virtue and holiness as their ultimate aspiration, and which we fear as children fear the dark; we must dispel it rather than evade it, as do the Indians through myths and empty phrases like reabsorption in *Brahma*, and as do the Buddhists through their *Nirvana*. Rather, we freely acknowledge that what remains after the will has been totally suspended is, for all those who are still full of will, nothing; but, conversely, too, to those in whom the will has turned about and has denied itself, this world of ours, real as it is, with all its suns and galaxies, is – nothing.

On the Metaphysics of Sexual Love

[...] One can doubt neither the reality nor the importance of the matter [*i.e.*, sexual love]: and so, instead of being amazed that a philosopher, too, should for once take up this theme, which is the perennial theme of all writers, one ought rather to be amazed that a subject which ordinarily plays so important a part in human life has till now barely been considered at all by philosophers, and is available to us as raw material. [...] So I have no predecessors either to make use of or to refute. The subject has forced itself upon me objectively, and has entered of its own accord into the context of my reflection on the world. Moreover, I can expect least acclaim from those who are themselves swayed by this passion, and who accordingly seek to express their immoderate emotions in the sublimest and most ethereal of figurative language. To them my view will appear too physical, too material, however metaphysical and even transcendent it really may be. Let them, for the moment, reflect that if the source of their inspiration for today's madrigals and sonnets had been born eighteen years earlier, they would scarcely have cast her a glance.

For the state of being in love, though it may pose as ethereal, is rooted in the sexual impulse alone; indeed, it is only a more closely determined, specialised, and (in the strictest sense) individualised sexual impulse. With this firmly in mind we will consider the important part played by sexual love in all its degrees and nuances, not only on the stage and in novels, but in the real world, too. Here it proves to be, next to the love of life, the strongest and most active of all motives, and continuously claims half the energies and thoughts of the younger part of mankind. It is the ultimate goal of almost all human endeavour, exerts an adverse influence on the most important affairs, interrupts the most serious business at any hour, sometimes for a while confuses even the greatest minds, does not hesitate with its trumpery to disrupt the negotiations of statesmen and the research of scholars, has the knack of slipping its love-letters and ringlets even into ministerial portfolios and philosophical manuscripts. Every day it contrives the worst and most intractable quarrels, destroys the most valuable relationships, ruptures the most durable bonds. It requires the sacrifice sometimes of life or health, sometimes of wealth, rank, and happiness. It makes unscrupulous those who were once honest, and makes traitors of those who have till now been loyal.

Generally, then, it plays the part of a malevolent demon who is trying to pervert, confuse, and overthrow everything. We will be forced to cry, What's all this noise about? Why the pushing, fretting, and fuming, the anxiety and distress? It is merely a matter of every Jack's finding his Jill.[1] Why should such a trifle play so important a part, and incessantly bring disturbance and confusion to this human life which is so well regulated? But to the serious researcher the spirit of truth gradually reveals the answer. What we are talking about here is no mere trifle; on the contrary, the importance lent to the matter is altogether appropriate to the seriousness and ardour of the activity itself. The ultimate purpose behind all love-affairs, whether played in sock or buskin, really is more important than all other purpose in human life, and is hence entirely worthy of the profound seriousness with which everyone pursues it. For what is decided by this means is nothing less than *the composition of the next generation*. The *dramatis personae* who will walk onto the stage when we have left it are determined here, in respect both of the life they will live and of their personal qualities, by these frivolous love-affairs. Just as the being, the *existentia*, of these future people is conditioned by our sexual impulse generally, so their nature, *essentia*, is entirely conditioned by individual choice in the gratification of the impulse, that is, by sexual love, and is in every respect irrevocably determined by this. This is the key to the problem. [. . .]

What presents itself to the individual consciousness as sexual impulse in general, and without being directed towards a specific individual of the opposite sex, is, in itself and over and above the phenomenon, simply the will to life. But what is manifest in consciousness as a sexual impulse directed to a specific individ-

---

[1] I have not ventured to express myself distinctly here: the courteous reader must therefore translate the phrase into Aristophanic language.

ual is in itself the will to live as a quite specific individual. In this situation the sexual impulse, although in itself a subjective need, has the knack of skilfully assuming the mask of objective admiration and thereby deceiving our consciousness; for nature requires this stratagem to achieve its own purposes. But whenever two people fall in love, however objective and touched even by the sublime their admiration may seem, nature's sole intention is the procreation of an individual of specific qualities. This is confirmed first and foremost by the fact that the essential element is not, as we might expect, reciprocal love, but possession, that is, physical enjoyment. To be confident of the first cannot console us at all for our being deprived of the second; on the contrary, in such a situation many a one has shot himself. On the other hand, people who are deeply in love content themselves, when they cannot gain love in return, with possession, that is, with physical enjoyment. All forced marriages offer evidence of this, as does the buying of a woman's favour, in spite of her aversion, by means of generous gifts or other offerings; and so, even, do instances of rape. The true purpose behind the whole love-story – although the parties concerned do not know it – is the production of this particular child; how this purpose is attained is a secondary consideration. Here highminded people, those of superior sensibility, and especially those who are in love, may object noisily to the gross realism of my view, but they are mistaken. For surely the precise determination of the individual personalities of the next generation is a much nobler and more deserving purpose than those exuberant emotions and soap-bubbles of theirs. Can there, indeed, of all the purposes on earth, be any which is greater or more important? It alone corresponds to the depth with which passionate love is felt, to the seriousness with which it presents itself, and the importance which it attributes even to the trifling details of its own time and place. Only in so far as this purpose is assumed to be the true one, do the difficulties, the endless exertions and annoyances endured for the attainment of the love-object, seem appropriate. For it is the future generation, in all of its individual determinateness, that is struggling into existence by means of those efforts and exertions. This future generation is already astir in that wary, specific and capricious choice made to satisfy the sexual impulse – the choice which we call love. The increasing affection between two lovers is, even now, really the will to life of the new individual which they can and would like to engender. From the moment when their eyes first meet with longing, this new life is kindled, and it announces itself as a future individuality, harmoniously and well integrated. They feel the longing for an actual union and fusion into a single being, in order to live henceforth only as this; and this longing is fulfilled in the child they engender. In this child the qualities passed on by both parents are fused and united in one being, and so they will live on.

APPENDIX

Abstract[1] of Schopenhauer's essay *On the Fourfold Root of the Principle of Sufficient Reason*

This essay is divided into eight chapters. The first is introductory. The second contains an historical review of previous philosophical doctrines on the subject. The third deals with the insufficiency of the previous treatment of the principle, and prescribes the lines of the new departure. The fourth, fifth, sixth and seventh treat of the four classes of objects for the subject, and the forms of the principle of sufficient reason which respectively characterise these classes. The eighth contains general remarks and results. It will be convenient to summarise these chapters severally.

Chapter I

Schopenhauer points out that Plato and Kant agree in recommending, as the method of all knowledge, obedience to two laws: – that of homogeneity, and that of specification. The former bids us, by attention to the points of resemblance and agreement in things, get at their kinds, and combine them into species, and these species again into genera, until we have arrived at the highest concept of all, that which embraces everything. This law being transcendental, or an essential in our faculty of reason, assumes that nature is in harmony with it, an assumption which is expressed in the old rule: 'Entities should not be multiplied unnecessarily.' The law of Specification, on the other hand, is stated by Kant in these words: 'The number and variety of entities is not to be limited without good reason.' That is to say, we must carefully distinguish the species which are united under a genus, and the lower kinds which in their

---

[1] Reprinted from Haldane and Kemp's translation.

turn are united under these species; taking care not to make a leap, and subsume the lower kinds and individuals under the concept of genus, since this is always capable of division, but never descends to the object of pure perception. Plato and Kant agree that these laws are transcendental, and that they presuppose that things are in harmony with them.

The previous treatment of the principle of sufficient reason, even by Kant, has been a failure, owing to the neglect of the second of these laws. It may well be that we shall find that this principle is the common expression of more than one fundamental principle of knowledge, and that the necessity, to which it refers, is therefore of different kinds. It may be stated in these words: 'There is nothing without a reason why it should be rather than not be.' This is the general expression for the different forms of the assumption which everywhere justifies that question 'Why?' which is the mother of all science.

Chapter II

Schopenhauer in this chapter traces historically the forms in which the principle had been stated by his predecessors, and their influence. He points out that in Greek philosophy it appeared in two aspects – that of the necessity of a ground for a logical judgment, and that of a cause for every physical change – and that these two aspects were systematically confounded. The Aristotelian division, not of the forms of the principle itself, but of one of its aspects, the causal, exemplified a confusion which continued throughout the Scholastic period. Descartes succeeds no better. His proof of the existence of God, that the immensity of His nature is a *cause or reason* beyond which no cause is needed for His existence, simply illustrates the gross confusion between cause and ground of knowledge which underlies every form of this ontological proof. 'That a miserable fellow like Hegel, whose entire philosophy is nothing but a monstrous amplification of the ontological proof, should dare to defend this proof against Kant's criticism of it is an alliance of which the ontological proof itself, little as it knows of shame, might well feel ashamed. It is not to be expected I should speak respectfully of people who have brought philosophy into disrespect.' Spinoza made the same confusion when he laid it down that the cause of existence was either contained in the nature and definition of the thing as it existed, or was to be found outside that thing. It was through this confusion of the ground of knowledge with the efficient cause that he succeeds in identifying God with the world. The true picture of Spinoza's 'Causa sui' [cause of itself] is Baron Münchhausen encircling his horse with his legs, and raising himself and the horse upwards by means of his pigtail, with the inscription 'Causa sui' written below. Leibnitz was the first to place the principle of sufficient reason in the position of a first principle, and to indicate the difference between its two meanings. But it was Wolff who first completely distinguished them, and divided the doctrine into three kinds: *principium fiendi* (becoming) *principium essendi* (being), and *principium cognoscendi* (knowing). Baumgarten, Reimarus, Lambert, and Platner added nothing to the work of Wolff, and the next great step was Hume's question as to the validity of the principle. Kant's distinction of the logical or formal principle of knowledge – Every *proposition* must have its ground; from the transcendental or material principle, Every *thing* must have its ground – was followed out by his immediate successors. But when we come to Schelling we find the proposition that gravitation is the *reason* and light the *cause* of things, a proposition which is quoted simply as a curiosity, for such a piece of nonsense deserves no place among the opinions of earnest and honest inquirers. The chapter concludes by pointing out the futility of the attempts to prove the principle. Every proof is the exhibition of the ground of a judgement which has been expressed, and of which, just because that ground is exhibited, we predicate truth. The principle of sufficient reason is just this expression of the demand for such a ground, and he who seeks a proof, *i.e.*, the exhibition of a ground for this principle itself, presupposes it as true, and so falls into the circle of seeking a proof of the justification of the demand for proof.

Chapter III

In the third chapter Schopenhauer points out that the two applications of the principle of sufficient reason distinguished by his predecessors, to judgements, which must have a ground, and to the changes of real objects, which must have a cause, are not exhaustive. The reason why the three sides of a certain triangle are equal is that the angles are equal, and this is neither logical deduction nor a case of causation. With a view to stating exhaustively the various kinds into which the application of the principle falls it is necessary to determine the nature of the principle itself. All our ideas are objects of the subject, and all objects of the subject are our ideas. But our ideas stand to one another as a matter of fact in an orderly connection, which is always determinable *a priori* in point of form, and on account of which nothing that is in itself separate and wholly independent of other things can be the object of our consciousness. It is this connection which the principle of sufficient reason in its generality expresses. The relations which constitute it are what Schopenhauer calls its root, and they fall into four classes, which are discussed in the four following chapters.

Chapter IV

In the fourth chapter Schopenhauer deals with the first class of objects for the subject and the form of the principle of sufficient reason which obtains in it. This first class is that of those complete ideas of perception which form part of our experience, and which are referable to some sensation of our bodies. These ideas are capable of being perceived only under the forms of space and time. If time were the only form there would be no coexistence, and therefore no persistence. If space were their only form there would be no succession, and therefore no change. Time may therefore be defined as the possibility of mutually exclusive conditions of the same thing. But the union of these two forms of existence is the essential condition of reality, and this union is the work of the understanding (see *World as Will and Idea*, § 4). In this class of objects for the subject the principle of sufficient reason appears as the law of causality or the principle of sufficient reason of becoming, and it is through it that all objects which present themselves in perception are bound together through the changes of their states. When a new state of one or more objects makes its appearance it must have been preceeded by another on which it regularly follows. This is causal sequence, and the first state is the cause, the second the effect. The law has thus to do exclusively with the *changes* of objects of external experience, and not with things themselves, a circumstance which is fatal to the validity of the cosmological proof of the existence of God. It follows also from the essential connection of causality with succession that the notion of reciprocity, with its contemporaneous existence of cause and effect, is a delusion. The chain of causes and effects does not affect either matter, which is that in which all changes take place, or the original forces of nature, through which causation becomes possible, and which exist apart from all change, and in this sense out of time, but which yet are everywhere present (*e.g.* chemical forces; see *supra*, § 26). In nature causation assumes three different forms; that of cause in the narrow sense, of stimulus, and of motive, on which differences depend the true distinctions between inorganic bodies, plants, and animals. It is only of cause properly so called that Newton's third law of the equality of action and reaction is true, and only here do we find the degree of the effect proportionate to that of the cause. The absence of this feature characterises stimulation. Motive demands knowledge as its condition, and intelligence is therefore the true characteristic of the animal. The three forms are in principle identical, the difference being due to the degrees of receptivity in existence. What is called freedom of the will is therefore an absurdity, as is also Kant's 'Practical Reason'. These results are followed by an examination of the nature of vision, which Schopenhauer sums up in these words: 'I have examined all these visual processes in detail in order to show that the understanding is active in all of them, the understanding which, by apprehending every change as an effect and referring it to its cause, creates on the basis of the *a priori* and fundamental intuitions or perceptions of space and time, the objective world, that phenomenon of the brain, for which the sensations of the senses afford only certain data. And this task the understanding accomplishes only through its proper form, the law of causality, and accomplishes it directly without the aid of reflection, that is, of abstract knowledge through concepts and words, which are the material of secondary knowledge, of thought, thus of the Reason.' 'What understanding knows aright is reality; what reason knows aright is truth, *i.e.*, a judgement which has a ground; the opposite of the former being illusion (what is falsely perceived), of the latter error (what is falsely thought).' All understanding is an immediate apprehension of the causal relation, and this is the sole function of understanding, and not the complicated working of the twelve Kantian Categories, the theory of which is a mistaken one. A consequence of this conclusion is that arithmetical processes do not belong to the understanding, concerned as they are with abstract conceptions. But it must not be forgotten that between volition and the apparently consequential action of the body there is no causal relation, for they are the same thing perceived in two different ways. Section 23 contains a detailed refutation of Kant's proof of the *a priori* nature of the causal relation in the 'Second Analogy of Experience' of the *Critique of Pure Reason*, the gist of the objection being that the so-called subjective succession is as much objective in reality as what is called objective by Kant: 'Phenomena may well follow one another, without following *from* one another.'

Chapter V

The fifth chapter commences with an examination of the distinction between man and the animals. Man possesses *reason*, that is to say, he has a class of ideas of which the animals are not capable, *abstract* ideas as distinguished from those ideas of perception from which the former kind are yet derived. The consequence is, that the animal neither speaks nor laughs, and lacks all those qualities which make human life great. The nature of *motives*, too, is different where abstract ideas are possible. No doubt the actions of men follow of necessity from their causes, not less than is the case with the animals, but the kind of sequence through thought which renders choice possible *i.e.*, the conscious conflict of motives, is different. Our abstract ideas, being incapable of being objects of perception, would be outside consciousness, and the operations of thought would be impossible, were it not that they are fixed for sense by arbitrary signs called words, which therefore always indicate *general* conceptions. It is just because the animals are incapable of general conceptions that they have no faculty of speech. But thought does not consist in the mere presence of abstract ideas in consciousness, but in the union and separation of two or more of them, subject to the manifold restrictions and modifications which logic deals with. Such a clearly expressed conceptual relation is a judgement. In relation to judgements the principle of sufficient reason is valid in a new form: that of the ground of knowing. In this form it asserts that if a judgement is to express knowledge it must have a ground; and it is just because it has a ground that it has ascribed to it the predicate true. The grounds on which a judgement may depend are divisible into four kinds. A judgement may have another judgement as its ground, in which case its truth is formal or *logical*. There is no truth except in the relation of a judgement to something outside it, and intrinsic truth, which is sometimes distinguished from extrinsic logical truth, is therefore an absurdity. A judgement may also have its ground in sense-perception, and its truth is then material truth. Again, those forms of knowledge which lie in the understanding and in pure sensibility, as the conditions of the possibility of experience, may be the ground of a judgement which is then synthetical *a priori*. Finally, those formal conditions of all thinking which lie in the reason may be the ground of a judgement, which may in that case be called metalogically true. Of these metalogical judgements there are four, and they were long ago discovered and called laws of thought. (1) A subject is equal to the sum of its predicates. (2) A subject cannot at once have a given predicate affirmed and denied of it. (3) Of two contradictorily opposed predicates one must belong to every subject. (4) Truth is the relation of a judgement to something outside it as its sufficient reason. Reason, it may be remarked, has no material but only formal truth.

Chapter VI

The third class of objects for the subject is constituted by the formal element in perception, the forms of outer and inner sense, space and time. This class of ideas, in which time and space appear as pure intuitions, is distinguished from that other class in which they are objects of perception by the presence of matter which has been shown to be the perceptibility of time and space in one aspect, and causality which has become objective, in another. Space and time have this property, that all their parts stand to one another in a relation in which each is determined and conditioned by another. This relation is peculiar, and is intelligible to us neither through understanding nor through reason, but solely through pure intuition or perception *a priori*. And the law according to which the parts of space and time thus determine one another is called the law of sufficient reason of *being*. In space every position is determined with reference to every other position, so that the first stands to the second in the relation of a consequence to its ground. In time every moment is conditioned by that which precedes it. The ground of being, in the form of the law of sequence, is here very simple owing to the circumstance that time has only one dimension. On the nexus of the position of the parts of space depends the entire science of geometry. Ground of *knowledge* produces *conviction* only, as distinguished from *insight* into the ground of *being*. Thus it is that the attempt which even Euclid at times makes, to produce *conviction*, as distinguished from insight into the ground of being, in geometry, is a mistake, and induces aversions to mathematics in many an admirable mind.

Chapter VII

The remaining class of objects for the subject is a very peculiar and important one. It comprehends only one object, the immediate object of inner sense, the subject in volition which becomes an object of knowledge, but only in inner sense, and therefore always in time and never in space; and in time only under limitations. There can be no knowledge of knowledge, for that would imply that the subject had separated itself from knowledge, and yet knew knowledge, which is impossible. The subject is the condition of the existence of ideas, and can never itself become idea or object. It knows itself therefore never as *knowing*, but only as *willing*. Thus what we know in ourselves is never what knows, but what wills, the will. The identity of the subject of volition with the subject of knowledge, through which the world 'I' includes both, is the insoluble problem. The identity of the knowing with the known is inexplicable, and yet is immediately present. The operation of a motive is not, like that of all other causes, known only from without, and therefore indirectly, but also from within. Motivation is, in fact, causality viewed from within.

Chapter VIII

In this, the concluding chapter, Schopenhauer sums up his results. Necessity has no meaning other than that of the irresistible sequence of the effect where the cause is given. All necessity is thus conditioned, and absolute or unconditioned necessity is a contradiction in terms. And there is a fourfold necessity corresponding to the four forms of the principle of sufficient reason: – (1) The logical form, according to the principle of the ground of knowledge; on account of which, if the premisses are given, the conclusion follows. (2) The physical form, according to the law of causality; on account of which, if the cause is given, the effect must follow. (3) The mathematical form, according to the law of being; on account of which every relation expressed by a true geometrical proposition is what it is affirmed to be, and every correct calculation is irrefutable. (4) The moral form, on account of which every human being and every animal must, when the motive appears, perform the only act which accords with the inborn and unalterable character. A consequence of this is, that every department of science has one or other of the forms of the principle of sufficient reason as its basis. In conclusion, Schopenhauer points out that just because the principle of sufficient reason belongs to the *a priori* element in intelligence, it cannot be applied to the entirety of things, to the universe as inclusive of intelligence. Such a universe is mere phenomenon, and what is only true because it belongs to the form of intelligence can have no application to intelligence itself. Thus it is that it cannot be said that the universe and all things in it exist because of something else. In other words, the cosmological proof of the existence of God is inadmissible.

SCHOPENHAUER AND HIS CRITICS

The following extracts from both critics and admirers of Schopenhauer present a range of responses to his work. This survey should also give some indication of the vicissitudes of his philosophical fortunes over the past 150 years.

J. Oxenford, 'Iconoclasm in German Philosophy' (1853):

... while Schopenhauer's teaching is the most genial, the most ingenious, and – we would add, the most amusing that can be imagined, the doctrine taught is the most disheartening, the most repulsive, the most opposed to the aspirations of the present world ... We only wish we could see among the philosophers of modern Germany a writer of equal power, comprehensiveness, ingenuity and erudition, ranged on a side more in harmony with our own feelings and convictions, than that adopted by this misanthropic sage of Frankfurt.

Richard Wagner, Letter to Liszt, December 1854:

Apart from progressing on my music, I have of late occupied myself exclusively with a man who has come like a gift from heaven, although only a literary one, into my solitude. This is Arthur Schopenhauer, the greatest philosopher since Kant ... The German professors ignored him very prudently for forty years; but recently, to the disgrace of Germany, he has been discovered by an English critic. All the Hegels, etc. are charlatans by the side of him. His chief idea, the final negation of desire of life, is terribly serious, but it shows the only salvation possible.[1]

Friedrich Nietzsche, *The Birth of Tragedy* (1872):

The extraordinary courage and wisdom of Kant and Schopenhauer have succeeded in gaining the most difficult victory, the victory over the optimism concealed in the essence of logic – the optimism that is the basis of our culture.

Nietzsche, *Twilight of the Idols* (1888):

Schopenhauer, the last German worthy of consideration ... is for a psychologist a first-rate case: namely, as a maliciously ingenious attempt to adduce in favour of a nihilistic total depreciation of life precisely the counter-instances, the great self-affirmations of the 'will to life', life forms of exuberance. He has interpreted art, heroism, genius, beauty, great sympathy, knowledge, the will to truth, and tragedy, in turn, as consequences of 'negation' ... – the greatest psychological counterfeit in all history, not counting Christianity.[2]

William James, 'German Pessimism' (1875):

It was reserved for Schopenhauer to show his countrymen that the cursing and melting moods could be kept alive permanently, and extended indefinitely by making proper theoretic deliberation; and Schopenhauer's disciple [E. Von] Hartmann, whose work [the *Philosophy of the Unconscious*] has met with one of the greatest literary successes of the time, and carried the new gospel into regions where the torch of metaphysics had never yet begun to glimmer ...

[Schopenhauer] is assuredly one of the greatest of writers. When such a one expatiates upon the texts of *Homo homini lupus* and Woman the focus of the world's illusion, he will have all the cynics with a taste for good literature for his admirers. And when he preaches compassion to be the one cardinal virtue, and morbidly reiterates the mystic Sanskrit motto, *Tat twan asi* – This (maniac or cripple) art thou – as the truth of truths, he will of course exert a spell over persons in the unwholesome sentimental moulting-time of youth. But the thing which to our Anglo-Saxon mind seems so outlandish is that crowds of dapper fellows, revelling in animal spirits and conscious strength, should enroll themselves in cold blood as his permanent apostles ...

George Moore, Preface, *Confessions* (1889):

I owe much of my mind to Schopenhauer; but I will not say here that if these confessions induce any one to turn to *The World as Will and Idea*, they will have effected their purpose. My book was written to be read, not to help another book to be read.

C. Lombroso, *The Man of Genius* (1891):

The most complete type of madness in genius is presented to us by Schopenhauer ... [He] told Frauenstädt that at the time when he was writing his great work [*W. W. I.*] he must have been very strange in his person and behaviour, as people took him for mad ... He was contradiction personified. He placed annihilation, nirvana, as the final aim of life, and predicted (which means that he desired) one hundred years of life. He preached sexual abstinence as a duty, but did not himself practise it.

Josiah Royce, *The Spirit of Modern Philosophy* (1892):

The way to meet Schopenhauer's pessimism is, not to refute its assertions, but to grapple practically with its truths.

V. I. Lenin, *Materialism and Empirio-criticism* (1909):

But on the question of the will [Ernst Mach] is not content with confusion and half-hearted agnosticism: he goes much further. '... Our sensation of hunger', we read in [his *Mechanics*], 'is not so essentially different from the pressure of the stone on its support ...' [So] there is possible an idealism which recognizes the world as will.... [He is] not averse to coquetting with an idealism like Schopenhauer's!

Hans Vaihinger, *The Philosophy 'As If'* (1924):

Schopenhauer's pessimism became in me a fundamental and lasting state of consciousness, and all the more so because of my own sad and difficult experience. Even in earlier days I had been deeply affected by Schiller's lines 'Who can enjoy life, if he sees into its depths!' I have not found that this outlook tends to weaken biological and moral energy. On the contrary, I am one of those whom only pessimism enables to endure life, and to whom pessimism gives the ethical strength to work and fight for themselves as well as to help others. On the other hand, I believe that pessimism has given me a more objective view of reality.

Sigmund Freud, 'A Difficulty in the Path of Psychoanalysis' (1917):

... above all [our forerunners] is the great thinker Schopenhauer, whose unconscious 'Will' is equivalent to the mental instincts of psychoanalysis. It was this same thinker, moreover, who in words of unforgettable impressiveness admonished mankind of the importance, still so greatly under-estimated by it, of its sexual craving.

Sigmund Freud, *New Introductory Lectures*, xxxii (1933):

You may perhaps shrug your shoulders and say; 'That [theory of the death instinct] isn't natural science, it's Schopenhauer's philosophy!' But, Ladies and Gentlemen, why should not a bold thinker have guessed something that is afterwards confirmed by sober and painstaking detailed research?[3]

Thomas Mann, *The Living Thoughts of Schopenhauer* (1939):

This [account of the aesthetic state] is one of the greatest and profoundest of Schopenhauer's perceptions and however frightful the accents he commands in describing the tortures of the will and the domination of the will, in equal degree his prose discovers seraphic tones, his gratitude speaks with surpassing exuberance, when abundantly and exhaustively he discourses on the blessings of art.

Albert Einstein, *The World as I See It* (1940):

Schopenhauer's saying, that 'a man can do as he will, but not will as he will', has been an inspiration to me since my youth up, and a continual consolation and unfailing well-spring of patience in the face of the hardships of life, my own and others.

Bertrand Russell, *History of Western Philosophy* (1945):

[Schopenhauer] began the emphasis on will which is characteristic of much nineteenth and twentieth century philosophy ...

In one form or another, this doctrine that the will is primary has been held by many modern philosophers, notably, Nietzsche, Bergson, James and Dewey.

C. G. Jung, *Memories, Dreams, Reflections* (1961):

But the great find resulting from my researches was Schopenhauer ... Here at last was a philosopher who had the courage to see that all was not for the best in the fundaments of the universe ... Schopenhauer's sombre picture of the world had my undivided approval, but not his solution of the problem.

G. E. M. Anscombe, *Introduction to Wittgenstein's Tractatus* (1959):

As a boy of sixteen Wittgenstein had read Schopenhauer and had been greatly impressed by Schopenhauer's theory of the 'world as idea' (although not of the 'world as will'); Schopenhauer then struck him as fundamentally right, if only a few adjustments and clarifications were made ... If we look for Wittgenstein's philosophical ancestry we must ... look to Schopenhauer; specifically to his 'solipsism', his conception of 'the limit' and his ideas on value will be better understood in the light of Schopenhauer than of any other philosopher.

M. O'C. Drury, 'Some Notes on Conversations with Wittgenstein' (1976):

There are two words which were frequently used by Wittgenstein, 'deep' and 'shallow'. I remember him saying: 'Kant and Berkeley seem to me to be very deep thinkers. But in Schopenhauer I seem to see to the bottom very quickly.'

Karl Popper, *The Open Society and its Enemies* (4th ed. 1962):

... I wish to show how difficult and, at the same time, how urgent it is to continue Schopenhauer's fight against this shallow cant [of Hegelianism] ...

Max Horkheimer, 'Schopenhauer Today' (1967):

What Schopenhauer declared about individuals – that they are an expression of the blind will to existence and well-being – is at present becoming apparent with regard to social, political and racial groups in the whole world. That is one of the reasons why his doctrine appears to me as the philosophic thought that is a match for reality. Its freedom from illusions is something it shares with enlightened politics . . . There are few ideas that the world needs more than Schopenhauer's – ideas which in the face of utter hopelessness, because they confront it, know more than any others of hope.[4]

George Lukas, *The Destruction of Reason* (1973):

. . . with Schopenhauer begins the fateful role of German philosophy: to be the ideological guide of extreme reaction.

J. P. Stern, *Hitler* (1975):

Hitler's deadly seriousness, his singlemindedness and his commitment all issue from this notion of 'my adamant Will'. The origin of this notion and of its vocabulary in Schopenhauer and Nietzsche is a commonplace in the history of ideas . . . although it is very unlikely that Hitler ever read Schopenhauer at all extensively (in spite of repeatedly claiming that 'in the trenches I read and re-read the little volumes until they fell apart') . . .

References

1. Quoted in B. Magee, *The Philosophy of Schopenhauer* (1983).

2. From translations by W. Kaufmann, *The Birth of Tragedy* (New York, 1967) and *The Portable Nietzsche* (New York, 1962).

3. From the *Standard Edition*, gen. ed. J. Strachey (London, 1964) xxii.

4. Printed in M. Fox (ed.), *Schopenhauer* (1980).

SUGGESTIONS FOR FURTHER READING

After the *The World as Will and Idea*, Schopenhauer's most important works are:

On the Fourfold Root of the Principle of Sufficient Reason, trans. by E. F. J. Payne (La Salle, 1974).

On the Basis of Morality, trans. by E. F. J. Payne (La Salle, 1965).

On the Freedom of the Will in Nature, trans. by K. Kolenda (La Salle, 1960).

The Will in Nature, trans. by E. F. J. Payne (New York, 1993), ed. by D. E. Cartwright.

Manuscript Remains, 4 vols., ed. by A. Hübscher, trans. by E. F. J. Payne (Oxford, 1985).

Parerga and Paralipomena, 2 vols., trans. by E. F. J. Payne (Oxford, 1974).

Secondary Works

H. Zimmern, *Arthur Schopenhauer: His Life and Philosophy* (London, 1876).

W. Wallace, *Life and Writings of Arthur Schopenhauer* (London, circa 1890).

T. Whittaker, *Schopenhauer* (London, 1909).

Patrick Gardiner, *Schopenhauer* (Penguin: Baltimore, 1963); probably still the best general book on Schopenhauer.

F. Copleston, *Arthur Schopenhauer, Philosopher of Pessimism* (London, 1975).

M. Fox (ed.), *Schopenhauer: His Philosophical Achievement* (Brighton, 1980).

D. W. Hamlyn, *Schopenhauer*; in the series 'Arguments of the Philosophers' (London, 1980).

B. Magee, *The Philosophy of Schopenhauer* (Oxford, 1983).

J. Young, *Willing and Unwilling: A Study in the Philosophy of Arthur Schopenhauer* (The Hague, 1987).

E. von der Luft (ed.), *Schopenhauer: New Essays in Honor of His 200th Birthday* (Lewiston, 1988).

R. Safranski, *Schopenhauer and the Wild Years of Philosophy*, trans. by Osers (London, 1989).

C. Janaway, *Self and World in Schopenhauer's Philosophy* (Oxford, 1989).

C. Janaway, *Schopenhauer* (Oxford, 1994).

C. Janaway (ed.), *Willing and Nothingness: Schopenhauer as Nietzsche's Educator* (Oxford, 1998).

C. Janaway (ed.), *The Cambridge Companion to Schopenhauer* (Cambridge, 1999).

INDEX